*Opening Financial Markets*

A VOLUME IN THE SERIES

*Cornell Studies in Political Economy*

EDITED BY PETER J. KATZENSTEIN

A full list of titles in the series appears at the end of the book

# Opening Financial Markets

## BANKING POLITICS ON THE PACIFIC RIM

### LOUIS W. PAULY

CORNELL UNIVERSITY PRESS

*Ithaca and London*

First published 1988 by Cornell University Press.
First printing, Cornell Paperbacks, 1990.

International Standard Book Number 0-8014-2080-6 (cloth)
International Standard Book Number 0-8014-9928-3 (paper)
Library of Congress Catalog Card Number 88-47740
Printed in the United States of America
*Librarians: Library of Congress cataloging information
appears on the last page of the book.*

⊗ The paper in this book meets the minimum requirements of the American National Standard for Information Sciences—Permanence of Paper for Printed Library Materials, ANSI Z39.48-1984.

FOR GERMAINE ROSE PAULY

There was nothing natural about *laissez-faire*; free markets could never have come into being merely by allowing things to take their course. . . . *Laissez-faire* itself was enforced by the state.

Karl Polanyi, *The Great Transformation*

# Contents

# Preface

This book represents the culmination of a twelve-year involvement with the banking industry. For over half of that period, I worked in the international divisions of two banks, one in the United States and one in Canada. During much of the balance, I studied the political economy of international finance in graduate programs at Fordham University, New York University, the London School of Economics and Political Science, and Cornell University. From the beginning, I was struck by the constraints that at virtually every point surround institutions popularly depicted as exceptionally powerful. This impression was reinforced as I studied what I now take to be the source of those constraints. It is not by chance, then, that this book is about the state, and the interaction of states, in the banking sector.

In this book I attempt to explain why advanced industrialized nations have moved so consistently during recent decades to open their traditionally protected national banking markets to foreign institutions. Extending access rights to foreign banks is essentially a matter of changing existing regulatory policies and is hence a matter of politics. My research reconstructs the manner in which those policies changed in four distinctive national contexts and identifies the fundamental political forces driving their evolution. I argue that a specific set of such forces, although embedded in unique configurations of regulatory power, impelled a broadly liberal convergence of market access policies in the banking sector between the late 1950s and the late 1980s and created a normative foundation for international coordination in the sector. During that period competition intensified between multinational banks and between the states that charter them. Converging patterns of domestic regulatory politics, however, simultaneously shaped an emergent interstate consensus on basic rules governing access to national markets. During a period of retrenchment that began in the middle of the 1980s, banks operated in markets now intrinsically linked. Technological advances and economic pressures affected the operational possibilities of those banks, but political forces and intentional political decisions fundamentally determined the more open market structures in which their actual strategic choices were made.

Modern banking is a complicated business with many interrelated aspects. A range of governmental policies — macroeconomic, prudential, sectoral adjustment, and market access policies, to name a few — have important consequences for the markets in which banks and related financial intermediaries operate. In my research on one particular aspect of contemporary banking, I undertook extensive fieldwork in the United States, Japan, Canada, and Australia — each an important part of the Pacific Rim, a region now emerging as the financial linchpin of the interdependent international economy. The four constitute a reasonable cross-section of the advanced industrialized world, and, in each case, policy debates on the issue of foreign bank regulation achieved a degree of salience sufficient to generate an accessible record and manifest legislative or administrative decisions.

For the United States, Canada, and Australia, with their Anglo-Saxon legal cultures, the evidence of legislative histories supplemented by corroborating interviews adequately elucidated underlying policy-making patterns. Moreover, an established comparative political literature on the latter two countries assisted in isolating parallel policy determinants. In Japan, however, the letter of the law often appeared to codify decisions actually taken at a more obscure level. Uncovering subtle mechanisms of policy development through a more extensive series of interviews was therefore critical in this case. I did not extend the research to member-states of the European Community because their regulatory policies are complicated by a larger effort to create a fully integrated financial market. In view of their collective importance, however, the last chapter reviews aspects of that effort relevant to my argument.

Following a research method associated with the work of Alexander George, I focus on comparable regulatory decisions and organize four case studies around questions aimed at determining the sources of those decisions. What was the character of the overarching regulatory context in which access policy evolved? What private interests were most keenly engaged in policy debates? How and to what effect were those interests organized? What were the specific goals of governmental actors? How distinctive were those goals, and what capacity did public officials have to achieve them? Did policy outcomes reflect a movement in the direction of improved access for foreign institutions to national markets? What combination of factors best explains specific policy shifts? What was the normative basis of policies ultimately adopted?

Conventional empirical analysis adequately reveals the articulation of market access policy within specific cases. In exploring the implications of parallel policy movements across cases, however, I have adopted a processual and interpretive approach to normative development, an approach associated in legal theory with the work of such seminal thinkers as Lon Fuller. This approach encompasses both the causes of policy reform within each country and the meaning of convergent change. Increasingly shared normative standards become evident when the four cases are viewed together. Because market access policies have a direct impact on institutions licensed by other states, they establish the basis for reciprocal adjustments between states. Changes in domestic laws and practices by their nature initiate processes of interstate communication and accommodation. Behavioral norms arise as states convey mutual expectations and give evidence by their actions over time that those expectations are being met. Reciprocal state interaction can thus establish patterns of obligation. In the banking sector of the advanced industrial world, such patterns gradually coalesced over a thirty-year period around mutual openness and nondiscrimination combined with regulatory adjustments to ensure roughly equivalent access to markets that remained structurally distinct.

International normative development in this sense is analogous to one of the processes Philip Jessup posited for the formation of transnational law (the simultaneous adoption of equivalent domestic legislation by national governments). It is also analogous to the types of routinized customary practice that provide a basis for order in the developing societies studied by legal anthropologists. By assenting to the mutual interpenetration of their banking markets and by forging compatible domestic policies, states create an understanding that frames continuing bilateral and multilateral relations. Common norms may ultimately feed back into domestic decision-making arenas and make it difficult for governments to reverse course. Norms may, for example, strengthen the claims of foreign institutions operating domestically, encourage domestic banks to enter open foreign markets, and cast a shadow of illegitimacy or unfairness over regressive policy options. Because those norms are now only incipient, however, it is too early to make definitive assessments of their ultimate impact. But what can be done, by focusing on converging domestic policies, is to bring to light the development of a framework that legitimates a new structural openness in an imporant sector of modern capitalism.

I gathered most of the material for this book between 1984 and 1987 from primary and secondary sources in the countries examined. A number of scholars contributed to my thinking on the subject as I prepared for fieldwork. For formative comments, I am grateful to Jonathan Aronson, John Barcelo, Ralph Bryant, Kent Calder, Benjamin Cohen, John Fayerweather, Jeffry Frieden, Ernst Haas, Miles Kahler, Robert Keohane, Stephen Krasner, Ellis Krauss, Charles Lipson, Michael Mochizuki, John Odell, Nicholas Onuf, Abraham Rotstein, John Ruggie, Michèle Schmiegelow, Joan Spero, Andrew Spindler, Marc Triebwasser, Philip Wellons, Mark Zacher, and especially Peter Katzenstein.

For valuable assistance in Washington, D.C., and New York, I thank Samuel Abram, James Ammerman, George Clark, Frederick Dahl, Jane d'Arista, William Glidden, Stewart Goddin, Douglas Kruse, Steven Lucas, Lamar Smith, Sydney Key, and especially Gary Welsh. In Canada, I benefited greatly from the help and comments of Joan Cait, William Curran, Barbara Dance, George Douglas, Anthea Downing, Jane Dysart, Jennifer McKeon, Adelaide Richter, and my colleagues at the University of Toronto. In Japan, special assistance came from Yuichiro Nagatomi, Seizaburo Sato, Tomomitsu Oba, Toyoo Gyohten, Masaki Omura, Heizo Takanaka, Mariko Fujii, Kozo Yamamoto, Eisuke Sakakibara, John Clayden, Takashi Inoguchi, Yoshio Okubo, Kazuo Nukazawa, Minoru O'uchi, Tait Ratcliffe, Frances McCall Rosenbluth, Sonja Ruehl, Kim Schoenholtz, Yoshio Suzuki, Soichiro Tahara, and Keiichi Tsunekawa. The same came in Australia from Peter Abelson, Edna Carew, Keith Carpenter, Gregory Crough, Sol Encel, Ross Gittins, Ian Harper, John Hewson, James Horne, Warren Hogan, John Howard, Brian Metcalfe, Jan Munro, James Perkins, John Rose, Ian Sharpe, John Stone, Laura Tingle, Thomas Valentine, Michael Waterhouse, and Edward Wheelwright. In Europe, Paolo Clarotti, Jürgen Fitzenreiter, Joachim Henke, Robert Ley, Rinaldo Pecchioli, Stuart Robinson, and Peter Troberg helped a great deal. I also acknowledge with gratitude some three hundred bankers, government officials, and market observers who provided background interviews. Without their insights and their time, my work would not have been possible.

Much-appreciated support came from several institutions. The Center for International Studies of Cornell University, the Royal Bank of Canada, and the Sicca Foundation made various field trips

possible. The Institute of Fiscal and Monetary Policy of the Japanese
Ministry of Finance generously sponsored me during a fascinating
summer in the ministry's Tokyo headquarters. Access to useful
libraries, archives, and other facilities was provided by the Bank for
International Settlements, the General Agreement on Tariffs and
Trade, the Bundesbank of the Federal Republic of Germany, the
Office of the U.S. Special Trade Representative, the Australian
Labor Party, Citibank, Massey College of the University of Toronto,
the Royal Bank of Canada, the Toronto-Dominion Bank, Irving
Trust Company, Westpac Banking Corporation, the Organization
for Economic Co-operation and Development, the Commission of
the European Communities, the Australian embassy in Washington,
the Canadian embassy in Tokyo, the U.S. Senate Banking Committee, and the U.S. Department of the Treasury.

For constructive comments in the final stages, I am indebted to
Peter Katzenstein, Theodore Lowi, Helen Milner, T. J. Pempel,
Richard Rosecrance, Lawrence Scheinman, George Staller, Jennifer
Holt, Robert Keohane, and an anonymous reviewer. Roger Haydon
and Richard Rose provided excellent editorial advice.

Earlier and more detailed versions of the Australian and Japanese
case studies were published as monographs: *Foreign Banks in Australia: The Politics of Deregulation* and *Regulatory Politics in Japan:
The Case of Foreign Banking*. For permission to use some of that
material in this book, I thank Australian Professional Publications
and the China-Japan Program (East Asia Papers Series) of Cornell
University, respectively.

My wife, Caryl, contributed to this book in the innumerable ways
known to any happily married author. I treasure her patience, optimism, determination, and enthusiasm. Tessa arrived when the man-
uscript was first accepted for publication and Reid arrived just as the
finishing touches were being put on the book. More cooperative
babies would be difficult to imagine; nevertheless, only their grand-
mothers' unstinting help made it possible to complete the project on
time. Finally, their great-grandmother, to whom the book is dedi-
cated, continues to inspire her growing family with her love of life
and passion for learning.

Louis W. Pauly

*Toronto, Canada*

*Opening Financial Markets*

CHAPTER ONE

# Banking, Politics, and Rules

In banking circles, "global village" has become a common metaphor to depict the consequences of contemporary changes in international financial markets. Technological innovation, market deepening, and capital mobility are widely credited with linking formerly discrete markets so inextricably that a truly global financial marketplace has finally emerged. That marketplace, it is often said, now overwhelms the political forces that once clearly controlled it. National governments are seen to be fundamentally constrained.

Though increasing interdependence is a fact in the financial sector, the common wisdom exaggerates the changes that have occurred. Consider the reactions to the physical expansion of financial institutions across national borders. When a bank from Hong Kong moves to acquire a major American bank, when foreign institutions attempt to expand the range of their activities in Tokyo, when the market share of foreign banks rises rapidly in Canada, when Japanese institutions bid for prominent market positions in Germany and California, headlines are generated, governmental assent is requested, investigations are triggered, regulatory policies are scrutinized, and the continuing political foundations of financial markets are exposed. The conventional global village metaphor suddenly looks simplistic. This book is about those political foundations.

## THE ARGUMENT

Through an examination of a key aspect of increasing international financial interdependence — the institutional interpenetration of banking markets in advanced capitalist countries—this book demonstrates that considerable distance remains between the vision of a truly global market and contemporary reality. National markets, reflecting unique histories and deep political relationships, remain the building blocks of the international banking system. Since World War II markets have opened to greater foreign participation—not because of inexorable economic revolutions, however, but because of the decisions and actions of states motivated by similar but not identical processes of domestic political change. International pressures are mediated by idiosyncratic configurations of domestic power. A vital element of intentionality must therefore be taken into account. A global village does not spontaneously spring up; it must be created. Politics within distinct state structures remains the axis around which international finance revolves.

This book explores how intentional linkages between financial markets are created through parallel developments in domestic policies. Its empirical focus is a comparison of policies regulating the direct operations of foreign institutions in the markets of advanced capitalist countries. The book argues that such market access policies have in recent years been converging in the direction of increasingly common regulatory standards. It concludes, however, that the processes encouraging this evolution rest not on ineluctable economic forces but on political will. In showing how convergent policies have developed in this specific arena, the study contributes to work in political economy on the manner in which coordinating norms and rules may emerge between interactive, interdependent, but fundamentally autonomous states.

In 1921, during the second session of the nascent League of Nations, the Swedish banker-statesman Marcus Wallenberg proposed a multilateral agreement that would guarantee the openness of the banking markets of member states on the basis of reciprocity.[1] Wallenberg's plan specifically aimed at easing establishment problems confronting the branches of national banks in foreign markets and at bringing some consistency to idiosyncratic national regulatory structures. But his idea proved contentious and quickly sank into the oblivion that some years later swallowed the League itself. Nevertheless, following the war the ill-fated League was intended to prevent, Wallenberg's goal would be realized in substantial part, albeit not in the way he had originally envisaged.

Between the late 1950s and the late 1980s, the advanced states of the capitalist world moved steadily toward a mutual understanding as to the appropriate regulatory treatment of foreign banks in their domestic markets. This understanding rested not on formal multilateral negotiation but on a tacit convergence of national policies. It organized itself around core concepts of liberalization (or openness) and reciprocal national treatment (or mutual nondiscrimination), and increasingly it coordinated the expectations and behavior of like-situated states, even though their fundamental political autonomy kept it tentative. This understanding did not obviate continuing competition at the level of the state or the level of the firm, nor did it guarantee that such competition would never lead to deteriorating interstate relationships. As the understanding became clearer in the course of bilateral and multilateral interaction, however, it did serve to legitimate an increasing institutional interpenetration of national markets. The incipient framework for relations continued to fall short of Wallenberg's original plan for a formally binding treaty, but this imperfection could be viewed as a strength and not a weakness in the contemporary era, for informal consensus helped reconcile a continuing tension between the economic logic of competition and the political necessity of control in markets still intrinsically national in their foundations.

The next chapter proposes a general explanation for the reform of market access policies. Detailed case studies of the United States, Japan, Canada, and Australia follow. On the basis of the convergent paths evident in these cases, the concluding chapter compares them and elucidates the normative framework that has thereby evolved. Some introductory comments on regulatory politics in this sector provide an orientation to the subject.

## OPENNESS AND THE POLITICS OF FOREIGN BANK REGULATION

States, and competition between states, pervade the financial markets in which banks participate. All banks are creatures of states. Their legal charters are granted by their home states; their principal regulators are officials of those states; the bulk of their capital bases come from markets under the purview of those same officials; their executive managements are almost always dominated by nationals of their home states; their ability to expand into external markets is a function of host state law; the direction of their international lending responds to subtle cues from their home states; in times of crisis, they are dependent on the supervisory policies of home and host states alike. In essence, the very possibility of the financial intermediation services that banks provide is a function of incentives and accommodating policies adopted by home and host states alike. The

*3*

structures of national banking markets that result from such policies are constantly changing but remain distinctive.

The impact of state involvement in banking markets is especially evident when banks attempt to expand physically across borders. Most banks aiming to develop business with nationals in another country below the level of the major corporate enterprise, and even at that level to nurture long-term relationships, continue to find it necessary to maintain formal presences in target markets. In recent years technological innovations and cost pressures have encouraged banks to develop such operations selectively, but they have not obviated the need to function directly within diverse legal and political environments. Similarly, economic transformations in interdependent markets have made it more difficult to differentiate between banks and other kinds of financial institutions, but they have not persuaded any governments to abandon fundamental regulatory prerogatives.

Since the late 1950s states have allowed national financial boundaries to become more porous; especially after the collapse in the early 1970s of the Bretton Woods system of fixed exchange rates and the subsequent marked rise in the international mobility of capital, the states of the advanced industrial world found it difficult to retain absolute control over their domestic monetary economies. All states, however, retained preponderant influence over a key channel through which their monetary policies have traditionally been implemented, their domestic banking markets. The political architecture sustaining these markets, the historically rooted structure of regulation in a sector always regarded as sensitive, essentially reflected unique relationships between governments and participants in those markets, between participants themselves, and between the constituencies affected by policy change.

In all advanced market-economy countries, in short, in the two dozen countries comprising the Organization for Economic Cooperation and Development (OECD), banking remains a vitally important economic sector and is closely monitored by national governments. A subset of the array of policies affecting banking within national borders regulates the entry of foreign banks and the conditions of their operation after entry. The maintenance of national control over local banking markets, especially over access to domestic deposits, is a traditional concern of governmental overseers. Of all the reasons for regulating banking differently from other industries, such as those related to macroeconomic, antitrust, and prudential considerations, the insistence that control be *national* is invariably, if subtly, viewed as important. Money and power are perceived as intimately linked, and the right to dominate trading in a national currency—accepted as a basic store of value, means of exchange, and unit of economic measurement—is still viewed as a sovereign prerogative, a public trust granted by the state. So when foreign interests threaten to become significant in domestic banking markets, even the most open-minded of governments have historically assessed the implications in terms not just of economic stability or competitive efficiency but of national sovereignty as well. Often they have chosen to regulate the entry and expansion of foreign banks in a manner distinctly different from that applied to domestic institutions.

Immediately following World War II the market access policies applicable to foreign banks remained illiberal in most countries of the developed world; domestic markets were effectively protected and reserved for indigenous institutions. Because most banks did not particularly want to develop direct, long-term relationships with foreign customers, except through nascent wholesale and traditional correspondent networks, and because most governments, in keeping with the principles of the Bretton Woods monetary system, sought to control the mobility of capital, such illiberal policies and practices caused little tension. This situation began to change following the establishment of the European Common Market in 1957, the return to full multilateral currency convertibility in 1958, the concurrent initial expansion of American multinationals and their banks in Europe, and the rise of the Eurodollar market in the 1960s. Governments thereafter gradually allowed entry and operating barriers to erode, and over time foreign banks began to capture increasing shares of domestic markets. During the 1960s the market shares of foreign banks began growing to significant, if varied, levels in many OECD countries.[2] A controlled "liberalization" of national market access policies facilitated this growth. Deliberate movement toward expanding competitive opportunities for foreign institutions occurred in virtually all OECD countries.[3]

The consistency of this movement toward greater openness is striking. If relevant policies are grouped and compared along a theoretical spectrum ranging from closure and discrimination to openness and nondiscrimination, by the 1980s most states of the OECD moved decisively in the latter direction. Entry restrictions loosened and, after entry, foreign banks were increasingly treated as domestic banks for regulatory purposes.[4] Moreover, most states did not insist on strict reciprocity from the home states of entering or expanding banks. They appeared instead to have acted on the looser presumption, sometimes more and sometimes less explicitly stated, that more

5

generous regulatory treatment would in some fashion be fairly reciprocated. The results have tended toward effectively reciprocal nondiscriminatory policies with adjustments across markets to provide a
rough equivalence of new competitive opportunities.[5] Equivalent
access gradually emerged as a guideline against which to measure a
fundamental, but liberally interpreted, reciprocity. Moreover, even
when recriprocal expectations were made explicit, by the late 1980s
the general effect was to encourage broader openness and not closure. The latter course remained a possibility, especially in reaction
to developments in Japan and several newly industrializing countries. Events showed, however, that protectionist impulses could be
mitigated in a sector that can often be kept somewhat separate from
broader trade frictions, partly because the key political actors are
relatively few in number and have cross-cutting priorities.

Invariably, it is the domestic political environment that decisively
shapes rules governing foreign bank entry and operation after entry.
Of course, the domestic environment may be affected by external
developments. This is, in fact, a dominant theme of contemporary
financial history. The acceleration of the pace of financial innovation in OECD markets, the decontrol of interest rates and exchange
rates in various countries, the development of new technologies, and
variable national inflation rates, for example, all have potential
spillover effects. Nevertheless, it remains the case that particular
governments react to exogenous changes and adjust operative regulatory policies only when such effects are finally internalized, when
the problems they engender become domestic political problems.
Economic analysis may perhaps demonstrate why policies should
change, but only detailed examinations of domestic policy making
can explain how and why changes actually do occur.

DOMESTIC POLICY REFORM AND THE DEVELOPMENT
OF REGULATORY STANDARDS

A broad range of such policy reforms facilitated the growth of
international banking during the 1960s.[6] Regulatory acquiescence,
for example, allowed private commercial banks to become key channels for cross-national financial transfers. The refusal of states to
initiate adequate official alternatives for the recycling of oil revenues
subsequently stimulated the expansion of banks throughout the
1970s.[7] Opportunities to participate in offshore currency markets
(actually liberally regulated offshoots of traditional national markets
created by states in competition with one another) further encour-

aged the international ambitions of bank shareholders and managers. On the basis of the resulting growth of their balance sheets, many banks sought to establish or reinforce institutional footholds in foreign national markets themselves. Few host countries initially welcomed such penetration, the financial sector equivalent of foreign direct investment.[8] In most, an array of explicit or implicit policies hindered expansion strategies. Restrictions included outright prohibitions on entry, discriminatory regulatory requirements, limits on cross-border personnel movement, and other measures denying foreign banks the right to compete with indigenous institutions on an equivalent basis. These are the types of policies that have been changing in recent years.

Market access policies gradually converged in the direction of a set of basic regulatory standards across the banking markets of the OECD. Those standards did not create a binding order above states; rather, they organized relations across a particular group of similarly situated states. Despite broadening economic interdependence, states remained responsible for the fundamental structures, the political architecture, of markets under their purview. Financial interpenetration did not necessitate homogenization and did not necessarily imply increasing international harmony. Dis-integration, as opposed to continued integration of national markets, remained conceivable.[9] Only effective coordination of regulatory policies on an essentially reciprocal basis would permit the institutional interpenetration of markets to persist.

Among the countries examined in the following chapters, a tacit consensus emerged around regulatory norms that allowed enduring pressures of nationalism, competition, and integration to coexist in the banking sector. Comparable domestic regulatory policies converged toward an acceptance of market openness. They did so by extending the scope of nondiscriminatory treatment for foreign institutions operating in national markets and by rendering more equivalent the conditions of access across those markets. By the late 1980s effectively reciprocal developments created a normative base that helped sustain the institutional interpenetration of markets still structurally distinct. The character of those developments provided evidence that states remained the central actors in the real global village.

CHAPTER TWO

# Foreign Banking in Four Countries: The Regulatory Contexts of Policy Making

Because banking is a regulated industry in all advanced industrial countries, the principal actors in domestic policy making include those regulated, those doing the regulating, and those seeking to benefit from regulatory change. Accordingly, in the four countries examined in this book, there are important variations in the roles played by domestic banks, domestic governments, foreign banks, and foreign governments. In the United States, a long debate on foreign bank regulation came to a stable conclusion only after those domestic banks most affected by actual and potential foreign competition had reached a tacit agreement on the need for legislative change. In Canada, the activities of foreign bankers as market innovators and political lobbyists encouraged national decision makers weakened by the peculiarities of confederalism to formulate increasingly liberal policy initiatives. In Japan, the centralization of regulatory power and the intensity of competition within a rigidly segmented market precluded effective responses to the claims of foreign banks until foreign governments intervened; when domestic conditions were right, these foreign governments often provided the final push needed to reconcile conflicting domestic interests. In Australia, national political leaders within cohesive official institutions dominated a lengthy effort to restructure the political foundations of a traditionally protected domestic banking market.

Four principal factors—shifting domestic governmental assessments of the appropriate balance between competition and control in national markets, strategic reevaluations within domestic banking communities of the trade-off between protection and reciprocity, foreign bank market and political activity, and foreign governmental pressure—account for shifts in the market access policies of all

Figure 1. Principal political catalysts to policy change on banking market access and four ideal-typical cases

|  | Banks | Governments |
|---|---|---|
| Foreign | Canada | Japan |
| Domestic | United States | Australia |

four countries. The factors were involved to some degree in all cases, but within each case the action of one particular set of actors served as a critical catalyst to policy change. Each case, then, may be seen as a kind of ideal-type that brings to light one important aspect of a general process of policy development (see Figure 1). This chapter sets the stage for a comparison of the respective roles played by these catalysts. It does so by introducing the regulatory settings of national debates on foreign banking in the four countries.

## THE UNITED STATES

The question of the proper place of foreign banks in American financial markets forms part of a perennial debate over the regulation and supervision of banking in general. A key element of that debate concerns the division of responsibilities for bank regulation between federal and state governments, a division that has historically diffused political power and thereby provided a significant degree of flexibility for private interests. The American constitution left ambiguous the precise separation of financial regulatory powers between federal and state governments. Over time, both levels of government claimed the prerogative of chartering banks.[1] By the middle of the nineteenth century, American banks had a clear option as to the identity of their principal governmental overseer. In this dual system, however, federal law remained silent on the question of foreign banks, and they originally had a state chartering option only.

Early in the twentieth century the shared regulatory responsibility of federal and state governments became more contentious as technological and economic developments encouraged the innovation of branch banking. Because most state and all federal banks were unit banks prior to this time (that is, they were forbidden to operate out of more than one physical location), an important barrier existed to the tendency toward bank expansion and financial concentration so evident in other countries. Unit banking, however, became increasingly untenable as some state banks were permitted by local law to create branch systems and federally regulated national banks pushed for the right to compete on an equal footing. The subsequent battle between federal and state regulators, and between national and state banks, culminated in the McFadden Act of 1927 and the Banking Act of 1933. These laws allowed national banks to set up branches first in their home cities and then in their home states provided state chartered banks in the same territory were allowed similar privileges under state law. More importantly, they also banned branching across state lines by either national or state banks. This proscription was later reinforced by the Bank Holding Company Act of 1956 and its 1970 "Douglas" amendment, which extended federal supervisory authority over bank holding companies and forbade them to acquire banks outside their home states unless specifically authorized by host state law.[2]

Foreign banks were an anomaly within this regulatory environment as long as they avoided the organizational form of subsidiaries. In effect, because federal law did not cover the establishment of foreign branch or agency networks and because a few states allowed foreign offices within their borders, notwithstanding the existence of sister offices in other states, foreign banks were often able to operate directly across state lines. This anomalous privilege became politically significant when overall foreign bank growth accelerated in the 1960s.

In addition to geographic constraints on their expansion, beginning in the 1930s American banks had to contend with certain functional limitations on their business powers. The most important of these related to prohibitions on mixing commercial banking and investment banking and on bank ownership of nonfinancial companies. Federal rules were most clearly articulated in sections of the Banking Act of 1933 (often referred to separately as the Glass-Steagall Act) and the Bank Holding Company Act of 1956.[3] As in interstate banking, the situation of foreign banks with regard to nonbanking activities was an irregular one until 1978. Provided they did not establish operations in the form of subsidiaries within the United States, foreign banks were not legally classed as true banks in their domestic activities, did not fall within the ambit of either Glass-Steagall or the Bank Holding Company Act, and could therefore in certain states simultaneously operate nonbanking firms, such as securities houses, as well as bank branches or agencies. Once again, this anomaly was not seen as a serious matter in policy circles, or among domestic competitors, as long as such operations remained small and relatively innocuous.

Another regulatory matter affecting foreign banking was the mechanism of monetary control. Not until 1913 did the United States lay the permanent foundations for a central bank, and it took World War I and the Great Depression finally to provide the Federal Reserve system with a strong mandate to control the nation's monetary policy.[4] Traditionally, the Fed carried out its duties principally through commercial banks belonging to the system; these included all national banks and some state-chartered banks. Simply put, it executed monetary policy mainly through controlling the amount of reserves available to the system by engaging member banks in the purchase and sale of government securities, by changing the level of member bank reserve requirements, and by adjusting the rate of interest at which it lent reserves to member banks in need. To provide for the stability of the system, the Fed was also given a degree of supervisory authority over member banks and eventually over all bank holding companies. The ultimate macroeconomic effects of its monetary powers critically depended, therefore, on the acquiescence of those commercial banks accounting for the bulk of available reserves in the economy. During the 1960s and 1970s, this requirement became increasingly problematic. Given the dual banking system, Federal Reserve membership became an increasingly expensive and expendable option for most commercial banks. Until passage of the Monetary Control Act of 1980, banks could, and did, opt out by choosing less onerous state regulation. Foreign banks, for their part, were able to avoid Fed controls altogether as long as they shunned the subsidiary organizational form and therefore avoided falling under the federal Bank Holding Company Act. In the same manner, foreign banks could avoid the expensive obligation of carrying insurance from the Federal Deposit Insurance Corporation (FDIC).

Finally, jurisdictional overlap within the federal government itself, and resulting conflicts, affected the regulation of foreign banks. On banking matters, several federal institutions have separate interests and separate responsibilities. The Federal Reserve supervises and examines all state-chartered banks that are members of the Federal Reserve system and all bank holding companies. The Office of the Comptroller of the Currency, a semi-independent arm of the Treasury, supervises and examines all national banks, most of which are owned by holding companies. The FDIC supervises all insured state-licensed banks that are not members of the Federal Reserve system. The Department of Justice has authority to review bank mergers and acquisitions to ensure that antitrust statutes are not violated. In addition, state banking departments examine and supervise all state-licensed banks regardless of their status in the Federal Reserve system or with the FDIC; the states also oversee mergers involving state-licensed banks.[5] This overlap is compounded in international banking matters. The Fed is responsible for international prudential issues; a Fed officer, for example, sits on the committee of the Bank for International Settlements working on the development of multilateral supervisory standards. To the extent that such issues impinge upon the operations of national banks, the comptroller of the currency is also involved at this level. On the related matter of seeking fair treatment for U.S. banking operations overseas, the Treasury Department takes the lead, but insofar as more general foreign policy or international legal questions arise in this connection, the State Department often plays a role.

Despite periodic efforts to reform this complicated system of bank regulation, a lack of coherence and coordination can and often does arise from the differing priorities and goals of these various regulators on such matters as bank safety, competitive efficiency, monetary control, and international coordination. For example, the FDIC tends to be more conservative on questions of safety; the comptroller often gives priority to matters of market efficiency; the Fed frequently emphasizes monetary control issues; and state regulators at times appear to have as their chief objective the preservation of their own autonomy. Because individual banks retain some options regarding principal oversight regimes (for example, switching their charters from one level of government to another), the possibility for competition in laxity between supervisory agencies therefore exists.[6] During the period covered in the case study below, this jurisdictional confusion allowed domestic and foreign banks to pursue their own private interests within structures that made it extremely difficult for government officials to identify national interests and design appropriate policies.

## Japan

In contrast to the United States, financial regulation in Japan has long been centralized; it has not, however, been unchangeable, and a complex process of reform has been underway since the end of the high-growth era of the 1960s. Japan's regulatory structure has changed as the financial system has adjusted to a maturing domestic economy reshaped by slower growth, persistent trade surpluses,

*Table 1.* Relative shares of indirect and direct finance in Japan, 1973–82 (in percentages)

|                   | 1973 | 1975 | 1977 | 1979 | 1981 | 1982 |
|-------------------|------|------|------|------|------|------|
| Indirect          | 93.3 | 93.1 | 89.7 | 87.8 | 86.9 | 85.3 |
| Banks             | 64.1 | 58.8 | 49.6 | 48.0 | 49.8 | 42.2 |
| Trust/insurance   | 10.5 | 11.0 | 10.8 | 11.3 | 11.6 | 13.7 |
| Government related| 18.6 | 23.3 | 29.2 | 28.6 | 25.5 | 29.2 |
| Direct            | 7.2  | 7.1  | 9.9  | 8.9  | 11.6 | 11.4 |

SOURCE: Bank of Japan, Flow of Funds Accounts, cited in Federation of Japanese Bankers Associations, *Banking System in Japan*, 9th ed. (Tokyo: Federation of Japanese Bankers Associations, 1984), 16. (Rounding errors present in data.)

technological innovation, and the burgeoning external expansion of core industries. One aspect of regulatory reform concerns the access of foreign institutions to the changing financial system.

As Japan emerged from the wreckage of World War II, its banks regained their prewar role as the pivotal providers of funds for investment. Private sector decisions and the acquiescence of occupation authorities reconstituted a financial system based upon traditional indirect financing methods. A recovering government, content with an economic guidance mechanism based on a closely supervised interbank market, did its part to discourage the development of direct financing alternatives, such as equity and bond markets. Over time, indirect channels (saver to banker to borrower) declined somewhat in importance but persisted in dominating financial flows in the economy (see Table 1).

Reflecting the dual structure of the postwar economy as a whole, the banking system was concentrated and oligopolistic at the wholesale level and decentralized at the deposit-gathering retail level. At both levels, competition was intense. Profits of course were important, but market share was often the critical indicator of success. Government, in turn, sustained the system, worked with it to attain broad national goals, and sometimes attempted to accelerate market-defined outcomes.[7] On a continuous basis, however, government also played a regulatory role familiar in other industrialized countries as it sought to establish rules to mitigate what it deemed competitive excesses. In this role, the strength of centralized state institutions was evident, especially in comparison with the United States. In return for government's legitimation of property rights within the system and its confidence-generating prudential oversight, private market participants accepted extensive monetary controls and functional segmentation. Around this arrangement vested interests coalesced. Table 2 shows the major constituent groups of the resulting banking system and tracks their relative positions over time.

Table 2. Shares of total employable funds in major Japanese institutions, 1955-80 (in percentages)

| Group | 1955 | 1965 | 1975 | 1980 |
|---|---|---|---|---|
| City banks | 33.1 | 24.9 | 19.3 | 16.5 |
| Regional banks | 16.1 | 15.5 | 13.5 | 12.6 |
| Long term credit banks | 4.6 | 6.1 | 5.7 | 4.8 |
| Trust banks | 4.4 | 6.9 | 7.2 | 7.2 |
| Mutual banks | 5.7 | 7.2 | 6.2 | 5.7 |
| Credit associations | 4.0 | 7.5 | 8.2 | 7.7 |
| Rural institutions | 5.3 | 7.1 | 8.0 | 7.4 |
| Insurance companies | 3.5 | 6.0 | 6.6 | 7.1 |
| Post Office | 11.6 | 8.8 | 13.1 | 17.4 |
| Other (incl. foreign) | 11.7 | 10.0 | 12.2 | 13.6 |
| Total | 100.0 | 100.0 | 100.0 | 100.0 |

SOURCE: Bank of Japan, Flow of Funds Accounts, cited in Stephen Bronte, Japanese Finance: Markets and Institutions (London: Euromoney Publications, 1983), 15.

The governmental apparatus regulating these institutions, and effecting monetary policy through them, centers around the Ministry of Finance, which is principally responsible for policy formulation, and the Bank of Japan, which handles day-to-day policy implementation in the money markets.[8] Actual policy, however, reflects a subtle interaction between the ministry, the Bank, and the major players in the markets. Although the ministry clearly predominated at least until the end of the high-growth period, the balance of influence has changed over time. Combining the regulatory, supervisory, budgetary, tax, and customs functions often split in many other OECD governments, the ministry remains key. Nevertheless, under the pressure of governmental debt policies, expanding corporate liquidity, increasingly competitive market conditions, and the internationalization of core industries and banks, its power has been diminishing over the years.

Despite increasingly obvious limits on the power it wielded in the immediate aftermath of World War II, in bank regulation the Ministry of Finance remains more than just a broker between competing private interests.[9] The administration of the banking system, control over entry, ongoing supervision, and oversight of expansion abroad come almost entirely under the ministry's discretion. Policies relating to most of the functions of banks are designed within the ministry; only on rare occasions when a particular issue becomes highly politicized do parliamentarians or other ministries inject themselves into what usually seem to be highly technical matters. Indeed, subtle incentives and disincentives work to prevent such politicization from occurring by encouraging bureaucrats and private interests to compromise or acquiesce when matters are in dispute. For ministry officials, political intervention is painful, time consuming, and risky from the point of view of career advancement; for businessmen, garnering political favor can be very expensive, especially when rivals are competing financially either through legitimate channels or otherwise.[10]

Among the three ministry bureaus most directly engaged in financial regulation — covering banking, securities, and international finance — the Banking Bureau clearly enjoys primacy. But the traditional process of bottom-up decision making across bureaus, with its laborious mechanisms for seeking compromises on issues of dispute, helps prevent the imposition of unacceptable costs on any particular institutional groups. The intentional logic of this process requires that bureaus, sections, and departments represent the interests of their regulated constituents in such a way that the ministry as a whole does not lose an overarching sense of cohesive purpose.

Within the Banking Bureau, the Commercial Banks Division is solely responsible for supervising the activities of all major banks, including foreign banks. Approximately one thousand smaller banks and credit cooperatives are supervised by a separate division, as are insurance companies and government-affiliated institutions. Several hundred domestic and foreign securities companies report to the separately organized Securities Bureau. Insofar as the operations of domestic institutions abroad or of foreign institutions in Japan raise policy issues relating to foreign exchange, foreign capital flows, international organizations, and the like, the International Finance Bureau plays a role. Without direct line responsibility and without a powerful domestic constituency, however, the influence of the bureau remains of a second order.[11] Foreign banking matters often involve both the Banking Bureau and the International Finance Bureau. Policies emanating from the ministry may be administered directly or through the market operations of the Bank of Japan. Because the Bank is responsible for market safety and orderliness, its own prudential regulations also affect foreign banks. Both the ministry and the Bank, then, are the agencies principally responsible for regulating investment in the banking sector from abroad.

Perceptions of vulnerability lie at the root of Japan's historical response to foreign investment in its domestic markets. Efforts to preserve cultural distinctiveness and political autonomy have long been evident in Japan's relations with the West. Such national traumas as the imposition of the unequal treaties in the late 1850s and the Three-Power Intervention of 1895 are fundamentally related to the cautious regulation of foreign direct investment in the modern era. Indeed, even during the period of rapid modernization following the Meiji Restoration in 1867, a priority of government planning was to attract foreign technology and capital without necessarily attracting foreign control. Despite war and occupation, that policy objective did not change.

There were several distinct phases in the postwar movement of foreign enterprise to Japan and in the policies that controlled it. From 1945 to 1955 incoming investments were few mainly because of unattractive conditions in the economy; important entries into basic industries did occur, however, with the acquiescence of occupation authorities. After the occupation, the restrictive Foreign Investment Law, enacted in 1950, came fully into force; between 1955 and 1967 foreign entry was permitted on a limited basis in a range of basic and consumer industries in exchange for the critical technology that facilitated the country's switch to heavy goods exports. Continuing foreign exchange scarcity and a reluctance to allow wholly owned foreign companies to establish in the manufacturing sector underlay an ambivalent policy between 1964 and 1967 when Japan simultaneously accepted the liberalization obligations associated with membership in the OECD and tightened actual restrictions administered under the Foreign Investment Law.

Only in 1967, and under pressure from outside Japan, did a wary liberalization program really begin. In essence, the program allowed maximum foreign participation of 50 percent in joint ventures, except in specific industries where such participation was excluded entirely. In 1973 the government approved 100 percent ownership in principle but again with important exceptions. Significant foreign pressure, especially from the United States, accompanied the next phase of liberalization, which culminated in the 1980 Foreign Exchange and Foreign Trade Control Law. Officials in the Ministry of Finance, where it was drafted, viewed the new law as a codification of the liberalization that had already been taking place under informal administrative guidance; the law was a symbol of the direction of policy, a symbol largely for foreign consumption.[12] But it is clear that policy makers intended the law to be interpreted liberally by administrators, and this has generally been the case.[13] By virtue of requirements for prior notification, however, sufficient flexibility remained to stop any investment that threatened to be detrimental to national security, public order, and safety, or that appeared likely to harm domestic enterprises in the same industry. Administrators also retained the ability to hold up an investment on grounds of reciprocity.

*Table 3.* Foreign investment and foreign debt in Japan's private sector, 1979-85 (U.S.$ millions)

| Year | Direct investment | | Portfolio investment | | Loans | |
|------|--------|-------------|--------|-------------|----------|----------|
| | Abroad | From abroad | Abroad | From abroad | Extended | Received |
| 1979 | 17,227 | 3,422 | 19,003 | 22,606 | 14,938 | 1,815 |
| 1980 | 19,612 | 3,270 | 21,439 | 30,224 | 14,839 | 1,623 |
| 1981 | 24,506 | 3,915 | 31,538 | 47,852 | 18,944 | 1,478 |
| 1982 | 28,969 | 3,998 | 40,070 | 47,076 | 23,228 | 1,325 |
| 1983 | 32,178 | 4,364 | 56,115 | 69,948 | 29,266 | 1,320 |
| 1984 | 37,921 | 4,458 | 87,578 | 77,081 | 40,601 | 1,266 |
| 1985 | 43,974 | 4,743 | 145,748 | 84,847 | 46,870 | 1,211 |

SOURCE: Bank of Japan, *Economic Statistics Annual* (Tokyo: Bank of Japan, March 1985), table 132; (March 1987), table 136.

Although foreign pressure was always evident during these liberalization rounds, movement toward economic openness was still associated more with the maturity and competitiveness of Japan's core industries than with demands from abroad. But at important junctures such pressure reinforced the positions of liberal forces within decision making structures. Often, the essential requirement for policy change was to convince affected industries that their own fortunes would suffer if foreigners were not accommodated. This argument was more persuasive in an era when those firms were themselves expanding abroad and when resulting foreign claims directly affected future prospects.[14] In the decade after 1967 the annual flows of Japanese direct investment abroad rose from U.S. $275 million to $2,800 million. Similar increases occurred in portfolio investments overseas and in lending activity. By the 1980s outflows dwarfed inflows in all three categories. Table 3 gives an indication of the stock outcome over a seven-year period.[15]

The liberalization of inward direct investment in Japan has generally been characterized by a lag between the formal acceptance of international obligations and the adoption of fully consistent administrative procedures. There has been a further lag between the evolution of more liberal procedures and their codification in domestic statutes and regulations. The most relevant obligations are enshrined in OECD documents, including the Code of Liberalization of Capital Movements, which Japan accepted when it joined the OECD in 1964, and in a series of bilateral economic cooperation treaties, including one with the United States signed in 1953 and one with Britain signed in 1960.[16] Fundamental obligations thus incurred provided a limited right of establishment for certain foreign enterprises and national treatment after establishment.

Despite the obligations created by such agreements, incoming investment was often restricted throughout the 1960s and 1970s under an obscure protocol relating to the protection of monetary reserves. In reality, however, such constraints often resulted from a stultifying association between the caution of paternalistic bureaucrats and an array of narrowly focused domestic business interests, which was undoubtedly reinforced by widespread perceptions of economic weakness. Resistance to change has been especially evident in the banking sector, and yet in the contemporary era Japan has moved progressively to open its national banking market to foreign competition.

## CANADA

With its historically deep sensitivity to foreign involvement at the commanding heights of its domestic economy, Canada has long had an apparent incentive to keep its national banking market closed to the direct participation of foreign institutions. The fact that it eventually moved to open that market reflected persistent pressures initiated within Canada by foreign banks able to exploit weaknesses inherent in its confederal system of government.

Financial intermediaries were established in British North America during the early years of the nineteenth century, well before the foundation of an independent Canada. The first commercial bank, the Bank of Montreal, opened its doors in 1817 but, owing to political difficulties, waited until 1822 to receive its legal charter. The Bank of Nova Scotia followed in 1820. Near-bank intermediaries, such as mortgage companies specializing in the longer-term lending forbidden to the commercially oriented chartered banks, existed as early as 1845. In 1867 the British North America Act established the legal foundation for a newly confederated Canadian state. Section 92 of the act gave the central government, not the provinces, sole responsibility for banking and for regulation of the money supply. The government quickly began exercising its statutory authority over banking and in 1871 passed the first Bank Act, an act which subsequently has been reviewed and revised approximately every ten years.[17] The regulatory framework established by the act was very much a rule-oriented one that strictly defined entry conditions and bank operating powers. The first line of defense against potential financial instability was to be the integrity of a limited set of broadly based core institutions specifically authorized by Parliament to conduct the business of banking.

Stability did not come easily. The decades following confederation were marked by both a rapid rise in the number of banks (forty-one at the peak) and periodic financial crisis. Consolidation occurred in the pre–World War I period when outright liquidations or mergers left the system with twenty-two banks. The market remained regulated by ground rules specified in the Bank Act, but in practice a high degree of reliance was placed on self-regulation by the industry itself. The forum for joint stabilization of the system was often the Canadian Bankers' Association (CBA), a peak association that spoke for the industry whenever a consensus among the leading banks could be achieved.[18] Closer governmental supervision, over the objections of the CBA, came in 1923 in the wake of a major bank failure. In response the Office of the Inspector General of Banks was established under the aegis of the minister of finance. The supervisory functions of the inspector general were supplemented in 1935 when a central bank was created. Aside from its overall monetary and fiscal responsibilities, the Bank of Canada took over the role of lender of last resort to the chartered banks, a role traditionally filled by the minister of finance. As the banking system became more structured, and the role of political authorities more obvious, the maintenance of control by nationals became a clearer policy objective of successive governments.

Meeting this objective would have remained a fairly simple matter had it not been for the vagaries of the confederal system. Although banking, understood to be any activity involving both the taking of deposits from the public *and* the making of loans, had always been an undivided responsibility of the central government, financial operations that did not clearly entail one or the other function could fall under the autonomous regulatory authority of the separate provinces. The government of Ontario, for example, granted licenses to companies underwriting equipment leases. In the 1960s and 1970s such near-banking devices provided an attractive opportunity to aggressive foreign banks.

Unlike Canada's mining and manufacturing sectors, certain important parts of which have historically been well over 50 percent owned by foreign (mainly American) interests, the banking industry was traditionally owned and controlled by Canadians. The sensitivity to foreign involvement in this sector evident in most countries was heightened in Canada not only because foreign ownership loomed large in the economy as a whole, but also because the country depended upon American capital imports to finance economic development. To generations of Canadian leaders, this necessary linkage seemed to carry with it the seeds of unwanted political integration with the United States. Intentional institutional differences, such as less rigid functional segmentation and no geographic restrictions in the Canadian market, played an important part in preventing this linkage from bringing about that politically untenable consequence. Nevertheless, the vast size and dynamism of the American financial system exerted a complex influence on the structure of Canadian banking. A cogent analysis of policy responses to developments in the United States sums this up succinctly: "At times, the Canadian reaction was one of imitation. . . . At other times, the Canadian reaction was one of revulsion. On balance, the latter reaction has dominated. As a result, the Canadian financial system, and particularly the banks, developed along radically different lines from the American counterpart."[19]

Ambivalence engendered by the American connection has certainly been evident in controversies over bank regulation and deregulation in Canada during recent decades. Prominent policy inquiries at federal and provincial levels have regularly taken place and contributed to ongoing policy reforms. Experiments with deregulation even going beyond the American model have occurred, but so have countervailing movements toward reinvigorated regulation, mainly in response to prudential concerns. Notwithstanding direct and indirect foreign influences, domestic concerns have been primary causes of most policy changes.

Critical aspects of the Canadian banking market have long been deregulated. Chartered banks have been able to branch nationwide since confederation, and interest rate ceilings were removed in the mid-1960s following a major review of the financial system in anticipation of a Bank Act revision.[20] The findings of the royal commission that carried out the review, known as the Porter Report, laid the foundations for contemporary policy in this field. The report made four basic proposals: that interest rate ceilings be abolished, that the powers of the chartered banks be expanded to include the ability to engage in mortgage lending, that financial institutions licensed by the provinces be brought under federal purview, and that foreign banks be permitted to set up agencies in the Canadian market. The 1967 Bank Act, however, incorporated only the first two recommendations, both of which, despite some political controversy, seemed to flow from the natural evolution of the economy and the banking system. The latter two recommendations were viewed as much too radical in the 1960s and were therefore held in abeyance.[21]

Since 1967 Canadian regulators oversaw policy developments that followed a general trajectory dating back to World War I. After the war the number of chartered banks declined significantly and market concentration rose accordingly. Limitations on market access and expanded merger activity brought the number of banks to eleven in 1925. By 1966 there would be eight. Simultaneously, the proliferation of other types of financial institutions—some regulated by federal and some by provincial statutes—markedly changed the environment in which banks operated in Canada. Nevertheless, over a fifty-year period beginning in the 1930s, the proportion of total Canadian financial assets held by the chartered banks remained just below 50 percent, despite increases in the number of trust companies, cooperative societies, insurance companies, and other types of intermediaries. Because the institutions traditionally accounting for the bulk of this market share have been so few in number, this degree of concentration has long been a matter of public policy concern.[22] The issue became a focal point of debate during the Bank Act revisions of 1967 and 1980.

An effectively protected national market long satisfied the preferences of the domestic banking community and of economic nationalists in Ottawa. Nevertheless, around the time of the Porter Report, pressures for change mounted when an unusual set of circumstances left an American institution with a banking charter. Despite resulting restrictions imposed by the 1967 Bank Act, the bank managed to retain a presence. This presence provided a competitive stimulus for the bank's American, European, and Japanese rivals to seek even limited entry to an expanding and potentially lucrative market. What they lacked in the post-1967 environment was a legal means for establishing a banking branch or subsidiary. Although much less a problem than in the American system, jurisdictional confusion within Canada's confederal system of government here played a role. Confederalism gave foreign banks a foothold. On this fragile basis, they began to grow in a market long accustomed to the practices of effective oligopolists. Thereafter, they began to organize politically and were eventually able to exploit traditional Canadian hesitation over the choice between national autonomy and economic prosperity.

AUSTRALIA

Australia's policies on foreign bank access developed within a regulatory context informed, like Canada's, by long-standing concerns about foreign investment, but also by determined governmental efforts to reform a highly controlled financial system.

*Table 4.* Foreign investment in Australia's public and private sectors, 1969–85 (A$ billions)

| Year[a] | Investment in government securities | Investment in private enterprises | | | | Total |
|---|---|---|---|---|---|---|
| | | Direct | | Portfolio | | |
| | | Equity | Debt[b] | Equity | Debt[c] | |
| 1969 | 1.75 | 1.86 | 2.90 | 0.58 | 0.57 | 7.66 |
| 1970 | 1.64 | 1.95 | 3.33 | 0.65 | 0.72 | 8.29 |
| 1975 | 1.33 | 2.82 | 4.22 | 0.70 | 2.19 | 11.26 |
| 1978 | 3.77 | 3.93 | 4.89 | 0.77 | 3.60 | 16.96 |
| 1979 | 5.39 | 4.40 | 5.58 | 0.84 | 4.26 | 20.47 |
| 1980 | 5.52 | 4.74 | 6.20 | 1.05 | 5.01 | 22.52 |
| 1981 | 4.79 | 6.01 | 7.42 | 1.49 | 7.22 | 26.93 |
| 1982 | 5.66 | 6.84 | 9.12 | 1.82 | 14.26 | 37.70 |
| 1983 | 7.62 | 7.65 | 10.43 | 2.37 | 22.61 | 50.68 |
| 1984 | 8.62 | 8.00 | 12.28 | 2.65 | 29.41 | 60.96 |
| 1985 | 12.59 | n.a. | 14.61 | n.a. | 44.97 | 72.17[d] |

SOURCE: Reserve Bank of Australia, *Bulletin* (December 1984), 373; (January 1985), S97. (Data not compiled for 1986.)

[a] June year-end.

[b] Includes corporate borrowings, branch liabilities to head office, and intercompany debt.

[c] Includes borrowings by both public and private nonmonetary enterprises. Private sector debt represented over 80 percent of the total in 1978 and 70 percent in 1985.

[d] Exclusive of investments in equities.

Entry of a foreign bank represents but one type of capital import in a country long reliant on foreign capital inflows. From the time of the first permanent European settlement, Australia has been a net capital importer. Internal demand for investment funds has historically outstripped domestic savings; only in extremely unusual years has the country been a net international lender of capital. Beginning in the mid-1970s the capital account consistently registered inflows. Accordingly, Australia's net external debt rose from A$2 billion in 1970 to over A$70 billion by 1986. The cost of servicing this debt (principal and interest) increased significantly from 10 percent of total exports in 1969 to over 25 percent by the mid-1980s. In general, however, this cost was borne by an expanding economy. Between 1962 and 1972 a boom in the minerals sector pushed the average annual growth rate in GDP to 5.1 percent, but the following decade saw that rate cut to 2.2 percent.[23]

Private foreign investment typically comprised the bulk of net capital inflows, although in recent years burgeoning government borrowings added significantly to the total (Table 4). Behind the statistics lies the reality of a small population (15.5 million in 1984) in a land blessed with significant natural resources and an economy typically growing faster than would have been possible in the absence

Foreign Banking in Four Countries

*Table 5.* Foreign and domestic control of Australian industries and economic activities by sector, various years (in percentages)

| Sector, year | Measure | Foreign | Domestic | Joint |
|---|---|---|---|---|
| Mining, 1982–83 | Employment | 25.9 | 71.7 | 2.4 |
| Mining, 1982–83 | Value added | 27.6 | 52.5 | 19.9 |
| Large manufacturing, 1975–76 | Value added | 59.0 | 41.0 | — |
| Total manufacturing, 1972–73 | Value added | 34.3 | 65.7 | — |
| Mineral exploration, 1975–76 | Expenditure | 54.4 | 45.6 | — |
| Finance companies, 1976 | Balances | 48.2 | 51.8 | — |
| Life insurance, 1976 | Premiums | 18.7 | 81.3 | — |

SOURCE: For mining employment, *Year Book Australia,* 69 (1985), 585. All other entries from *Year Book Australia,* 65 (1981), 656.

of external financing. One consequence has been increasing foreign control in various industries. Estimates of control vary depending on the base used for calculation. Table 5 gives a rough idea of the magnitudes encountered.

As a political issue, foreign control became especially salient after World War II when the form and nationality of capital inflows changed. Straight loans and British portfolio investment were increasingly supplemented by direct investment, notably from the United States and later from Japan. Until the mid-1950s few observers expressed concern about the trend; indeed the American funds were welcomed by governments anxious to accelerate recovery and growth. Exchange controls rarely impeded inflows and aside from informal discouragement of investment in banks, news media, and civil aviation, official policy until the late 1960s essentially maintained an open door.[24] Earlier in the decade, however, well before the levels of control shown in Table 5 had been reached, debate on the consequences of direct investment became prominent in academic circles. Soon the left wing of the Labor party and a section of conservative opinion focused on the possibility that foreign direct investment carried with it unacceptable social costs. In the course of a broad inquiry into the nation's economic performance at the behest of a conservative government, the Vernon Committee considered the issue in 1965. It concluded that although "narrowly nationalistic objections to overseas investment should be heavily discounted," since the balance of benefits from such investment appeared clearly to lie with Australia, annual inflows had reached "desirable" levels and further increases were not to be encouraged.[25] The committee further recommended that takeovers of existing Australian companies should henceforth require government approval.[26]

Although little came of the Vernon Committee's specific recommendations, the open door in fact began to close several years later.

In 1968, without statutory authority, the conservatives intervened to prevent a foreign takeover of a large insurance company. During the next year the government established informal guidelines to limit domestic borrowings by foreign-owned companies and to prevent takeover attempts in certain sensitive sectors. Economic nationalism subsequently became an increasingly significant rallying point, especially within the Labor party.

Locked out of government at the federal level from 1949 until 1972, Labor finally won election on a platform that included an insistence on stricter controls over direct capital inflows. Before relinquishing power, however, the conservative coalition attempted to steal Labor's thunder by promulgating the first Foreign Takeovers Act, which set up a screening procedure for incoming direct investment.[27] Against a background of OPEC oil shocks and international monetary turbulence, the new Labor government devoted considerable attention to the balance-of-payments effects of foreign ownership and to the broader social and economic consequences of foreign control, especially in the minerals sector. Before it fell in 1975, the government had backed off initial attempts to subject investment in such areas as uranium exploration to extremely restrictive foreign participation limits. It nevertheless did succeed in passing strengthened foreign takeovers legislation.

A more rigorous policy on foreign investment was now bipartisan. The returning conservative coalition maintained the 1975 Takeovers Act and in 1976 established formal machinery for investment review. The conservatives declared that their policy was to "encourage foreign investment, provided such investment is consistent with Australia's national interests and meets the needs of the Australian community."[28] The new Foreign Investment Review Board (FIRB) proceeded to foster increased Australian equity participation in new businesses by requiring, for example, 50 percent local equity in new mining ventures (75 percent for uranium) and by limiting foreign investment in rural properties, real estate, radio and television, newspapers, and civil aviation. Investment in financial institutions was subjected to special restrictions.

Australia's foreign investment policy has always been deeply equivocal. Given traditional economic circumstances, expanded domestic control has not always been compatible with steady growth, especially after increases in debt became problematic. Conflicting desires have sometimes been all too evident. During the years policy was first being made explicit, Australia associated itself with the OECD Code of Liberalization of Capital Movements, albeit with important reservations, and with the OECD Declaration on International Investment and Multinational Enterprises.[29] More recently, when Labor regained power in 1983, the government softened an election pledge to strengthen the FIRB; after announcing the broad maintenance of existing policy, the government initiated a review aimed at bringing policy in line with its commitment to sustained economic growth.[30] The entire issue remained contentious, but the intensity of debate gradually lessened in the face of economic recession and burgeoning national debt.

Predating the more general policy on foreign investment, restrictions on participation in the Australian banking system have been enforced by consecutive governments and by the industry itself. Prior to World War II these restrictions were tacit, but effective. In the postwar years similar ends were served by increasingly formalized policy interpretations articulated mainly by the Treasury. Notwithstanding these restrictions, the participation of foreign institutions in the Australian financial system, broadly defined, became a prominent political issue by the early 1970s. The question of whether to allow foreign banks to build full-scale domestic banking operations went to the heart of the Australian system of financial regulation. As in other economic sectors, that system reflected a complex relationship between government and the business community developed over many years and through many crises. Research on that relationship is vast, but present purposes require only a sketch of early conclusions related to the financial sector.

The history of the Australian political economy shows a proclivity on the part of a fairly strong state to involve itself deeply in the development of a predominantly capitalist economy. The form of that involvement has varied, for example, from direct market participation in the country's early days and in periods of war to more subtle intervention aimed at influencing private production and distribution decisions, especially since World War II. The Great Depression of the 1930s was a crucial turning point. Contrary to the experiences of other Western countries during that period, Australia responded to economic shock with a marked, if incomplete, withdrawal of direct governmental participation in the domestic market, largely owing to a general repudiation of a developmental strategy of extensive and centralized public borrowing from foreign capital markets. A formerly weak private sector thereafter asserted itself, partly compensating for its small relative size by concentrating. But this concentration, involving both labor and capital, occurred not in a context of pure opposition to the old idea of activist government, but rather in a context of symbiotic interaction between increasingly capital-intensive industries and nurturing state institutions.[31]

Whereas the organization of economic interests had been directly encouraged by a strong state earlier in the century, the eventual cohesion of these interests did nothing to discourage continued indirect state involvement in the economy.[32] In this respect, the direct provision of, say, infrastructure facilities in the nineteenth century can be contrasted with the use of a uniform income taxation system after World War II to redistribute economic resources; similarly, import quotas and other direct trade controls were gradually replaced by more generalized tariffs. The striking exception to this transformation from direct to indirect involvement occurred in the monetary sphere.

Contrary to the experience of other industries, in banking a relatively unconstrained market was replaced by one extensively controlled by the state after the Great Depression. Although the most dramatic example of government intervention, the 1947 bank nationalization attempt, failed, direct controls became the central feature of the domestic banking system, especially during World War II. After the war, the controls remained as a Labor government sought to prevent a relapse into depression and to construct an economy more aligned with its social objectives. Monetary policy, directly administered through quantitative credit rationing (as opposed to indirect guidance by means of influencing the price of credit in an open market), became the principal tool for macroeconomic management. The policy entailed an extensive array of exchange controls, controls on public sector borrowing, volume and pricing restrictions on bank lending, and maturity constraints on bank deposits, all of which allowed the government, at least in theory, directly to control the money supply, and thereby aggregate economic output and the price level. It also originally permitted the government to ensure the allocation of a politically acceptable volume of credit to chosen sectors, such as housing, farming, and small business. Under its Westminster style of government, a strong Treasury Department grew up around these controls as it implemented policy decisions through a rather tractable Reserve Bank and, in turn, through the now-submissive domestic banks.[33] The banks formed the core of domestic financial markets, and in return for accepting a high degree of governmental control, their depositors received implicit protection against default, their employees could count on job security, their shareholders could anticipate a stable level of profitability, and their managers had several layers of strategic decision making lifted from their shoulders. Only the consumers of banking services were left out, although everything was done in their name.

In this environment, competition between existing banks shifted away from price differentials to distinctions in product delivery and service, a shift that accelerated the creation of extensive national branch networks. The success of the entire structure depended on the maintenance of market dominance by the banks, thus necessitating tacit limitations on entry. In addition, the durability of the system was fundamentally contingent upon compatible fiscal policies that ensured general price stability, upon the absence of disequilibrating exogenous economic shocks, upon enduring saving and borrowing habits, and upon a manageable rate of change in the technology of financial intermediation. With the benefit of hindsight, the mere statement of these conditions goes a long way to explain why the structure eventually broke down.[34]

As pressures on the regulatory structure mounted during the 1970s, foreign entry into banking was only one item on a crowded agenda of policy reform. Although a series of economic developments eventually pushed that agenda to the fore, decisions to dismantle the postwar architecture of financial regulation and replace it with a more indirect, market-oriented apparatus were deeply political.[35] As such, the timing of deregulation decisions often lagged far behind economic circumstances and differed in detail from what might have been considered optimal in a purely economic sense. The overall structure of financial regulation changed only when governments decided that the structure no longer facilitated the achievement of their political goals, including the goal of staying in power.

CHAPTER THREE

# The United States

After World War II, but especially after the mid-1960s, overseas activities of banks from the United States grew dramatically; the aggregate assets of their foreign branches increased from $9.1 billion in 1965 to $52.6 billion in 1970 and $160.2 billion in 1975. By the early 1980s international assets accounted for almost 15 percent of total American commercial banking assets (up from 3 percent in 1970), and for the largest banks, nearly 50 percent of total earnings were generated abroad. In a reciprocal and somewhat lagged fashion, foreign banks expanded their operations in the United States; from a base of $7 billion in 1965, the American assets of foreign banks grew to $43 billion ten years later.[1] In the late 1970s the growth of foreign banks in the American market exploded, and by 1982 their total assets exceeded $300 billion.[2] Long before that time, their presence had become a political issue of national importance.

## THE POLICY DEBATE: RECONCILING ECONOMIC INCENTIVES AND POLITICAL OPPORTUNITIES

Although a few foreign bank offices date back to the late nineteenth century, significant operations in the United States began only after World War I. As the level of international and capital market activity within the U.S. economy developed, foreign financial institutions followed their customers and set up (mainly in New York) representative offices, agencies, and trust companies.[3] In addition, during the 1920s several Canadian and Japanese banks initiated full branch operations in Illinois, California, Washington, and Oregon. The American market was a highly segmented one; entry privileges were severely limited at the state level, and a tendency toward sub-market protectionism was exacerbated by the absence of federal policy. Indeed, most states traditionally prohibited the entry of all foreign banks, a category originally understood to encompass even domestic banks that happened to be domiciled in other states. Of the five states initially open to foreign penetration, California, Illinois, and Washington subsequently rescinded the right to establish branches, and in 1923 New York turned down legislation that would have permitted branch operations in addition to more conventional (mainly trade and money-market oriented) foreign activities. The desire to protect smaller indigenous banks appears to have stimulated this movement, and because a federal chartering option was not yet available, foreign banks were left with few opportunities to expand into the domestic market. The financial collapse of 1929 further stifled foreign ambitions and prompted many to return home.

A new era in international banking began in the late 1940s when major American banks, principally from New York, accelerated their branching overseas. This external thrust on the part of money-center banks was to have important domestic repercussions during the next decade. In 1951 New York liberalized certain restrictions on foreign agencies and eight years later began again to consider the prospect of licensing foreign branches. Legislation was accordingly suggested by the First National City Bank and supported by Chase Manhattan, both of which were meeting resistance to expansion plans abroad, especially in Japan, the Philippines, Brazil, Venezuela, and Uruguay, on the grounds that reciprocity was not available within the United States. During 1960 the Association of New York Clearing House Banks, a professional association of the twelve largest money-center banks in the state, formally sponsored a bill to permit foreign branch licensing if reciprocity was available in the foreign parent bank's home country. After extended debate, which pitted the interests of the big banks against those of their smaller indigenous competitors, the bill finally passed and became law in 1961.[4] Three years later in California, Bank of America, facing serious pressure to close the state's banking market to increased foreign penetration and fearing the new international competitive advantages of its New York rivals, managed to convince a reluctant legislature once again to permit the chartering of foreign branches. The victory was a hollow one, however, for the legislature made branch licenses contingent upon receipt of deposit insurance from the FDIC, a possibility precluded by existing federal law.[5]

By the late 1960s some form of direct foreign bank presence was allowed in six states—New York, California, Hawaii, Massachusetts, Oregon, and Washington—all of which required reciprocity from the home countries of the foreign banks. In reality, only New York and California were then considered important markets by most foreign institutions. In 1966, for example, New York hosted some sixty-two foreign bank representative offices and fifty-three agencies, branches, and subsidiaries; California hosted seven representative offices and eighteen agencies and subsidiaries; and only fourteen other foreign offices, all of limited scope, operated in other parts of the country. Although a lack of interest on the part of foreign banks accounted for the absence of foreign activity in many states, explicit state legislation sometimes specifically prohibited the entry of foreign branches (Delaware, Texas, Vermont) or any form of foreign banking office (Connecticut, Minnesota, Virginia, West Virginia, Rhode Island, Florida, Maryland, New Jersey, Ohio).[6]

Not surprisingly, the growth of foreign banks within the United States raised their political profile and attracted the attention of national policy makers. A number of events heightened this interest. First, in the wake of increasingly severe international payments imbalances and the attendant imposition of capital controls, including the 1965 Voluntary Foreign Credit Restraint Program, Congress wondered whether foreign banks in the United States had worsened the problem by funding overseas lending with domestic deposits. Second, the spectacular failure in October 1966 of the Intra Bank of Lebanon with an overexposed New York branch raised concerns about the adequacy of supervision over foreign operations within the United States. Third, America's largest trading partner, Canada, enacted legislation in 1967 designed to discourage the entry of American and other foreign banks, a move widely viewed in Washington and New York as discriminatory and retrograde, especially in light of Canadian bank expansion in several U.S. states. In response to these events the Joint Economic Committee of the Congress initiated studies aimed at assessing the overall impact of foreign bank operations in the domestic market (hereafter referred to as the Zwick Report) and the extent of foreign governmental restraints on American banks overseas.

## Early Congressional Activity

The Zwick Report was significant not only for its pioneering effort to gather data on foreign bank operations, which supported the view that such operations on the whole benefited the American economy and balance of payments, but also for its concluding policy recommendations. In essence the report built a case for extending federal regulatory control over foreign banks "so that foreign policy and the broader national and international implications of foreign bank activities can be adequately appraised."[7] At the same time, in order to encourage other countries to grant reciprocal privileges to all American banks wishing to operate abroad, the report recommended liberalizing conditions of establishment across the United States by allowing the federal government to license foreign branches and agencies in any location, regardless of statutory or implied prohibitions imposed by state governments. The rationale for such a policy is worth quoting in full:

> If U.S. foreign policy aims at seeking and according to foreign-owned enterprises operating in this country the same sort of treatment applied to American banks abroad, then conditions applying in most parts of the country should clearly be liberalized. In point of fact, it is an established economic policy of this country to attempt to obtain for U.S. enterprises operating overseas the same treatment from the local government as is accorded to enterprises owned by local citizens, and to accord in return similar treatment to foreign-owned enterprises operating in the United States. This policy applies in general and is an integral part of our friendship, commerce and navigation treaties with other countries. (P. 28)

This statement was a concise formulation of the national treatment standard, which would henceforth underpin federal policy development. By promoting it, the report implicitly rejected the strict reciprocity requirements imposed on foreign entry by state regulators. A tit-for-tat approach would be replaced by a broader openness that would tacitly, but more effectively, encourage reciprocal openness abroad. More specifically, the report recommended not only free entry but also equal market access, a notion that would entail providing foreign banks with regulatory advantages, such as deposit insurance, equal to those enjoyed by their domestic counterparts. The report concluded that foreign participation brought more advantages than disadvantages (in terms of financial innovation, the development of international financial centers, and the expansion of trade) and that there was "little evidence or complaints of competitive developments unfavorable to domestic banks" (p. 29).

Just as the Zwick Report was being published, the first bill to tackle some of the issues it raised was introduced in the Senate by Jacob Javits of New York; the bill called for the extension of federal authority over foreign banks but insisted on a reciprocity test for federal licensing. In March 1967 Wright Patman of Texas, chairman of the Banking Committee, introduced a similar bill in the House.[8] Although neither bill reached the hearing stage because the issue was simply not seen as important enough to require immediate action, both signaled the beginning of a long national debate on the subject.

In 1969, Patman focused again on foreign bank growth in the context of a bill designed to expand the 1956 Bank Holding Company Act.[9] The original act had extended federal authority over all bank holding companies that owned two or more banking subsidiaries. Patman's new bill aimed at bringing one-bank holding companies within the same purview. Because this organizational structure was a primary vehicle for foreign bank entry into certain states, the bill threatened to bring many foreign banks under federal control for the first time and simultaneously to restrict their powers to engage in nonbanking activities. Although the control of purely domestic one-bank holding companies was the principal intent of the bill, this foreign bank side effect raised serious questions about the extraterritorial application of U.S. law; technically, it would have forbidden foreign parent banks designated as holding companies from carrying on certain types of business inside or outside the United States. For many foreign banks, especially those from European countries where it had long been common practice for financial institutions to own shares in industrial concerns, such a restriction threatened to force abandonment of the American market.

The foreign banking community as a whole was slow to mobilize against Patman's bill. Although a trade association, the Institute of Foreign Bankers (IFB), had been formed in the early 1960s, it functioned mainly as a social club for expatriate bankers living in New York City. On political matters, the IFB preferred to have its interests looked after by key correspondent banks, principally the clearing banks of New York.[10] Unhappy with this arrangement in the wake of Patman's proposals, twenty-one banks broke away from the IFB and founded the Committee of Foreign-Owned Banks (CFOB). Through retained Washington counsel, the new organization began lobbying Congress and the Federal Reserve on the holding company issue and other matters of direct concern to its member banks. Despite this effort, the CFOB did not succeed in fully exempting foreign institutions from the new legislation finally passed in late 1970. They did, however, succeed in ensuring that the law included sufficiently ambiguous wording to allow the Federal Reserve a degree of interpretive flexibility with regard to distinctly foreign operations. Subsequent Fed regulations and decisions under the amended act did in fact show some sensitivity to unique foreign circumstances. Foreign bank subsidiaries were expected to conform to the act's provisions in their operations within the United States, but exceptions for their nonbanking activities elsewhere avoided the danger of retaliation against American banks abroad. Notwithstanding the new holding company rules, however, foreign banks operating domestically as branches or agencies, as opposed to subsidiaries, remained unaffected and outside federal jurisdiction.

The foreign bank issue reemerged in 1973 on several fronts. As foreign, especially Japanese and British, penetration of the California banking market accelerated, a new effort was mounted in the state legislature to restrict further growth. A bill to this effect was only narrowly defeated after Bank of America, concerned about foreign reprisals against its overseas network, lobbied intensely against it. At around the same time, in the course of studying the monetary implications of the rapid expansion of American banks in the Euromarkets, Federal Reserve Governor George Mitchell became increasingly interested in related questions involving foreign bank growth in the United States. On February 1, 1973, the Fed announced the formation of a steering committee under Mitchell's direction with the purpose of formulating comprehensive legislative recommendations on this issue. Several factors motivated this step, including a rapid rise in foreign bank assets in the U.S. market ($32 billion in 1973 as compared with $7 billion in 1965), the desire to preempt protectionist actions by state or federal lawmakers and thereby avoid retaliatory moves by other countries, and the desire to enhance the ability of the Fed to control domestic monetary aggregates. The problem of monetary control became especially salient during 1973 when the Fed, as part of an effort to curtail a rapid expansion of total bank credit, asked all foreign-owned banks (about one hundred at the time) voluntarily to maintain reserves equivalent to those held by Fed member banks.[11]

Late in 1973, before the Mitchell Committee released its report, the foreign bank issue again entered the congressional agenda when two bills were proposed in the House, one by Wright Patman, the other by Thomas Rees of California.[12] Although the bills differed in certain respects, the Patman bill being generally more restrictive, their essential purposes were similar. In essence, the bills attempted to create a federal regulatory structure that would strictly limit foreign banks to the subsidiary form of organization, restrict their operations to only one state, and impose federal reserve requirements. More dramatically, they also aimed at establishing a ceiling on aggregate foreign participation in the U.S. market and prohibiting foreign acquisitions of American banks. Reactions to these proposals were quick in coming.

In a letter to Patman, Federal Reserve Chairman Arthur Burns objected strenuously to the discriminatory thrust of his bill. While conceding the desirability of clarifying the legal position of foreign banks, Burns called for an approach that would ensure treatment more comparable to that of domestic peer institutions based on the principle of nondiscrimination. "Implementation of this principle in the U.S.," he wrote, "would not only offer public benefits in the domestic context, it would also set a standard for other countries on the treatment we would expect to be afforded to American banks operating within their territories."[13] Patman responded that his bill was not restrictive but was merely intended to compensate for structural differences between domestic and foreign banking systems and reflected "the traditional American view that a decentralized, responsive and competitive banking structure is essential to any concept of economic democracy."[14]

Foreign bankers themselves disagreed strongly with Patman but only uneasily supported the Burns counterproposal. Not surprisingly, they preferred no new legislative action at all. For the present, existing state regulation served most of their interests and implicitly exempted them from more onerous federal limitations. The one salutary result of the Patman and Rees bills, however, was to bring the disparate group of expatriate bankers together in a common cause. Armed with a clearer view of their mutual interest, the IFB approached the CFOB with a proposal for reunion. On the condition that the new IFB would now become politically active, the CFOB accepted, and work began on crafting a joint position.

Unlike the response of the foreign banks, the reaction of domestic banks to the Patman and Rees bills was mixed. Although there is no evidence to suggest that any group among them promoted the drafting of either bill, some banks clearly favored a more restrictive approach to foreign participation in the U.S. market. Quite commonly during this period, domestic bank executives, especially from regional or medium-sized banks, made speeches pointing out inequities resulting from the special treatment of foreign-owned operations. But it was not entirely clear whether foreign advantages (such as the ability to operate in more than one state) overbalanced their disadvantages (such as the inability of foreign branches to hold FDIC insurance or borrow from the Federal Reserve).

For smaller banks in most states except California, foreign banks were simply not yet an issue. For the larger banks, on the other hand, the Patman and Rees bills did raise serious concerns, and their collective position was clear. The New York Clearing House Association sent a letter to federal officials opposing any new federal legislation on this matter and favoring the continued authority of state regulators over foreign banks. Furthermore, the association unanimously endorsed the view that any legislation, especially if it required a strict reciprocity test for foreign entry into the United States, risked harming the offshore operations of American banks and provoking outright retaliatory measures from foreign governments.[15] Within the domestic banking community as a whole, however, a sharper divergence of views would later emerge.[16] In later years certain banks, such as regional banks in California, where foreign competitors had begun to develop retail operations, increasingly felt threatened by foreign entry into the United States. For these banks, proposals like those of Patman and Rees promised protection.

In the spring of 1974 the Mitchell Committee completed the first phase of its work and, after extensive discussions with foreign central bankers, circulated draft legislative proposals to interested parties within the United States. The proposals endorsed the principles of mutual nondiscrimination and equal treatment and brought foreign branches and agencies within the ambit of the Bank Holding Company Act, thereby forcing them to choose a home state and limiting their interstate and nonbanking activities to those permitted domestic peer institutions. They also made membership in the Federal Reserve system and in the FDIC compulsory for all foreign banks, but granted permission for foreign bank holding companies to establish Edge Act subsidiaries and to adopt a federal charter, thus allowing some limited foreign operations in ostensibly closed states. Finally, the proposals included a grandfathering clause that would allow the continuation of existing irregular activities, such as foreign interstate operations, but would forbid any new establishments.[17]

When IFB representatives met with the Mitchell Committee to discuss the proposals, their first reactions were to oppose any and all legislation and to ally themselves more closely with the New York Clearing House banks.[18] The first test of this tacit alliance occurred at the April 1974 convention of the Bankers' Association for Foreign Trade (BAFT), a professional association founded in 1921 to facilitate trade financing and now an influential lobby for U.S. banks involved in international business.[19] As the convention began, it appeared that a draft resolution calling for strict controls on foreign banks (as in the Patman and Rees bills) would carry because it clearly had the support of a majority of BAFT's members (mainly regional and smaller banks). The biggest banks, however, opposed the resolution vehemently.[20] To their chagrin, and despite intense campaigning at the convention (especially by Chase Manhattan and Citibank, which had large stakes overseas and significant correspondent business with the foreign banks), the big banks lost the battle and the resolution passed. Continued campaigning at a subsequent BAFT board meeting, however, succeeded in watering down the wording of the resolution. In essence, the larger banks opposed not only the Patman and Rees bills, but also the more moderate Mitchell Committee proposals.

In preferring no legislation at all, the money-center banks were joined by the influential Committee of State Bank Supervisors (CSBS). This Washington-based lobby for state banking authorities saw any federal legislation in this area as a direct threat to states' rights and to the traditional dual banking system. Insofar as such legislation expanded the role of the Federal Reserve, the CSBS saw it as a step toward mandatory Fed membership for all state-chartered banks. Interestingly, another supporter of the Clearing House and CSBS position appeared within the Federal Reserve itself when officials at the Federal Reserve Bank of New York came out publicly opposing the proposals of the Mitchell Committee.[21]

Despite this diversity of views, the Fed formalized the Mitchell proposals and submitted draft legislation during the closing days of the Ninety-third Congress.[22] Even though action was not expected during the current session, the board was clearly interested in preempting the reintroduction of more restrictive bills. The Fed knew that inaction on the Patman and Rees bills did not imply a lack of interest in Congress; in fact, key legislators (including Patman) were actually waiting to see what the Fed would propose. The possibility of some kind of congressional move was heightened by the collapse of New York's Franklin National Bank in May 1974 amidst a scandal involving its partial foreign ownership.[23]

Before the Ninety-fourth Congress came into session, the major points of controversy on the foreign bank issue were already clear: foreign multistate and nonbanking operations, federal oversight, monetary control, international reciprocity, the safety of domestic deposits in foreign-owned banks, and possible limits on foreign ownership and control of the American banking system. In 1975 Congress began studying these matters in light of the Fed's proposed bill. After preliminary hearings before the House Subcommittee on Financial Institutions Supervision, the entire issue became part of a major research effort sponsored by the House Committee on Banking, Currency, and Housing.[24]

*Congress Weighs the Options*

The resulting study attempted to provide the committee with broad background information and specific legislative proposals for the reform of various aspects of the nation's financial system. The study tried to come to grips with the prudential and balance-of-payments issues raised by the participation of U.S. banks in the Eurocurrency markets and with the related issue of foreign bank participation in the U.S. market. As part of this latter task, in August 1975 a congressional delegation visited central bankers and other government officials in England, France, Germany, Italy, and Switzerland to discuss the Federal Reserve proposals for foreign bank regulation and to assess the potential for retaliation against U.S. bank operations abroad. In part, the study represented a comprehensive attempt to deal with the public policy dilemmas posed by the growth of foreign banks in the domestic market.[25]

The congressional study team finally recommended eliminating any competitive advantages enjoyed by foreign banks operating domestically and argued for equalizing regulatory regimes between these institutions and their domestic peers. Moreover, they recommended imposing federal reserve requirements on the foreign banks, requiring mandatory federal chartering, establishing guidelines on optimal foreign participation, and forbidding joint interlocks and investments with domestic banks in the same banking submarkets. These recommendations quite intentionally left out two key provisions of the Fed bill: some form of grandfathering for existing foreign bank interstate and nonbanking offices and mandatory membership in the Federal Reserve system. The absence of support for grandfathering was especially curious in that foreign concerns about retroactive legislation in this regard were well known and repeatedly expressed to the congressional delegation during its European tour. Nevertheless, the study team held that it was already too late simply to legitimate all existing foreign operations in the United States; their current size represented too much of a threat to the overarching policies of geographic and functional segmentation and to existing antitrust policies.

Following completion of the study, the House Committee on Banking drafted a bill and reported it out to the full House in the spring of 1976. But attention had shifted to the Senate, where in January 1976 a subcommittee of the Committee on Banking, Housing, and Urban Affairs held three days of public hearings on the original bill proposed by the Federal Reserve. As the hearings of the Subcommittee on Financial Institutions began, the chairman, Senator Thomas McIntyre of New Hampshire, gave an indication as to why a full year had slipped by before the Senate began considering the Fed proposals. McIntyre, known to be a strong proponent of greater freedom in the banking sector, mentioned in his opening statement that the Banking Committee was reviewing possible changes in the entire federal financial regulatory apparatus, as well as amendments to the Glass-Steagall Act and to the statutes prohibiting interstate branching. It made more sense, in his view, to address the foreign bank issue in the context of these other considerations rather than separately. Nevertheless, he claimed to approach the hearings with "no preconceptions."[26]

George Mitchell, now Fed vice-chairman, and Stephen Gardner, deputy treasury secretary, were the first to testify. Mitchell defended S.958 (as the Fed-proposed bill was numbered) by pointing to the rapid recent growth of foreign banks and the "patchwork" dual regulatory system that resulted in illogical differences in the treatment of domestic and foreign banks. Summing up the final rationale for the bill, he stated:

> Federal legislation providing national standards for the treatment of foreign banks in the United States would make for a stable environment in this country. Since U.S. banks are leaders in international banking, it would also contribute to an emerging pattern by which foreign banking authorities could be guided in their treatment of banking interests originating outside of their countries. Such a common approach would facilitate cooperation between national banking authorities and promote the development of international standards of banking soundness and competition.[27]

Mitchell reinforced this position by citing the general endorsement of various central banks of the thrust of S.958. He alluded, however, to the fact that this support was contingent on a suitable grandfathering clause that would avoid penalizing existing foreign operations; inclusion of such a clause would become increasingly problematic as foreign bank growth continued, but the present level of foreign penetration was considered manageable.[28] Mitchell concluded, therefore, that grandfathering was a small price to pay for insurance against foreign retaliation.

Secretary Gardner supported these views and emphasized that legislation mandating Fed membership for all foreign banks was needed to bolster the Fed's ability to control monetary aggregates. Further, Gardner affirmed the view of the administration that a policy of national treatment as embodied in S.958, which included no reciprocity provision, was in the best interests of the United States and in conformity with the regulatory policies of most major trading partners. A more stringent policy based on reciprocity risked restrictions on U.S. banks abroad and would prove exceptionally difficult to administer, given existing structural differences between national banking systems.[29]

Disagreement with certain provisions of S.958, although not with the overall intent of the bill, came from other federal agencies. FDIC officials asserted that mandatory insurance coverage for foreign branches and agencies would subject the insurance fund to unacceptable risks because foreign parent banks could not be adequately supervised. In addition, the element of compulsion entailed by this provision, notwithstanding the opinion of the Federal Reserve, was judged by the FDIC to contravene the principle of national treatment. Related objections came from spokesmen for the State Department who contended that several provisions of the proposed bill, for example, the requirement for mandatory membership in the Federal Reserve system, did not to conform strictly with obligations contained in treaties of friendship, commerce, and navigation.[30] In a similar vein, the comptroller of the currency, having recently returned from meetings with financial leaders in Europe, testified that precipitate action on S.958 as drafted might invite retaliation. He therefore recommended delaying passage until "current reviews of 1930s policies" were completed.[31]

During the hearings, outright opposition to S.958 as a whole came from the Conference of State Bank Supervisors, the Institute of Foreign Bankers, and the New York Clearing House Association. The CSBS favored optional federal or state licensing for foreign banks and vigorously opposed the right of any bank choosing a federal license to establish within a state that normally would have refused a state license. Similarly, on the question of interstate branching, the CSBS favored allowing individual states to decide whether they wanted out-of-state foreign banks to branch internally (as Illinois had done in 1973 in a bid to make Chicago an international financial center). The CSBS also remained unconvinced about the need for the extension of federal reserve requirements to foreign offices or of Glass-Steagall restrictions to foreign securities affiliates. A split among the membership, however, precluded a firm position on the extension of FDIC coverage.[32] In general, the CSBS view represented a deliberate attempt to preserve the integrity of the dual banking system and thereby to protect state regulatory prerogatives. For the CSBS, the central battle was over governmental turf.

For its part, the IFB, now claiming an institutional membership of 116 banks, maintained that S.958 was unjustified by the pattern of growth of the foreign sector. Moreover, it was fundamentally unfair and threatened to cause significant uncertainty among legitimate participants in the American banking market. Because there seemed to be little evidence of injury among domestic competitors, and hence a lack of significant complaint, the IFB concluded bluntly that foreign banking was beneficial to the United States and that this "discriminatory" bill had its impetus simply in the centralizing ambitions of the Federal Reserve. At the same time, its spokesmen assiduously avoided any discussion of potential retaliatory actions by their respective home countries. Less reticent on the subject of retaliation, however, were spokesmen for the New York Clearing House Banks and for the Banking Federation of the European Economic Community. Both groups argued that reprisals were conceivable, especially if a permanent grandfathering provision was excluded from any final bill.

The contentions of the IFB and the Clearing House were criticized by the Bankers' Association for Foreign Trade. BAFT's spokesman, a regional banker from Rhode Island, strongly supported S.958 and viewed it as a measure to equalize the competitive advantages and disadvantages of participants in the American banking market. He noted, however, that BAFT was split on the subject with a significant minority seeing no need for new policy initiatives and a majority calling for quick federal action to fill an accidental regulatory void.[33] Senator McIntyre and the subcommittee remained unconvinced. Given the lack of consensus within the government and the banking community, McIntyre felt free to follow his prointerstate banking instincts by refusing to move S.958 after the hearings. To the dismay of the Fed, the bill died. Later that year, however, the issue reemerged in the House of Representatives.

The House Banking Committee was then considering its own legislation to bring foreign banks within the federal regulatory structure.[34] The Subcommittee on Financial Institutions Supervision held additional hearings in March, the Banking Committee itself (by a vote of 29-3) reported a resulting bill out to the floor, and the House ultimately approved it on July 30, 1976. Although the substance of the bill was similar to that of S.958, several significant differences were incorporated. Dubbed the International Banking Act of 1976 (IBA), the bill authorized the Federal Reserve to impose reserve requirements on foreign banks but did not mandate formal membership. Moreover, it required federal screening of new foreign entries, extended a federal chartering option, and devised a mechanism for foreign parent banks to indemnify the FDIC for deposit insurance coverage. Finally, while it grandfathered existing interstate banking operations (if established before May 1, 1976), it mandated that foreign banks divest themselves of securities affiliates by 1985.

During debate on the bill in the House, Representative St. Germain (then chairman of the Subcommittee on Financial Institutions Supervision) described a "broad consensus" supporting the legislation. The ensuing discussion did indicate a good deal of bipartisan agreement on the principle of extending federal regulation, in some fashion, to foreign banks. Clearer lines were drawn, however, when Representative Stephens of Georgia proposed an amendment, explicitly supported by state banking regulators, that would have allowed states to permit unlimited foreign entry notwithstanding continuing interstate branching prohibitions on domestic banks.[35] Clearly this amendment would have contradicted a major rationale for the bill, but by a closer vote than expected (185-205), the amendment was defeated. Although there was no rigid partisan split on the vote, ranking Republicans from the Banking Committee supported the amendment, as did representatives from states aspiring to create international financial centers within their borders. Another amendment, proposed by Representative Rees of California, would have moderated the effect of the limited grandfathering provision for foreign securities affiliates. Despite much discussion on the question of retaliation against U.S. banks overseas, this amendment was also defeated (142-240). The final bill carried by voice vote and was sent to the Senate. Senator McIntyre's subcommittee reopened hearings in August.[36]

During the hearings, the views of the new Carter administration were presented by the Treasury Department. The spokesman agreed that a new law was required but objected to the lack of permanent grandfathering for securities affiliates, to special federal screening procedures for new prospective entrants, and to mandatory deposit insurance guarantees. The administration was convinced that the House bill would rightly be interpreted by trading partners as retroactive and intrusive. In order to avoid a counterproductive retaliatory cycle, it advocated preserving an open door policy on the foreign entry question and a policy of national treatment, with full grandfathering, for all established foreign offices. The position of the Federal Reserve differed only marginally from that of the administration. Stephen Gardner, now a governor of the Fed, acknowledged in his testimony that the Fed was now prepared to accept a compromise on the matter of monetary control; in exchange for the right to impose reserve requirements on foreign banks, it would not insist on formal membership. For its part, the FDIC too showed a greater degree of tractability during this new set of hearings. Its official position now countenanced insuring foreign operations structured as subsidiaries with distinct capital bases and engaged mainly in domestic retail business.

The CSBS, on the other hand, again opposed crucial elements of the proposed legislation. The prohibition on new foreign bank branches in more than one state, as well as compulsory subjection of all foreign banks to Fed controls, continued to be unacceptable. The state regulators adamantly insisted on autonomy in the determination of which foreign banks, if any, could enter their markets, a right that obviated any general screening or oversight procedures initiated by the federal government. The CSBS continued to see no real need for new federal legislation in this area. In support of this view, the conference ironically marshalled extensive evidence that interstate banking (for example, through Edge Act corporations and nonbank affiliates of banks) had already become a reality. To impair the ability of states to strengthen their own financial infrastructures by encouraging the entry of foreign banks, they argued, mistakenly countered this trend. As an example, the commissioner of banks for Massachusetts outlined the efforts made in his state to reinvigorate the Port of Boston, partly by transforming the city into an international financial center. Passage of the International Banking Act in its present form threatened to undermine these efforts, for when forced to choose a home state, most foreign banks would surely remain in New York, Illinois, or California. Without the presence of some of the major established foreign banks, however, it would be doubly difficult to attract new foreign entrants to Boston. The commissioner emphasized to the senators that the attempt to renew a city like Boston in this manner was at base a matter of job creation, and he laid heavy emphasis here on the support his views had received from the Greater Boston Labor Council (AFL-CIO).

Further opposition to the House bill came from the regional stock exchanges. Contrary to the views of the New York Stock Exchange, which favored restrictions on foreign bank ownership of securities firms at least until Congress decided to modify the Glass-Steagall Act, the regional exchanges now favored the continued participation of foreign bank affiliates in their markets, mainly to help them compete more effectively with their New York rival.[37] This testimony was buttressed by statements from three European securities firms and by a delegation of senior German and French bankers representing the European Banking Federation. The Europeans described the increasing distress building on the Continent as the provisions of proposed U.S. legislation became better understood. They now viewed any change in the legal status quo as discriminatory if it impaired their abilities to participate fully in American investment banking. The legislation as drafted, they argued, inadequately took into account the different structures of overseas banking markets. In an effort to avoid giving offense, however, the Europeans shied away from any reference to retaliation and concluded that it was simply mistaken to seek equal treatment for inherently different institutions.[38]

This position was now obviously coordinated with that of the Institute of Foreign Bankers, which itself remained in total opposition to the bill. The IFB continued to look upon various aspects of the bill, including those now modified, as patently discriminatory. Its spokesman contended:

> The conclusion seems inescapable that equal treatment has been the rhetoric carrying this legislation as far as it has come but [its] real thrust is indiscriminate federalization of foreign bank regulation which is effectively administered at present by three state banking administrations [New York, Illinois, California]. . . . If the trend of the times is to preserve the American system of restraints on the power of central government and to slow down the expansion of Federal power in recent decades, it would appear that this bill bucks that trend. It does so without identification of specific offsetting public benefits and without any clearly defined justification.[39]

Warned by one Banking Committee member that failure to pass the House legislation might lead to a more restrictive bill in the future, the spokesman concluded, "In view of the unresolved differences of opinion among bank regulators and among the domestic banks which have concerned themselves with this subject, we are inclined to take our chances on the future."[40]

The last word in the hearings went to the domestic banks. Once again, BAFT testified in strong support of the bill but, indicative of an emerging compromise within its membership, recommended that a permanent grandfathering provision be included. The spokesman for the association admitted that most of its members had come to this position because they considered it unacceptable for foreign banks to be permitted to expand their multistate networks while they themselves were restricted; at the same time they believed that it would be unfair to require divestiture of existing investments made in good faith. The New York Clearing House, not surprisingly, demurred. Its spokesman called the bill unnecessary and undesirable. He excoriated the House for not including permanent grandfathering, downplayed the impact of foreign interstate branches, and rejected mandatory FDIC coverage and federal reserve requirements. In contrast to the BAFT representative who minimized the possibility of foreign retaliation, the spokesman for the New York banks concluded his testimony with a lengthy discussion about the high probability of reprisals.[41] Faced with this continuing divergence of views and constrained by an imminent dissolution of the Ninety-fourth Congress, Senator McIntyre and his colleagues concluded once again that the time had not yet come for the International Banking Act.

## Moving toward a Policy

Although no decisive action was yet taken, in retrospect the early Fed proposals, initial congressional study and debate, and continuing discussions with other governments constituted an important stage in the development of a national American policy on foreign banking. They also represented the formative steps of a deliberate strategy to encourage a liberal policy convergence among other countries. What slowed both developments down was a traditional problem for the American state in situations where the need for action was not urgent — an unwillingness to move much faster than the underlying support of those domestic interests most involved would allow. Definitive action would wait on the emergence of consensus among domestic banks. In the meantime, foreign institutions continued their growth in the American market.

The Federal Reserve began collecting data on the size and scope of foreign banking operations in late 1972. The data showed that both the absolute and the relative expansion of those operations was dramatic during the period of debate on federal legislation. The aggregate assets of foreign bank offices grew by 176 percent between 1972 and 1977 (compared to 38.1 percent for domestic banks), while their liabilities increased by 282 percent (39.7 percent for domestic banks). In terms of market share, foreign banks accounted for 5 percent of U.S. bank assets in 1972 and 10.4 percent in 1977. Of total loans made to American corporate borrowers, they held 14.5 percent in 1972 and 39 percent five years later. The number of foreign offices carrying on this business expanded from 101 to 210 over the same period. Japan accounted for 28 percent of these offices in 1972 and 25 percent in 1977; Canada for 21 percent in 1972 and 12 percent in 1977; and Europe, for 33 percent in 1972 and 37 percent in

*Table 6.* Foreign direct investment in the United States, 1965–82 (U.S.$ billions)

| Country | 1965 | 1970 | 1975 | 1976 | 1977 | 1978 | 1979 | 1980 | 1981 | 1982 |
|---|---|---|---|---|---|---|---|---|---|---|
| Canada | 2.4 | 3.2 | 5.4 | 5.9 | 5.7 | 6.2 | 7.2 | 10.1 | 9.9 | 9.8 |
| Britain | 2.9 | 4.1 | 6.3 | 5.8 | 6.4 | 7.6 | 9.8 | 12.2 | 15.6 | 23.3 |
| Netherlands | 1.3 | 2.2 | 5.3 | 6.3 | 7.8 | 10.1 | 12.7 | 16.9 | 23.1 | 21.5 |
| Switzerland | 0.9 | 1.5 | 2.1 | 2.3 | 2.7 | 2.9 | 3.4 | 3.9 | 4.3 | 4.8 |
| Other European | 1.0 | 1.7 | 4.9 | 5.8 | 6.9 | 8.6 | 11.5 | 12.8 | 17.5 | 18.9[b] |
| Japan | 0.1 | 0.2 | 0.6 | 1.2 | 1.8 | 2.7 | 3.5 | 4.2 | 7.0 | 8.7 |
| Other | 0.2 | 0.4 | 3.1 | 3.5 | 3.5 | 4.4 | 6.4 | 8.3 | 13.0 | 14.8 |
| Total[a] | 8.8 | 13.3 | 27.7 | 30.8 | 34.8 | 42.5 | 54.5 | 68.4 | 90.4 | 101.8 |

SOURCE: U.S. Department of Commerce, Bureau of the Census, *Statistical Abstract of the United States* (Washington: GPO, 1984), 822.

[a] Book value at year-end. Prior to 1975, covers U.S. firms in which foreign interest was 25 percent or more; after 1975, covers U.S. firms in which foreign interest was 10 percent or more.

[b] The major components of the 1982 figure include: Belgium and Luxembourg, 2.4; France, 4.7; Germany, 8.2; Italy, 0.9; Sweden, 1.5.

1977. The bulk of this activity remained concentrated in New York, California, and Illinois; in 1977 foreign banks controlled 27 percent, 14 percent, and 4 percent, respectively, of total banking assets in these states. Twenty-three foreign banks operated in two or more states in 1972; over fifty did so by 1977.[42] Although different foreign banks maintained different market strategies, several common factors helped explain this tremendous expansion of activity. Principal among them was the marked growth of foreign investment in the United States (Table 6).

Reports of market participants and circumstantial statistical evidence indicate that banks moved with their clients to the American market.[43] But other factors were also at work. The expansion of the Eurocurrency markets since the 1960s and the collapse of the fixed exchange rate system in the 1970s transformed bank strategies by providing incentives to establish diversified international networks. Within that context the dynamic overseas thrusts of American banks in previous years made the task of diversification more urgent. As banks felt compelled to compensate for incursions into their own home markets, and simultaneously discovered new sources of earnings abroad, defensive and offensive marketing strategies moved in tandem. Banking competition became internationalized to an extent previously unknown.

At the same time, despite periodic vicissitudes, the U.S. dollar remained the pivotal currency in international trade and investment and many global banks saw a U.S network as a tool for building a more stable base of dollar deposits. Further stimulus in this direction came from the relaxation of U.S. capital controls in January

1974, a move that allowed banking offices resident in America once again to extend dollar-denominated credit directly to offshore borrowers.[44] Once the process of foreign entry had begun, market dynamics only accelerated foreign bank growth. The sheer size and diversity of the domestic American market provided opportunities for business expansion unrelated to initial strategies. Moreover, the peculiarities of American banking law and business practice created a demand for certain retail and securities capabilities of foreign institutions, while growing import and export activity generated a need for trade financing expertise. Finally, although the existence of all of these incentives makes it impossible to gauge accurately its discrete impact, another factor at work throughout the 1970s was the urge on the part of foreign parent banks to establish or expand in the United States before possible enactment of restraining legislation. Despite its indecisiveness, the tone and duration of the debate on the subject surely made an impression in the boardrooms of international banks.

With all of these developments occurring in the marketplace, a full year passed before Congress resumed consideration of the International Banking Act. In July 1977 the House Subcommittee on Financial Institutions Supervision took up the issue again in another set of hearings after a new version of the IBA, virtually identical to the one passed in 1976, had been resubmitted.[45] As he opened the hearings, Chairman St. Germain admitted the fragility of what seemed last year a "broad consensus" underpinning the bill, and he noted that "considerable apprehension had been voiced by an increasing number of individuals and the foreign institutions they represent as to the impact of this bill on their existing, and I must emphasize, their contemplated future operations in the United States."[46] Nevertheless, he reaffirmed the need for the legislation, particularly in view of the Federal Reserve's insistence that this was its top legislative priority. In his own opening statement, the ranking minority member of the subcommittee, Representative Rousselot, reintroduced two major points of contention by supporting the Stephens amendments to permit states to license branches of foreign banks established elsewhere (even if interstate prohibitions remained for domestic banks) and to limit Federal Reserve authority strictly to those foreign banks opting for federal charters.

A familiar lineup of witnesses testified at the hearings. Leading the pro-IBA forces, Governor Gardner of the Fed began by asserting that the continuing escape of foreign institutions from federal control undermined the effectiveness of monetary policy. Fed oversight in this sphere was justified for reasons of equity among comparable institutions and by ample precedent in other countries. He contended, however, that criticism of the clause providing temporary grandfathering for existing foreign securities affiliates deserved greater weight; for such activities, the majority of the Fed's Board of Governors favored permanent grandfathering.[47] On two other issues the board proposed compromises. First, a formal federal screening authority over new foreign entries would not be sought. Instead, continuing informal consultations between state regulators and relevant federal departments would suffice. Second, the Fed would seek to limit the extraterritorial reach of U.S. law by explicitly exempting the off-shore activities of foreign banks from any nonbanking prohibitions included in the IBA as long as the on-shore dealings of foreign banks with related clients (such as between a branch of a European bank and the U.S. subsidiary of an industrial concern partly owned by its parent bank) were carried out on an arm's length basis.[48] The board was not prepared to compromise, however, on the two central provisions jeopardized by the Stephens amendments, and it continued to favor mandatory FDIC coverage at least for the domestic deposits of foreign banks.[49] During questioning, Gardner was repeatedly asked if the IBA contemplated by the board would provoke retaliation or be seen as abrogating any treaty commitments. He dismissed such fears, saying, "No other sovereign nation lacks the kinds of controls over foreign banks in their jurisdictions that we lack over foreign banks in ours."[50]

Also strongly supporting the IBA was the Bankers' Association for Foreign Trade. Once again a BAFT spokesman stated, "The vast majority of our members support passage of legislation this year which would effectively equalize the operating environment for both foreign and domestic banking activities in the U.S."[51] Certain details of the BAFT position had been modified slightly. But BAFT's core concern remained unchanged: the existing and future operations of foreign banks subverted traditional geographic restrictions on banking in the U.S. market. If new national policy was to be designed in this area, it should occur after open debate on this central issue, and any resulting interstate banking privileges should be extended to all.[52] The other major trade association now favoring the bill was the Securities Industry Association, the major lobby for American investment banks. This group supported the IBA as drafted and opposed any move to extend the ten-year grandfathering clause for foreign securities affiliates. Simply put, they wanted all commercial banks, whether foreign or domestic, to stay out of investment banking, and they were very explicit in saying so.[53]

The administration generally endorsed the IBA. Officials from the Treasury Department and the State Department, after previously coordinating their testimony with that of the Federal Reserve, testified in favor of passage of the bill with certain amendments. The Treasury was particularly concerned with upholding the principle of nondiscrimination and therefore opposed a section instituting a federal screening apparatus, which could lead to a tacit reciprocity test contrary to U.S. open door policies. Such screening, its spokesman contended, "could reduce permissible international banking activities to the least common denominator, as countries tighten regulations to achieve strict reciprocity. Furthermore, it could be an administrative nightmare to enforce different sets of rules for different foreign banks operating in this country."[54] The State Department agreed with this view and again added that certain provisions of the IBA, such as mandatory FDIC coverage, federal screening, and temporary grandfathering of securities affiliates, appeared to violate international obligations. Given suitable modifications in these areas of the bill, however, the administration had no difficulty supporting passage.

The most significant opposition to the IBA came once again from the Conference of State Bank Supervisors, the New York Clearing House, the Institute for Foreign Bankers, and the EEC Banking Federation. Joining them this time was the governor of the state of Georgia. By now the respective views of the major lobbying groups were familiar. For their own reasons, all disliked the erosion of the dual banking system represented by the IBA. The CSBS, supported by the governor, wanted to preserve flexibility for states to pursue their own development and regulatory plans.[55] This desire to preserve options resonated with the foreign bankers and the Clearing House. The IFB, now speaking for 142 institutional members, held that although the IBA appeared to be nondiscriminatory in principle, it would in practice penalize foreign banks. A spokesman again pressed for no legislation at all, but in the first indication of a willingness to bend slightly, he concluded that a potentially acceptable bill would be one leaving licensing discretion to the states, making federal controls and oversight optional, and permanently grandfathering existing nonconforming operations.[56]

This latter point remained the principal concern of the European Banking Federation, although its representatives continued to be highly circumspect in any discussion of potential retaliation.[57] Less restrained, however, were the New York banks. Given American bank assets of $225 billion overseas at that point, the Clearing House maintained that the risk and potential cost of retaliatory moves by other countries was simply too high. More specifically, any movement in the United States toward more restriction might drive international banking standards away from national treatment in the direction of strict reciprocity policies, a development that would harm American interests abroad. In view of this possibility, the New York bankers concluded, foreign interstate and investment banking activities should be permitted to continue and federal controls should be extended on an optional basis only.

Following the hearings, lobbying continued behind the scenes.[58] On October 12, 1977, the subcommittee completed the mark-up of the bill after approving several major changes. Before consideration by the full Banking Committee, Chairman Henry Reuss and Representative St. Germain sent the amended bill to the Federal Reserve for comment.[59] It took three months but Fed Chairman Arthur Burns finally responded with a blunt and detailed repudiation of the proposed bill. As amended in the House, the new IBA limited Fed control to those foreign banks opting for federal charters, allowed states to override interstate branching restrictions, restricted FDIC coverage, and placed a ten-year limit on grandfathered foreign bank securities affiliates. Inasmuch as each of these amendments directly contradicted the recommendations of the Fed, Burns stated that the board could not support enactment of the bill. On the matter of possible foreign retaliation, he noted that Governor Gardner had again visited with banking leaders in the EEC and concluded that the absence of permanent grandfathering "could do great harm to U.S. interests abroad." He concluded that the bill's provisions served "neither the overriding federal interest in regulating foreign banking in the U.S. nor any legitimate concerns of federalism."[60] Other interested parties, however, obviously had another view of those "legitimate concerns." The subcommittee bill clearly reflected successful lobbying efforts by the CSBS and various state governments.

Despite the impasse with the Fed, the House Banking Committee continued to work on the legislation, and quiet lobbying intensified. The resulting bill was introduced in the House on February 9, 1978, and referred back to the Banking Committee for final consideration. On February 28 the committee sent it again to the floor by a vote of 46-0.[61] At this point the bill reflected several major concessions to the Fed. First, the Fed was given authority to impose reserve requirements on state-chartered foreign branches, agencies, and investment companies (but not banking subsidiaries) "after consultation" and "in cooperation" with state authorities provided that the offices were owned by foreign parents having worldwide assets in excess of $1 billion.[62] Second, with regard to interstate branching, the subcommittee amendment was reversed and foreign banks were not allowed to branch outside their "home states" (the state where the bank initially decided to accept domestic deposits) until such time as domestic banks could do so. Third, foreign securities affiliates operating before May 23, 1977, were permanently grandfathered. Finally, the committee watered down original proposals for federal screening by simply directing the secretary of the treasury to issue guidelines that would "take into account the treatment by foreign governments of U.S. banks which do business in their respective countries."[63]

The underlying tug-of-war between state regulators and the Fed continued when the full House debated the new bill on April 6, 1978. Much of the debate focused on the interstate branching prohibition; the central dispute remained the Fed's call for competitive equality between like-situated competitors versus the insistence of state regulators on a satisfactory degree of regulatory autonomy. Following extended discussion on this matter several floor votes were taken. The first rejected an amendment to strengthen the bill's interstate branching provision. The second reversed the restrictive wording that came out of the Banking Committee and restored the subcommittee's more liberal clause permitting individual states to determine whether to allow foreign branches, notwithstanding McFadden Act prohibitions. Other changes made by the Banking Committee stood, and the bill was passed by a vote of 367–64.[64] The revised bill was sent to the Senate for another hearing before Senator McIntyre's subcommittee.

As soon as that hearing began on June 21, 1978, it became evident that something had changed. From Senator McIntyre came the opening statement:

> For my part, I am now of the opinion that the climate is now ripe for enactment of this legislation. In previous years, I had some reservations about the necessity for the various proposals before us at that time. I now feel, however, that the continuing growth of foreign banking activity in this country has generated sufficient interest to establish better Federal monitoring. . . . Moreover, I believe that the political climate is still relatively calm which, hopefully, will enable us to fashion a rational bill. Further delay may very well result in a more restrictive piece of legislation which, in my opinion, would serve nobody's interest.[65]

In the subcommittee, which had heretofore been the graveyard of the IBA, several factors were now motivating action. The rapidly accelerating growth of foreign banks in the American market could no longer be ignored. According to evidence presented by the Fed, 60 foreign banks with $37 billion in assets in 1973 had become 122 banks with assets over $90 billion by April 1978. Their aggregate share of commercial and industrial loans now represented over 20 percent of similar loans by large U.S. banks. In selected markets, especially California and New York, these formerly marginal and specialized institutions were now aggressively diversifying into small business lending and retail banking.[66] The implication of this activity, which McIntyre failed to bring out, was that these institutions now represented significant competition to a broad range of domestic banks across a wide range of geographic and functional submarkets. Of those domestic banks, the most vulnerable were the middle-sized regional banks; foreign banks had targeted their important domestic corporate clients, and they had limited ability or inclination to compensate for such inroads by expanding abroad. The larger domestic banks, of course, had this option and had long been pursuing foreign market shares. Conversely, the majority of small local banks across the country still operated in relatively protected retail markets, for most states remained closed or financially unattractive to foreign banks. As one foreign banker noted at the time, "The regional banks are feeling the pinch and are pushing very hard on the International Banking Act."[67]

Another changing factor was the public profile of the foreign banks. Not only had they grown significantly in quantitative terms, but their new strategies for penetrating the American market raised new and sensitive political questions. The initial growth of the foreign sector had usually come about by way of de novo establishment and expansion (wholly owned, start-up offices). For some banks this was a slow and painful process entailing unsustainable price-cutting strategies to build market share. As their domestic counterparts became more competitive, many were left with their "foreign" labels and higher funding costs.[68] Faced with this increasingly competitive market, some foreign banks chose a new strategy: growth by means of acquiring existing domestic institutions. The number of such acquisitions picked up markedly in 1977, and foreign investors (of which 90 percent were themselves banks) had purchased controlling interests in forty-two existing American banks by late 1978 and seventy-one by mid-1979.[69] The takeover of Franklin National by European-American in 1974 had already brought this method of expansion into public view. But two spectacular foreign bids in the spring of 1978 heightened awareness of its possibilities both inside and outside banking circles. Hongkong and Shanghai Banking Corporation bid for 51 percent of the shares of Marine Midland Bank, and National Westminster of Britain sought 75 percent of National Bank of North America; the domestic targets were then, respectively, the seventh and tenth largest banks in New York State, and both were clearing banks. Fears that these developments signaled the beginning of a massive foreign takeover of the American banking system had already been mooted during the recent House debate on the IBA, and proponents of the bill had had to fight tenaciously to keep them in the background in order not to disrupt consideration of the more manageable issues already addressed in the bill.[70]

Another factor helps explain the subcommittee's new-found enthusiasm for the IBA. Under its new chairman, William Miller, and after enduring its recent setbacks in the House, the Federal Reserve had become noticeably more amenable to compromise. Very quickly in what turned out to be his short tenure in office, Miller had forged close alliances on Capitol Hill; in particular, he had established good working relationships with key senators on the Banking Committee. Other changes in the legislative environment became evident during the course of the hearing.

The list of witnesses began with Miller, who offered an important concession on the contentious interstate branching issue. He maintained that restrictions on interstate branching by foreign banks were fully consonant with the principle of national treatment; similar banks required similar regulatory consideration. He therefore recommended reversing the House amendment on this matter (section 5 of the bill) and imposing existing federal and state geographic restrictions on foreign banks until such time as comparable domestic banks obtained formal interstate branching powers. Further cross-state expansion could be permitted, however, by amending the Edge Act to allow foreign-owned banks to establish Edge corporations. Should this still not be enough to satisfy those states wishing to create international financial centers, Miller allowed, the Fed would reluctantly go along with enabling foreign banks to establish agencies on a multistate basis. In addition, Miller conceded on the question of mandatory Fed membership for all foreign banks, but he insisted that the Fed needed authority to impose reserves not just on foreign branches and agencies chartered federally, but on all state-chartered foreign offices, including subsidiaries. Fighting his own intrabureaucratic battles, Miller also asserted that foreign banks should be forced to carry FDIC insurance on domestic deposits and that the Fed should be given primary, not residual, supervisory and examining authority over all foreign banks.

As usual, the antithetical view came the CSBS, which supported section 5 as written and vigorously disputed the Fed's need to impose reserve requirements on state-chartered foreign banks. He also categorically rejected Miller's request for primary supervisory authority over any state banks and argued for optional deposit insurance.[71] Although for different reasons, the comptroller of the currency and the chairman of the FDIC also testified in opposition to certain recommendations of the Fed. As the principal supervisor for all national banks, the comptroller naturally held that he, and not the Fed, should have primary responsibility for supervising the foreign peers of the national banks. On the interstate branching issue, however, the comptroller agreed that national treatment required competitive equality, and he therefore endorsed Miller's position. On the matter of most concern to him, the chairman of the FDIC again stated his preference for optional deposit insurance, also on the grounds of national treatment, but expressed his willingness to go along with mandatory insurance if it could be waived whenever the FDIC determined that home country insurance of parent banks adequately covered U.S. operations. Nevertheless, he averred, under either scheme the FDIC would have to assume the major supervisory role over institutions that it insured.[72]

Sensing that the IBA now had a stronger chance of passage than in previous years, a greater number of organizations from the private sector submitted opinions. BAFT was no longer alone in its call for a stronger set of restrictions on foreign banks. Contrary to those who called the IBA discriminatory, spokesmen for BAFT argued that the current regulatory treatment of foreign banks translated into effective discrimination against domestic institutions. Consequently, the concession to state regulators, mistakenly included in section 5 of the draft bill during debate on the House floor, should be excised, and interstate branching restrictions should be imposed on the foreigners. Although grandfathering of existing offices was acceptable, all new establishments should conform to domestic practice. Changes in the McFadden Act should not occur by default.

Joining BAFT for the first time in this stance were two other bankers' associations, the Association of Reserve City Bankers and the American Bankers' Association (ABA). The former group represented over 160 banks located in the principal banking cities of the United States. In a statement calling for a tightening of section 5 of the draft bill, these banks labeled foreign financial institutions as an increasing economic threat to the domestic banking system. The ABA, the largest banking lobby in the country, had long been reticent about taking a public position on the foreign bank issue, both because of splits among its membership and because many of its members with strong interests in the matter felt adequately represented by BAFT or the Clearing House. But now the majority of its directors believed the time had come for an official contribution to the debate. On section 5, the ABA agreed with BAFT and called for a tightening of restrictions. As the association's president put it, "We believe foreign and domestic banks should compete on a level playing field and abide by the same rules and regulations."[73] Further, the association acceded to the Fed's desire to impose monetary controls and federal supervision on foreign banks but only with the proviso that state-chartered banking subsidiaries be exempted. Because the affected foreign offices were seen as unique, the ABA concluded that the extension of this authority would not jeopardize the dual banking system. An intensive national lobbying campaign focused on key legislators quietly complemented the ABA's public pronouncements.

The testimony of the Institute of Foreign Bankers flatly contradicted the domestic bank associations. Unconvincingly, but unabashedly, its spokesman asserted, "We can find very little to justify enactment of this bill.... There appears to be no domestic bank outcry against interstate wholesale banking or related financial services." But finally seeing the wisdom of beginning as graceful a bow as possible before what was looking inevitable, the spokesman concluded, "We hear speculation that the several large recently proposed foreign bank acquisitions may stimulate new protectionist concerns about foreign bank participation in the U.S. market.... In deference to this reported mood that something must be done at this time, we will include in our comments proposals for improvements in the bill."[74]

Conspicuously absent from the banking fraternity during this phase of the debate were the New York Clearing Banks. The former allies of the foreign banks did not even submit a written statement to the subcommittee this time. The growing scope of competitive pressures from foreign bank activity could no longer be treated as a peripheral matter even for major banks. Unity among them on this score had lessened, and whatever rationale there had been for supporting exceptional treatment for foreign banks was quickly evaporating. The threat of retaliation abroad had evidently receded; more importantly, such bids as that of Hong Kong's quasi-central bank for a member institution (Marine Midland) were profoundly disturbing and had helped convince the banks at least to acquiesce in, if not publicly to support, passage of the International Banking Act. After many years of contention, there now existed a tacit consensus between larger and smaller domestic banks, a consensus reflected in the public position of the ABA. The stage was therefore set for final legislative action, and the time had come for compromise.

The most promising move in this direction came from Senator Stevenson of Illinois. Seeking a way to break the logjam over interstate branching after the latest hearing of the Senate subcommittee, Stevenson and his staff developed the concept of the limited branch and tied this to a liberalization of the Edge Act. Stevenson proposed that foreign banks designate a home state but remain able to establish special branches in other states where permitted by state law. Although these branches outside the home state would have unrestricted powers on the lending side, their deposit-taking powers would be limited to those of an Edge Act corporation; that is, they could only accept deposits related to international transactions. At the same time, the Edge Act itself would be changed to allow domestic banks to engage in a wider range of lending activities with fewer technical restrictions and foreign banks to open Edge Act subsidiaries, an option formerly precluded by citizenship requirements for directors. Stevenson's compromise proved to be a critical turning point in the legislative history of the IBA. Immediately it received support from the Fed, the Treasury, and BAFT.[75] Although the FDIC, CSBS, IFB, and EEC Banking Federation initially expressed misgivings, all eventually decided that they could live with it.[76] Other compromises were made during the mark-up of the House bill in the full Senate Banking Committee.

While intense lobbying efforts continued, the Banking Committee worked on the IBA in July and unanimously reported an amended bill to the Senate floor on July 26. The bill required foreign banks to choose a home state and allowed them to apply for federal charters.[77] In the name of national treatment, the bill included the Stevenson amendment to limit the ability of foreign banks to accept deposits in states other than their home states without impairing their ability to undertake other types of business across state lines.[78] The bill also made FDIC insurance available but voluntary unless retail deposits were involved. On the issue of monetary control, the Fed was given the ability to impose reserve requirements on all federally chartered foreign branches and agencies as well as on those chartered by states after consultation with the states involved. Foreign banks were held not to be eligible for Fed membership, but those subject to such requirements were given access to the Fed's discounting and clearing facilities.[79] On the supervisory question, the bill split primary examination functions between the comptroller, the FDIC, and state supervisors, depending on how the foreign bank to be supervised was chartered. The Fed was given residual authority to conduct special examinations of foreign bank offices, but only in consultation with the primary examiner.[80] The bill also permanently grandfathered existing nonbanking affiliates of foreign banks, but gave the Fed the right to review the situation after seven years. Glass-Steagall prohibitions and other traditional rules were applied to new operations.[81] As for future foreign bank entry, the bill explicitly excluded reciprocity tests, but in an intentional effort to encourage the adoption of national treatment in other countries, it mandated a study by the administration on the treatment of U.S. banks abroad.[82]

## THE POLICY OUTCOME: THE INTERNATIONAL BANKING ACT OF 1978

As intended, the compromise bill did not make anyone entirely happy, but it did successfully foster a welcome spirit of resignation. The Federal Reserve certainly received less than it had hoped for in 1973, but it could live with its disappointment. Some members of the domestic banking community would have preferred tighter restrictions on foreign banks but were satisfied with their new competitive powers under a liberalized Edge Act. The IFB grumbled about the restrictions on limited branches but ultimately accepted the bill with relief. The CSBS never came out in support of the bill, but it ultimately acquiesced in the new balance struck within the dual banking system. Similarly, the FDIC continued to resist certain details but now lacked any capability of changing them.[83]

The International Banking Act of 1978 came before the full Senate on August 15. Without dissenting opinion the bill passed and was sent back to the House. House leaders were prepared to accept the amendments of the Senate without the need for a joint conference, and the bill went to the floor on August 17. After summary debate the bill passed without objection and was signed into law one month later.[84]

The IBA may be seen as an explicit expression of a normative standard that American officials would now much more assertively promote in other countries and against which they would evaluate the treatment of American institutions abroad. Passage of the act signaled a new phase in the activism with which certain segments of the government, notably the Treasury Department and congressional banking committees, would push for policy movement overseas. This would not, in the end, determine that movement, for overriding domestic political interests were as important in other countries as they had been in the United States itself. But the clearer articulation of increasingly shared expectations would move in the same direction as those interests and subtly encourage the development of a broader normative framework to sustain openness and freer international competition in banking.

Those observers who contended that the IBA was on balance a liberalizing and not a protectionist piece of legislation appeared vindicated by the continued expansion of foreign banks within the United States after 1978.[85] By May 1979, 144 foreign banks were operating 315 offices (up from 210 in 1977) and maintaining assets of $97 billion, an increase of 92 percent in two years. Of the 136 foreign parent banks operating agencies and branches, more than half had offices (with total assets of $16 billion) in states other than their designated home state.[86] This continued expansion rekindled public and congressional interest in several policy areas left open in the delicate compromises of the IBA. As implemented, for example, the IBA further eroded traditional constraints on interstate banking by making it easier to establish Edge Act subsidiaries and branches.[87] Similarly, the formal exemption of foreign bank securities operations in existence before 1978 contributed to rising pressures for reform of functional constraints associated with the Glass-Steagall Act. One of the most contentious policy issues, however, involved the direct acquisition of domestic banks by foreign interests.

## Aftermath of the IBA

During final congressional deliberations on the IBA, disquiet about foreign bank expansion by way of acquisition had barely been contained. The drafters of the final bill itself had avoided the subject. As foreign acquisition activity subsequently accelerated, however, the highly sensitive and symbolic issue became openly controversial. The bid by the Hongkong and Shanghai Banking Corporation (HSBC) for Marine Midland, in particular, brought policy concerns into sharper focus by raising concrete questions about the proper role and scope of foreign institutions in the domestic banking system, about the ability of single governments to supervise and stabilize banks that were becoming increasingly cosmopolitan, and about international reciprocity. As the takeover attempt proceeded, it also focused attention once again on the question of the appropriate relationship between state and federal regulators in America's dual banking system. A brief review of the transaction will therefore be useful.

In 1978 Marine Midland Bank, with over $10 billion in assets, was the seventh largest bank in New York State and the single most important bank in the market outside New York City. It was also seriously troubled and in need of capital. Since union with a domestic bank capable of taking on its problems would probably have raised antitrust challenges (and surely would have limited the autonomy or long-term employment of the existing Marine management), the bank looked favorably on the April 1978 offer from HSBC to take control of 51 percent of its shares (and to retain existing management) in exchange for a capital injection of $200 million. Since Marine was a state-chartered bank holding company, both the New York Banking Department and the Federal Reserve Board had to approve the transaction.

Owing to the complexity of the proposal, state regulators required an extended period of time for analysis. Initial studies completed by the New York Banking Department noted the benefits to be derived from the acquisition, especially the healthy capital injection and stimulus to competition.[88] Further consideration, however, brought up troubling doubts about the ultimate implications of the transaction. State officials wondered if the initial capital inflow would quickly be reversed by the payment of excessive dividends, and they worried that local communities might suffer if the new foreign owners refused to reinvest a fair share of their profits in the local economy. In view of difficulty encountered in obtaining financial information from HSBC, they also became concerned about the adequacy of HSBC's supervision in Hong Kong. But perhaps more important than any of these uncertainties were the concerns Muriel Siebert, the New York State banking superintendent, highlighted in a letter to Henry Reuss, chairman of the House Banking Committee. "I cannot reconcile the fact that our own banks operate under statutory and regulatory restrictions which place them at a distinct disadvantage relative to their foreign competitors in these proposed acquisitions, [and] opening the U.S. banking system to foreign acquisitions will not create equivalent acquisition opportunities for our banks abroad."[89] Siebert called, therefore, for an immediate review of national policy before existing bids were approved. The banking committees of both the House and the Senate agreed.

Just prior to the announcements of such a review, however, the Federal Reserve declared that it had approved the HSBC-Marine transaction under the Bank Holding Company Act.[90] All that was needed now was concomitant assent from New York. By then, however, pressure was in fact rapidly building within the state to deny approval.[91] To circumvent this impending deadlock, the managers of Marine decided to relinquish their bank's state license and apply to the comptroller of the currency for a federal charter. Events thereafter moved rapidly. Immediately upon hearing of Marine's plan, Siebert released her department's final study of the HSBC application, which outlined the reasons for denial or delay.[92] She then carried her battle to Washington. The effort proved fruitless, however, for the comptroller quickly announced approval of Marine's application for a federal charter.[93] Marine thereby became a national bank outside the jurisdiction of New York State, and its Fed-approved acquisition by HSBC was automatically consummated.

Senate hearings on foreign acquisitions and a range of related banking issues began in the summer of 1979.[94] Setting the stage, a proposal was put forward by Senator John Heinz of Pennsylvania to place a six-month moratorium on foreign takeovers of American banks, during which time Congress would conduct its policy review.[95] In the now familiar pattern, federal and state regulators disagreed as they testified before the Senate Banking Committee. The Fed, supported by the Treasury and the comptroller, opposed the moratorium on the grounds that it would impede healthy capital flows and hinder competition. To the contrary, Muriel Siebert held large bank acquisitions to be of a different order from most foreign investment. Moreover, she contended, if foreign banks were to be permitted to continue such activities, then domestic institutions should be accorded the same privilege.[96]

A CSBS spokesman appeared with Siebert, but for him the issue was not quite so clear. Reflecting the wishes of his membership, the spokesman preferred to spend most of his time discussing another subject under review, a Fed proposal to provide greater operational flexibility for Edge Act corporations, an idea not surprisingly viewed by state regulators as another threat to the dual banking system. For the same reason, while not necessarily relishing the prospect of increasing foreign takeovers, many CSBS members had great difficulty accepting Siebert's conclusion that out-of-state banks should be able to bid on banks within their jurisdictions. Nevertheless, in deference to Siebert, who had recently engaged in a celebrated struggle with federal regulators, the CSBS spokesman took no definitive position one way or the other.[97]

The domestic banking community was itself not of one mind on the issue of foreign acquisitions. The Clearing House banks did not take a formal position, and BAFT did not testify. But spokesmen for several individual banks, including Citibank, Morgan, and important regional banks in California and Texas, did testify against the moratorium. The American Bankers' Association agreed with this view but requested relaxation of restraints on domestic banks, especially in cases where a takeover of a failing bank was necessary.

Besides, according to the ABA, regulators already possessed enough authority to prevent unwise or unwanted foreign intrusions. Most foreign acquisitions that had gone ahead were seen to be healthy, and foreign acquirers had shown themselves to be good corporate citizens, obeying the spirit as well as the letter of American law. A dissenting voice came, however, from the Independent Bankers' Association, an organization of small local banks. A spokesman for this group strongly endorsed the moratorium and called for further efforts to limit foreign penetration of the banking system.[98]

The hearings did not lead to the immediate adoption of the moratorium proposal but did intensify debate on the proper scope of foreign participation in the banking system. An acceleration of foreign acquisition activity following the hearings, however, was a more successful stimulant to policy change. Headlines were generated as National Westminster Bank, Standard and Chartered Bank, Algemene Bank Nederland, and other major foreign institutions aggressively bid for control of existing American banks in New York, California, Illinois, and Florida.[99] Concerned that this continuing wave of activity was being artificially stimulated by unusually depressed bank stock prices and an undervalued dollar, Congress attached a six-month moratorium provision to the omnibus Depository Institutions Deregulation and Monetary Control Act of 1980. At the urging of the Federal Reserve, however, the moratorium was not renewed when it expired.[100] Nevertheless, congressional concerns did not entirely abate.

In the House of Representatives, Congressman Benjamin Rosenthal of New York and others on his subcommittee of the Government Operations Committee became keenly interested in the acquisition issue during the Hongkong and Shanghai negotiations. After the Fed approved the Marine takeover, Rosenthal requested a reversal of the decision. The Fed refused, the deal later went through, and Rosenthal held public hearings in the spring of 1980 to investigate the matter.[101] The same motivation prompted the House Banking Committee's Subcommittee on Financial Institutions to request a comprehensive review of the situation from the General Accounting Office.[102] Although the resulting GAO report took seriously the matter of ensuring equal treatment for domestic banks potentially interested in acquisitions, it did highlight the positive effects of most completed foreign acquisitions.

The more extravagant fears related to the foreign acquisition issue were also calmed by the simultaneous publication of a series of studies completed by the staff of the comptroller of the currency.[103] The studies pointed out that ninety-two foreign acquisitions had taken place between 1970 and 1980, thirty-six by foreign banks (accounting for 74 percent of the total assets acquired and 23 percent of all foreign bank assets in the United States) and fifty-six by foreign individuals (mainly purchasing small institutions). Despite this activity, the bulk of foreign bank growth in the United States reflected de novo expansion. Moreover, the banks acquired over the decade represented only 1 percent of all U.S. commercial banks and 4.5 percent of all insured commercial banking assets. Contrary to common fears, the reasons for acquisition strategies on the part of foreign banks were found to have more to do with domestic receptivity to capital infusions, legislative impediments to domestic acquirers, and perceptions of American political and economic stability than with depressed bank stock prices. The studies also identified two other factors that had now become determinants of acquisition strategies: the competitive incentive to counter moves made by rivals and the fear that future congressional action would preclude purchases not made immediately.[104] Finally, the studies presented evidence that foreign bank investment usually strengthened the balance sheets of the acquired bank and did not lead to a shift of assets out of the local market.

Although the comptroller's studies did not completely silence debate on the acquisition issue, they did temper the enthusiasm of those pushing for outright closure of the American market to this type of foreign investment. In early 1981 the Midland Bank of Britain (no relation to Marine Midland), to its later regret, bid for a majority interest in the troubled Crocker National Bank of San Francisco, and the takeover was approved with little difficulty. Later that year, however, new concerns arose when Banca Commerciale Italiana, a major institution indirectly owned by the Italian government, applied to the Fed for permission to acquire the Long Island Trust Company, a billion-dollar bank holding company in New York. The bid raised difficult questions about the applicability of the national treatment principle and the nonbanking restrictions of U.S. banking law. After much deliberation, the Fed approved the acquisition in June 1982 with several conditions to ensure continuing conformity with domestic law. But as it announced this decision, the Fed requested guidance from Congress on the broader question of the place of nationalized foreign banks within the U.S. system. The request apparently stymied the legislators, and although Congressman Rosenthal held further inconclusive hearings on the subject, the banking committees took no further action and provided no further guidance.[105] Foreign bank expansion slowed later in the year in the wake of global recession, the international debt crisis, a dramatic rise in the value of the dollar, and an intensification of competition within the American market. The foreign acquisition issue receded, but questions about the ultimate limits of foreign banks in the United States remained, as did concerns about reciprocity.[106]

One of the major choices Congress made in adopting the IBA was between standards of reciprocity and national treatment. State regulators and some domestic banks defended the idea of a reciprocity test for foreign entry. Such a test, they argued, would be fair and would provide a powerful lever for opening foreign banking markets to direct American participation. Conversely, federal regulators vigorously disputed the utility of such a test because of structural differences between national banking systems; more quietly, they also contended that true reciprocity in the context of the unique American dual and segmented banking system might actually harm American bank operations abroad. In the end, with the proponents of reciprocity having lost several attempts to block the federal approach, the national treatment standard prevailed.[107]

Although its supporters viewed national treatment as the more "liberal" standard, they shared an underlying presumption that such a policy in the United States should foster emulation abroad. More explicitly, reciprocal national treatment was expected for U.S. banks overseas, especially in those markets where their access was limited. Whereas a strict concept of reciprocity could be expected to lead countries toward the lowest common denominator of openness, as in the tariff wars of the Great Depression years, this broader notion of liberal treatment in the expectation of reciprocation was expected over time to facilitate maximum international openness. Congress underscored this intent, and implied that a more stringent standard could still be enacted, by instructing the administration to review the regulatory treatment of American financial institutions abroad.

The Department of the Treasury, in collaboration with other departments and agencies, completed what came to be known as the first National Treatment Study in September 1979.[108] The study began by spelling out the implications of a national treatment policy. In the IBA, it contended, Congress established a nondiscriminatory regulatory framework governing foreign bank entry and operation that afforded "equality of competitive opportunity" vis-à-vis domestic institutions in similar circumstances. Rather than carry out a narrow legalistic comparative analysis, the study took this as a benchmark against which to measure the performance of other countries. On this basis, it concluded that U.S. banks enjoyed a substantial degree of access to most foreign markets of importance to them except Canada, the Scandinavian countries, Japan, Australia, and certain developing nations. The study therefore recommended that informal diplomatic efforts continue to press for further progress toward national treatment abroad, albeit with the recognition that in certain countries, especially those in early stages of industrial development, structural constraints to complete openness would probably remain. On the basis of this analysis, the administration concluded that the embodiment of a reciprocity provision in national banking law was not justified.

After the National Treatment Study was completed, concerns about problems in specific countries became more prominent. In particular, in the context of other difficulties associated with bilateral trade and investment relations, questions about the treatment of American banks in Canada, Australia, Japan, South Korea, and Taiwan came to the fore.[109] In bilateral contacts with these countries, administration officials informally pressed hard for movement toward national treatment and used the possibility of reciprocal restrictions as a lever. Especially active in this area was Secretary of the Treasury Donald Regan, who gave the matter a high personal priority during the first four years of Ronald Reagan's presidency. Similarly motivated was the chairman of the Republican-controlled Senate Banking Committee, Jake Garn.

As we shall see, Regan gave special attention to the Japanese case and actively directed negotiations aimed at liberalizing Japan's capital market. In 1983 Garn became so agitated about Japan and other countries that he introduced a bill that would have amended the IBA to authorize the comptroller of the currency to "consider reciprocity" among other factors evaluated when a foreign bank applied for a federal branch or agency license.[110] Shortly thereafter, Garn also requested from the administration an update of the 1979 study to assess developments in problematic countries, some of which he had personally visited to dramatize the concern of the Congress. That update, covering sixteen nations, was released in July 1984; it concluded that significant progress toward national treatment had been made during the previous five years in Canada, Japan, Finland, Spain, Portugal, and Norway, and that minor improvements had taken place in Australia, Sweden, Korea, and Taiwan.[111] Convinced that even the possibility of enactment of his reciprocity bill served to maintain momentum in this direction, Garn held a hearing on it in September.[112]

The Banking Committee heard testimony on the proposal from Treasury Secretary Regan and from spokesmen for BAFT and Citibank. Garn himself opened the hearing by admitting that his motive in proposing the bill, as well as in calling for the National Treatment

Update, was to strengthen the position of U.S. negotiators abroad. Although passage of a moderate bill could probably be assured, he promised not to press for it during the current session of Congress. Instead, he would reintroduce it during the next session in order to keep up the pressure for liberalization overseas. The BAFT spokesman followed and called the bill "highly reasonable" but noted, "The problem with [such] legislation is that it is difficult to construct a universal legislative standard that is meaningful, pragmatic, and consistently helpful to U.S. bank interests abroad."[113] Since many of the impediments to national treatment abroad are informal and subtle, he continued, a more flexible response, including continuing negotiations and periodic updates of the National Treatment Study, was preferable. Citibank's representative agreed and recommended the bill be held in abeyance. Essentially the same position was put forward by Secretary Regan. Although he did not want to rule out firmer methods in the future, he remained satisfied with a pragmatic approach that relied on bilateral consultations supplemented by multilateral efforts in such forums as the OECD. He concluded that national treatment continued to be the best policy for the United States.[114]

As pressures for the general reform of American banking laws heightened in the late 1980s, debate on the wisdom of the national treatment approach persisted. To a considerable extent, attention focused on highly visible expansions of Japanese institutions. More broadly, the debate became entangled with governmental efforts to deal with particular bilateral trade imbalances and to encourage freer international trade in services. Financial services comprised an important part of this latter agenda and gradually came to be viewed in an integrated fashion. In tandem with evolving structural transformations in American financial markets, the debate refocused on whether national treatment provided an adequate standard for promoting openness abroad not just for American banks, as traditionally structured, but also for securities companies and a range of increasingly diversified financial institutions. With this background, in March 1986 Senator Garn requested the Treasury Department to undertake another national treatment study. The resulting report expanded prior reviews by examining separately regulatory conditions prevailing for banks in eighteen countries, half of which would be considered "newly industrializing countries," and for securities operations in eight countries, all OECD members.[115]

The new study generally reported a continuation of the same trend noted in its 1984 predecessor. Regulations discriminating against foreign institutions or essentially denying them "equality of competitive opportunity" were falling away in most OECD countries but remained a problem in a number of developing nations. With respect to both banking and securities markets throughout the OECD, little evidence could be found to support a general move by American policy makers away from national treatment or toward a stricter reciprocity approach. The study pointedly noted, however, that in a number of countries a "tendency toward selective reciprocity" was gathering strength. Nowhere was this being rigidly applied, but "administrative discretion" was increasingly being used to encourage openness abroad. A less overt approach by the United States, the study argued, remained advisable. This included continuing pragmatic efforts by the State Department and the Treasury Department in various bilateral and multilateral forums to encourage the removal of remaining explicit or tacit barriers.[116]

As if to forestall criticism for the lack of explicitness in the traditional American approach, the study underlined the difficulties posed by federalism and by certain rigidities in national financial policies. Although a general tendency toward openness to foreign institutions remained in the United States, and formerly closed states like Texas were opening while states like New York were doing away with explicit reciprocity requirements, states did retain an ability to contravene the spirit of federal policy.[117] At least with respect to countries without such a problem of subfederal autonomy, a stricter national policy on foreign access carried a real risk of backfiring on American institutions abroad. A similar threat continued to be posed by traditional functional barriers in American markets. American banks, for example, were often able to engage in a wider range of securities activities abroad than at home. In short, a lack of structural equivalence between diverse national regulatory systems, especially between segmented and universal systems, meant that comparing and contrasting competitive opportunities remained an imprecise task. A policy of national treatment with a degree of flexibility to ensure roughly equivalent access between competing markets, therefore, continued to be advisable because it preserved national structures without compromising the position of American institutions abroad. Nevertheless, as the study and continued congressional concern in the late 1980s made very clear, an expectation that such a policy would in fact be reciprocated remained central to that policy.[118] The only questions were whether countries with less liberal regulatory structures would respond to the subtle ways in which that expectation was expressed and whether countries with more liberal structures would continue to condone remaining rigidities within the American market.

CHAPTER FOUR

# Japan

During the 1980s aggressive Japanese banks moved into commanding positions in financial markets around the world. In aggregate terms, foreign banks in Japan were markedly less successful. This contrasting performance tended, however, to obscure the fact that foreign bank access to the Japanese market improved steadily, if slowly, from the 1960s onward. Never an easy market to penetrate, its political foundations have accommodated the same movement toward openness so evident in other advanced industrialized countries. The development of foreign bank regulatory policy in Japan has been shaped by factors similar to those operating elsewhere. Internal political incentives provided the necessary conditions for policy change. At critical points, however, these incentives were influenced in a distinctive manner by foreign governmental pressure.

## THE POLICY DEBATE: ENHANCING ACCESS IN A POLITICIZED, COMPETITIVE MARKET

Foreign banking in Japan began at the time of the Tokugawa Shogunate's collapse. Preceding the Meiji Restoration by a year, Hongkong and Shanghai Bank opened an office in 1866; the Chartered Bank of Great Britain followed in 1889. Twenty four years later, a predecessor institution to Citibank established the first American bank branch. These early foreign banks were few in number, concentrated their activities on trade financing, and relied heavily on cooperative correspondent relations with their Japanese counterparts. From a distance, other foreign institutions, mainly investment houses, participated in Japan's early industrial development by underwriting government bonds for onward sale in overseas capital markets. World War II severed these connections and temporarily closed all foreign bank branches. During the subsequent American occupation, eight banks reopened, including the above-mentioned and Bank of America, Chase Manhattan, and one bank each from France, the Netherlands, and Taiwan.

In 1949 the occupation authorities relinquished control over the banking sector, and responsibility reverted to the new Japanese government. Access policy thereafter became severely restrictive and was subordinated to broader foreign exchange and foreign investment policies. In effect, the residual American administration in Japan accepted measures aimed at protecting recovering domestic banks, which were themselves seen by the Japanese government as pivotal instruments for economic reconstruction. In the course of recovery the government wanted to avoid what it termed "overbanking." It also clearly wanted to regain and maintain domestic control. Between 1950 and 1967 only seven foreign banks, mainly from other Asian countries, were granted banking licenses, often under special circumstances.

Foreign banks received licenses under banking legislation dating from 1927. The brief text of the law mandated few specific regulatory distinctions between foreign and domestic institutions but did permit administrators wide discretion.[1] Much more important for the actual operation of foreign banks was the informal guidance received from supervisors in the Ministry of Finance and a subtle noncompetition understanding with domestic institutions. Until 1955 the result was a virtual monopoly for foreign banks over trade financing and foreign currency-related transactions and a prohibition on seeking purely domestic business, including retail deposits. For a time this arrangement suited everyone, but by the mid-1950s things began to change.

Starting in 1955 the Bank of Tokyo was permitted gradually to expand its overseas operations to facilitate trade and to support the activities of major clients. In a limited fashion, the city banks were gradually allowed to follow. The relationship between domestic and foreign banks in Japan remained cooperative, but the domestic banks slowly began to build foreign currency balances while the foreign banks started to extend limited amounts of yen-denominated loans to domestic clients. With the rise of the Eurodollar market and the growth in demand by Japanese corporations for foreign currency loans, however, the more important and most lucrative business of the foreign bank branches remained wholesale and dollar denominated. Over time, domestic banks made initial moves into this type of business, only to be pulled back abruptly by the ministry in the wake of financial problems associated with the first oil crisis.[2]

So evolved a curious and accidental monopoly by foreign banks over impact loans, that is, medium-term loans denominated in foreign currencies (usually U.S. dollars) and extended to domestic Japanese corporations.[3] Despite this anomaly, the Ministry of Finance ensured that foreign participation in the domestic market remained limited. Tacit prohibitions on foreign investment in mutual banks and trust banks dated from the 1950s; procedural mechanisms discouraged the opening of new subbranches in commercial banking markets; foreign exchange controls mandated Bank of Japan permission for each new impact loan; and informal guidance from the ministry discouraged terms of less than one year in the market for impact loans. In the field of yen lending, foreign access to the necessary yen deposits was severely constrained by informal guidance generally forbidding retail deposit solicitation and, more importantly, by limitations on amounts of foreign currency brought into Japan to be swapped into yen for onward lending.[4]

Until the late 1960s the rigidly controlled framework of Japanese banking drew little criticism domestically or internationally. For foreign institutions lucky enough to have established themselves in Japan before that time, the profits resulting from the system were large. Risks were limited by the quality of borrowing clients and often by government or domestic bank guarantees. Effective spreads between funding and lending costs were high, partly because limits on swapping assured arbitrage gains and partly because clients critically short of financing were willing to pay.[5] In such an environment, there was little incentive to press for change or to develop local management depth. Another reason for the lack of criticism from abroad at that time was the fixation of the most likely foreign critic, the United States, on geopolitical rather than economic priorities in its relationship with Japan, a stance that at the time implicitly condoned measures of economic control deemed unacceptable for other trading partners, such as Canada.[6] Sustaining such a situation was the fact that the American banks most aggressive internationally before the late 1960s—Citibank, Chase Manhattan, Bank of America, and American Express—were all established in Tokyo and were benefiting from entry barriers that kept out rivals. The one exception, Morgan Guaranty, was in fact lobbying energetically behind the scenes in its quest for a license.

Pressure for change slowly began to build around the time Japan joined the OECD and became a full member of the International

Monetary Fund. By 1965 it was becoming obvious that Japanese interests benefited greatly from openness abroad, especially Japanese banks, which now operated some one hundred offices in foreign countries. In the face of early foreign demands for reciprocal openness in Japan, the government initiated its first concerted liberalization round covering various areas of trade and investment. Although banking was often exempted from related commitments, an important signal of future intent came in 1969 when the Ministry of Finance finally acceded to Morgan's request for a branch license. Two years later seven other banks, including four from the United States, received licenses. Many more would follow during the next decade.

Foreign demands were not the only triggers for these initial moves. In the years of dollar shortage following the foreign exchange shock during the Nixon administration and the first oil shock, Japanese policy makers keenly sensed the continuing economic vulnerability of their country. For both business and government leaders this sense translated in part into parallel decisions aimed at ensuring future access to foreign capital markets. Capital from overseas borrowed directly or brought in by foreign institutions obviously played a critical role during the period of recovery and reconstruction; it still played an important role twenty-five years after the war's end. In 1970, for example, 12 percent of the total funding available to support the lending activities of domestic banks came from external sources, down only slightly from 16 percent in 1951.[7] As international credit conditions tightened in 1971, Japanese institutions suddenly found it difficult to raise the usual volumes on acceptable terms.[8] One response from the government was to allow more foreign banks into Japan. A complementary response from major domestic banks was to push for expanded penetration of foreign markets, a strategy that would eventually entail dramatic acquisitions of dollar-based American banks. The strategy was tacitly supported by Japanese regulatory authorities, as is evident from the pattern of foreign bank licensing decisions made by the Ministry of Finance. Foreign banks were allowed to establish branches in Japan only when their home governments provided reciprocal opportunities for Japanese banks.[9] On this basis, for example, branches of banks from Canada, Australia, Indonesia, and Texas were excluded.[10] The specific interests of domestic banks were, in this instance, seen as entirely compatible with broader national interests.

The market that new foreign banks entered remained tightly controlled. With informal constraints continuing to limit access to conventional yen deposits, foreign banks were relegated to three

Table 7. Number of Japanese banks abroad and foreign banks in Japan, June 30, 1976

| Country | Japanese banks abroad | | | | Foreign banks in Japan | | |
|---|---|---|---|---|---|---|---|
| | Banks | Branches | Subsidiaries | Representative Offices | Banks | Branches | Representative Offices |
| United States | 18 | 38 | 12 | 16 | 22 | 34 | 9 |
| Canada | — | — | — | 8 | — | — | 5 |
| Latin America | 1 | 3 | 4 | 16 | 2 | 2 | 5 |
| Europe | 19 | 38 | 8 | 19 | 18 | 25 | 39 |
| Asia | 7 | 24 | — | 32 | 10 | 14 | 10 |
| Other | — | — | — | 30 | — | — | 8 |

SOURCE: Ministry of Finance data, cited in Mainichi Daily News, October 30, 1976.

principal areas of activity: impact loans, short-term yen loans (largely financing trade), and foreign exchange. Bank of Japan controls operated extensively in each area. One of their effects was to limit customers of the foreign banks to top-tier corporate names, to other corporations whose obligations were usually guaranteed by domestic banks, and to domestic banks themselves.[11] Another effect, however, was to sustain profitability. As marginal suppliers of funds, the foreigners retained healthy premiums, especially during periods of tight money. Moreover, implicit or explicit guarantees still ensured that they took few loan losses.[12] Most incoming banks had no immediate aspirations in the retail or small business sectors, and few tensions regarding market access arose. Finally, because their swap limits were often proportionately more generous than those of domestic banks and they were excused from the more onerous obligations of domestic banks (such as requirements to buy government bonds at prescribed low rates of interest), for a time foreign banks delighted in their lot and enjoyed the fruits of positive discrimination. Institutional effects of the arrangement by the mid-1970s are shown in Tables 7-9.

For foreign bankers the times were too good to last, and indeed a few years after the number of new foreign entrants began to rise dramatically, overall profitability in the banking sector began a long slide. As marginal lenders in an economy that had now drastically slowed its former pace of growth, foreign banks faced a daunting new environment. The double-digit growth rates that made Japan the envy of the capitalist world during the 1960s ended with the new decade. In 1970 its gross national product advanced by a still healthy 8.3 percent in real terms, in 1973 by a more modest 5.3 percent. But in 1974 deep recession actually brought an annual decline of 0.2

*Table 8.* Market shares of foreign and domestic banks in Japan, 1971–76 (¥ 100 billions)

| | Deposits | | | Loans | | |
|---|---|---|---|---|---|---|
| Year | Japanese banks | Foreign banks | Foreign (%) | Japanese banks | Foreign banks | Foreign (%) |
| 1971 | 523 | 4.0 | 0.76 | 490 | 7.2 | 1.47 |
| 1972 | 612 | 4.4 | 0.72 | 570 | 8.2 | 1.44 |
| 1973 | 758 | 7.3 | 0.96 | 712 | 13.2 | 1.85 |
| 1974 | 847 | 8.9 | 1.05 | 807 | 19.8 | 2.45 |
| 1975 | 964 | 10.1 | 1.05 | 895 | 27.4 | 3.06 |
| 1976 | 1109 | 11.03[a] | 0.99 | 990 | 33.3[a] | 3.37 |

SOURCE: Ministry of Finance data, cited in *Mainichi Daily News,* December 15, 1977.
[a]Approximately 50 percent controlled by the three largest — Citibank, Bank of America, and Chase Manhattan.

*Table 9.* Earnings, return on assets, and asset growth of foreign banks in Japan, 1972–76

| Year | Gross earnings (¥ billions) | Return on assets (%) | Asset-growth rate (%) |
|---|---|---|---|
| 1972 | 15.7 | n.a. | 35.0 |
| 1973 | 18.1 | 1.03 | 13.3 |
| 1974 | 29.9 | 1.19 | 57.4 |
| 1975 | 40.6 | 1.12 | 27.9 |
| 1976 | 41.5 | 0.93 | 21.6 |

SOURCE: International Business Information, Tokyo, cited in Andreas Prindl, *Japanese Finance* (New York: Wiley & Sons, 1982), 71.

percent. During the next two years the growth rate bounced between 3 and 5 percent.[13]

As their liquidity increased because of slower growth, the requirements of corporate borrowers declined; many even accelerated repayment of existing debts. At the same time, changing conditions in the money markets and a strengthening of the yen deprived foreign banks of the easy funding profits often formerly available.[14] The accounting term "last in, first out" characterized well the plight of foreign lenders. Despite continued growth in the absolute number of foreign banks in Japan (sixty-one banks with eighty-one branches by the start of 1978), real portfolio growth ended in 1976.[15] During the following year outstanding loans stagnated and average pretax earnings fell by 18 percent.[16] Between 1976 and 1979 net earnings for all foreign banks fell from ¥41 billion to ¥18 billion; return on assets accordingly declined from 0.93 percent to 0.29 percent.[17]

Foreign currency loans comprised approximately half of foreign bank portfolios in 1975 when demand started to evaporate.[18] As they searched for substitutes to bolster their flagging positions, the for-

eign banks were stymied by a lack of adequate access to competitively priced yen funding. Swap limits, the absence of retail
branches, controlled interbank money markets, and a dearth of
sophisticated domestic depository instruments all constrained their
ability to raise yen deposits for onward lending. They could do little
about declining demand and increasing competition, but funding
restrictions appeared malleable. By 1978 a few prominent foreign
bankers were prepared to press for the extension of liberalization
programs to their areas of activity.[19] Contacts between foreign banks
and their home governments regarding regulatory treatment in
Japan first stepped up markedly in 1976 when the banks became
embroiled in a tax dispute with the Ministry of Finance.[20] Thereafter, such contacts increased steadily.

In policy-making circles in Washington and various European
capitals, the complaints of foreign banks operating in Japan slowly
came to be associated with the rapid overseas expansion of Japanese
banks. The overseas expansion of the city banks accelerated
throughout the 1970s. With the ministry's blessing, similar drives by
the long-term credit banks and regional banks began in 1973 and
1975, respectively. By the end of the decade, twenty-three Japanese
banks operated well over one hundred branches and dozens of subsidiaries in external markets, with particularly heavy concentrations
in New York, California, London, and Hong Kong.[21]

In their search for solutions, foreign bankers themselves were
divided. A few favored formation of a united front for purposes of
lobbying the Ministry of Finance. Others, especially the largest
American banks, preferred to go it alone because they believed their
own channels to the ministry would better advance their own interests. They also feared the possibility that the ministry would use a
formal association for the collective dissemination of "guidance."
Still others, mindful of the rapid growth of Japanese institutions
abroad, favored putting pressure on Japan through the auspices of
their home governments. But the vast majority of the foreign bankers, usually new to Japan and unsure of their situation, preferred to
avoid the political arena altogether and simply hoped the market
would turn in the near future.[22] Such hesitant stances were often
reinforced by differences of approach and understanding between
distant head offices and local representatives. In the case of the three
big American banks, for example, head office executives were
embroiled during the mid-1970s in a domestic debate over the place
of foreign banks within the United States itself and had adopted
positions favoring a policy of national treatment. Because this policy
implied nondiscriminatory regulation regardless of conditions pre-

vailing abroad, they were unable to provide forceful support for the view beginning to come from some of their Tokyo representatives that a more robust policy along lines of fully reciprocal treatment was required.

The first direct involvement of home governments came in 1978. Early that year a delegation from the European Economic Community went to Tokyo for trade talks. A group of European bankers approached the delegates and presented a series of complaints concerning their regulatory treatment in Japan. In April senior officers from the Federal Reserve Bank of San Francisco heard similar complaints during one of their regular visits to Tokyo and took them up informally with the Ministry of Finance. The more important grievances concerned yen-funding constraints, swap limits, restrictions on branching, tax treatment of off-shore funding, prohibitions on participation in subsidized trade financing schemes, rigidities in the interbank market, and restrictions on the acquisition of domestic banks. European banks also objected to regulations that prevented their engaging in securities-related business. A series of formal and informal meetings between governments followed these early contacts.

*Foreign Government Intervention*

In May 1978 a delegation from the Financial Institutions Division of the EEC Commission met in Tokyo with senior officials from the Ministry of Finance, the Bank of Japan, and the Ministry of Foreign Affairs.[23] Just before the meeting, the Bank of Japan had initiated a public campaign to disabuse market participants and observers of the idea that bank regulatory policy somehow discriminated against foreigners. The campaign continued after the Europeans left and focused on foreign "misunderstandings" of the intricacies of Japanese markets. Such requirements as were necessary for overall economic policy management were, according to the Bank, enforced without regard to nationality, except for the reciprocity test on entry. After entry, all comparable banks, whether domestic or foreign, were treated evenhandedly. The constraints pointed out by foreign institutions applied equally to domestic banks.

Even as the Bank's initial clarification campaign proceeded, foreign bankers noticed that incremental changes were beginning to take place. A tacit prohibition on foreign participation in Japan's Export-Import Bank financings, for example, turned out to be a "misunderstanding" on the part of domestic banks that put lending syndicates together and was now cleared up. Such small victories

73

encouraged some foreign banks to press for greater freedoms through whichever channels appeared promising. So began a process of quiet negotiation between governments, domestic banks, and foreign banks that would redefine the role of external actors in the Japanese financial system and help push ahead an overarching movement toward domestic regulatory liberalization.

Following the initiative taken by the EEC, early moves by the United States on bank regulation proved more complicated. For one, the issue fit uneasily in an economic policy agenda dominated by concerns over trade imbalances. Officials used to dealing with conventional tariff and nontariff barriers to trade were initially daunted by the complexities of financial regulation in Japan's highly segmented system. In addition, they were hampered by a tradition of not interfering in foreign regulatory matters unless American institutions were specifically and clearly being subjected to discrimination. They were also restrained by their government's own internal policy of not insisting on formal reciprocity.[24] Finally, jurisdictional rivalry and different views of strategic priorities within the American government made matters worse.[25] Gradually, the Treasury achieved dominance in this policy area, especially during the early years of the Reagan administration.[26] This change would not occur, however, before a vigorous initial thrust came from the Congress.

A congressional task force came to Tokyo in November 1978 to investigate rigidities in Japanese goods and money markets thought to contribute to a serious bilateral trade imbalance. During their visit members of the task force met with American bankers and, as a result, tacked a rough understanding of their complaints onto their subsequent report to Congress. The Jones Report, named for its principal congressional sponsor, concluded that Japanese regulatory treatment different from that imposed on domestic banks "discriminated against" American banks and inhibited them from promoting increased American exports to Japan. Prominent examples included restrictions on the issuance of certificates of deposit and debentures, on branching, and on the acquisition of domestic financial institutions.[27] In Congress, as well as in the Treasury, such allegations were instinctively, if confusingly, connected with calls for a revaluation of the yen. The Ministry of Finance rejected the allegations as groundless, a posture fully supported by both opposition and government members on the Diet Finance Committee.[28]

A more balanced and comprehensive review of the situation, although one that continued to use the vocabulary of trade liberalization, came from the Treasury during its 1979 study of U.S. bank treatment abroad. The process of drafting the section on Japan

*Japan*

appeared helpful in itself, as it engaged American financial attachés in extensive discussions with the Banking Bureau of the Ministry of Finance, thereby encouraging further "clarification." In the end, the Treasury concluded that Japan was making progress toward opening its banking system to effective foreign competition. Still, a "substantial lack of national treatment and equality of competitive opportunity" remained in practice.[29] In view of this finding, and seeking to head off further congressional intervention on trade policy matters, the administration decided to push ahead with financial diplomacy.

At this point American officials were not principally responding to pressures from American banks. Those pressures were there, but they were mixed with doubt concerning the wisdom of dealing with regulatory matters in the context of trade liberalization and yen internationalization. On the whole, despite the fact that some foreign bankers in Japan were going public with their complaints, government officials were actually ahead of most bankers. Government in this case was pushing more than it was being pushed.

## Japan's Response

Inside the Japanese government the rise of foreign pressure in the banking sector was a source of consternation. The perceived inaccuracies of the Jones Report in particular mystified officials in the Banking Bureau. Compounding the problem, from their point of view, was the apparent disagreement between some foreign banks and their governments and among the foreign banks themselves. Officials simply could not get a clear answer to the question: What do the foreigners want?[30] Despite the confusion, the need somehow to respond was certain. No one in the Ministry of Finance wanted to see the complexities of foreign bank regulation inextricably drawn into the very highly politicized, and therefore uncontrollable, arena of trade policy. As finance minister, Masayoshi Ohira had earlier come to the same conclusion. Upon his accession to the prime ministership in November 1978, he promised that Japan would move toward a more open financial system. In 1975 Ohira had initiated a comprehensive policy review of the banking system and of its now-outmoded legal framework. That review was still underway in the Council on Financial System Research, an advisory group to the finance minister (via the Banking Bureau) composed of retired officials, business leaders, and senior academics. Ohira's renewed commitment hastened their work.

Purely domestic pressures dominated the environment in which the financial system review took place. These pressures, and not foreign ones, had in fact set off the review process in 1975. In the highly unstable and inflationary period following the first oil shock, banks were widely accused of profiteering; the socialist opposition in the Diet had been particularly vocal on this score. The response from the government was the high profile council review. The council's wide agenda included the foreign bank issue but mainly concentrated on questions touching on the relationship between the Bank of Japan and the government, the establishment of a five-day workweek in banks, bank lending limits to single corporate groups, the government bond distribution system, and the "social responsibility" of banks. One issue — the division of functions between banks and securities companies — would in time come to the fore and bog down the council and the government for years in a frustrating search for compromise. In such a context, foreign banking issues had a very low priority. Only in November 1978, amid rounds of bilateral diplomacy, did the council find time to hear the testimony of four foreign bank leaders.

The general managers of Bank of America, Deutsche Bank, Morgan, and National Westminster then put forward their views and preferences.[31] Although steering clear of blunt charges of discrimination, the bankers contended that the effect of existing regulations on their uniquely structured operations amounted to tacit discrimination. Without a broad branch network, for example, restrictions on wholesale yen deposit raising hurt them more, even if applied equally to domestic and foreign institutions. The American bankers, in particular, argued that their operations offered great benefits to Japan in terms of economic efficiency. They did not, however, hesitate to allude to the growing market share of Japanese banks in the United States.

Even gingerly couched references to discrimination and possible retaliation were not well received by the council, and the onus was placed on the foreigners to substantiate their charges. In supplemental material sent to clarify their testimony, several of the bankers became more specific and listed their principal grievances as restrictions on holding open foreign exchange positions, prohibitions on offshore yen lending, limits on interbank deposit taking and access to Bank of Japan facilities, restraints on lending to government agencies, and branching restrictions. They added, "It is difficult to support charges of discrimination as they are largely effected through administrative guidance, which may or may not coincide with official policy and procedure.... In this environment foreign resident banks are leery of speaking frankly ... for fear of prejudicing their working relationships with regulatory authorities at the level where interaction is most frequent and crucial."[32] In its final report, the council responded:

> Criticism that there are differences in the treatment meted out to foreign banks in Japan and to Japanese banks has been raised in certain quarters. However, in actuality, foreign banks are treated equally in all fields, including branch office administration, transactions with the Bank of Japan, and foreign exchange control matters. No substantial differences exist in the treatment of the two types of banks. At the root of such criticism lies the fact that profits made by foreign banks have recently fallen. [This decline is due to general economic conditions and] profits made by foreign banks are not necessarily low compared to Japanese banks. There is another criticism to the effect that Japan's financial system and practices are narrow in scope. In reply ... it is necessary for foreign banks to get acquainted with Japanese systems and practices if they want to do business successfully in Japan. At the same time, Japan should liberalize and make its financial system more flexible in order to establish a good reputation internationally. We feel that such endeavors will contribute to the elimination of these and other similar criticisms.[33]

The council further recommended increased communication between foreign banks and the government, introduction of consolidated supervision for foreign banks (instead of branch-by-branch supervision), and introduction of a prudential guideline on adequate capitalization.[34]

In the domestic debate preceding and following the council's final report, the foreign bank issue attracted almost no attention. But the council's recommendations, especially those proposing such new controls as capital/asset ratios, did have the effect of unifying the foreign bankers themselves by putting them on the defensive. Although differences of view continued to hinder the establishment of a formal association, such groups as the Finance Committee of the American Chamber of Commerce henceforth played an increasingly active role. In addition, a conventional view was emerging among the disparate group of foreigners. As expressed by one banker in the light of the council's expected recommendations and the critical Japanese reaction to the Jones Report, "Even if it is said that we are treated on an equal footing with Japanese banks, the problem is that control over Japanese banks themselves is too strong.... [Without an easing of restrictions] it cannot be said that the doors of the market have been opened in the true sense of the term."[35] Tacitly conceding that the vocabulary of trade discrimination was serving little purpose and only exacerbating cross-cultural misunderstandings, a few foreign bankers began pushing for broader reform. In the mean-time foreign governments, especially the United States, continued pressing the Ministry of Finance to provide effective national treat-ment to foreign banks. Because the Banking Bureau was responsible for putting the council's recommendations into a new draft banking law, such pressures concentrated on it.[36]

## Legislative Reform and Administrative Change

As Banking Bureau officials began work on a new Banking Law, several developments affected the prospects of foreign banks in Japan. Although they remained concerned about "overbanking" in domestic markets, in 1979 the Ministry of Finance and the Bank of Japan took administrative steps to ease branching and retail deposit-taking restrictions for both foreign and domestic banks. They also allowed foreign banks into the consumer finance field and into the so-called *gensaki* market (a relatively free money market involving the sale and repurchase of qualifying securities) and moved to improve the efficiency of interbank markets. These changes initially appeared to help the foreign banks, but the more fundamental change in their operating environment came with the reform of exchange controls in 1979 and 1980.

Foreign exchange controls originally put in place in 1949 had been easing throughout the 1970s, when the position of Japanese banks in international markets had strengthened considerably.[37] This devel-opment gradually undercut the tenability of limitations on the abil-ity of Japanese banks to lend yen off shore or foreign currency on shore. The banks had in fact been lobbying strongly for greater flex-ibility since the mid-1970s. Ironically, the efforts of foreign govern-ments and some foreign banks now to encourage Japan to scrap residual elements of the exchange control system perfectly comple-mented this lobbying. In addition, all of the talk about equal treat-ment for domestic and foreign banks focused attention squarely on the anachronistic foreign monopoly over impact loans. In any case, partly responding to foreign criticism and eager to mitigate the monetary equivalent of existing trade controversy, Prime Minister Fukuda in February 1978 called on the Ministry of Finance to reform the Foreign Exchange and Foreign Trade Control Law.

After considerable bureaucratic infighting, especially between the Ministry of Finance and the Ministry of International Trade and Industry, the Diet passed a new Foreign Exchange and Foreign Trade Control Law in 1980. Before passage, however, the finance ministry continued liberalizing actual administrative practice. Early in 1979 one of the first things to go was the foreign monopoly over impact loans. Initially Japanese banks were permitted to lend foreign currency for short terms only and were requested by the ministry not to encourage clients to switch existing loans held by foreign banks. Eventually the term restriction was removed, and existing loans ran down of their own accord. After subsequent hectic activity in the domestic market, which witnessed small Japanese banks entering the market and bidding aggressively for initial market shares, the foreign-controlled proportion of this formerly protected and lucrative market fell to less than 50 percent by 1981. The ministry attempted to still the complaints of foreign bankers by increasing swap limits and providing several minor concessions.[38] As they watched their former mainstay disappear under the rubric of liberalization, the foreigners had little basis for specific complaint. Deeper changes in the Japanese economy, related to slowing growth and rising liquidity, had in any event been working to undercut the profitability of foreign currency lending, but foreign demands ironically helped accelerate the process. External pressure had helped push various deregulation measures that strengthened the competitive abilities of domestic banks. Foreign banks were the first to feel the pinch of equal treatment.

Further liberalization followed the decision of the Ministry of Finance in March 1979 to allow limited issuance of yen certificates of deposit (CDs) with pricing determined by the market. CDs, an important funding tool in other countries, had been a subject of debate in Japan for ten years. Foreign bank support only added to pressures from city banks and large corporations for a more efficient mechanism for handling surplus liquidity. Because of the potential threat to their own funding bases, the long-term credit banks in particular opposed the idea. A compromise that neatly avoided direct and immediate challenges to divergent interests was eventually reached within the Banking Bureau. As a starting point, only large denomination CDs with maturities of between three and six months would be permitted. Despite their pleasure with the direction of change represented in this decision, and with the ministry's further measure to compensate foreign banks for their lack of retail branches by granting them proportionally higher limits for CD issuance, foreign bankers found that the actual effect on profitability was negligible. Once again, liberalization unleashed powerful competitive forces within the domestic banking system, and foreign banks found themselves in an even tougher market.

The formal legal framework for this market was under review in the Banking Bureau when the CD and foreign exchange decisions

79

were taken. In addition to codifying the major recommendations made by the Financial System Research Council on credit limits, bank holidays, public disclosure, and so on, the drafters of a new law to regulate banking sought to clarify the position of foreign banks within the system. They took this to mean codification of the policy of national treatment already implicitly in place. For the domestic institutions most interested in the drafting process, other matters were of far more concern, especially the expansion of bank powers to include the sale of government bonds. A few foreign banks did hold occasional discussions with the drafting party, as did several foreign government officials, but most of the proposed terms could not be disputed.[39] No distinctions were made between domestic and foreign institutions in terms of official banking powers, and a loosening of effective restrictions, for example, on funding, branch expansion, and bank acquisitions, were to be applied without regard to nationality.

## THE POLICY OUTCOME: CONTINUING EVOLUTION

The Diet passed the new Banking Law in 1981. Although it left the government with sufficient flexibility to demand reciprocity for entry to the banking system, it came as close to meeting standards of openness and national treatment as had laws in most other countries in the OECD.[40] Moreover, in the actual implementation of parts of the law after enactment, the Ministry of Finance went beyond strict equivalence in several important respects: foreign banks were exempted for five years from a new lending limit applied to the domestic banks; no strict capital/asset limits were put in place; they were given proportionally more generous CD limits; and they continued to be exempted from government bond underwriting requirements.

In its design as well as its implementation, the foreign bank regulatory policy codified in the new Banking Law reflected more the internal workings of the ministry than specific nongovernmental pressures. Of course, Banking Bureau officials responsible for drafting the relevant sections of the law were well aware of the complaints of foreign governments and banks, even if they blamed them principally on misunderstandings. Similarly, they were aware that a liberal formal policy at home would assist the offshore growth of domestic banks and reduce the possibilities of foreign market closure.[41] But because the ministry had a high degree of autonomy in drafting this part of the law — owing mainly to the complexity of the issues, the absence of a split among domestic financial institutions over them, and the lack of interest among domestic industry groups—those considerations were filtered through a larger internal debate within the ministry over the appropriate balance between control and competition in the banking system as a whole. To simplify a complicated series of arguments, one view long dominant in the Banking Bureau had been averse to change, especially rapid change, and placed a high value on safety and stability. It had also shown a preference for the predominance of nationally owned institutions within the domestic market. Another view, coming to the fore especially in recent years within the International Finance Bureau, was more comfortable with the exigencies of market competition, oriented more toward efficiency criteria in policy making, and apparently unthreatened by the possibility of increased foreign penetration. The evolution of policy on foreign bank regulation between 1977 and 1981 actually reflected a very cautious balancing of these views. In the end, the supporters of the more outward-looking view argued for codifying the rules along national treatment lines, in the spirit of existing bilateral and multilateral commitments, and even for going beyond a strict reading in order to alleviate pressures from abroad.[42] Despite some hesitation, tradition-minded officials went along, partly because they were distracted by more pressing domestic banking issues, but mainly because they saw little harm. The maturity of the domestic banking market, its obvious competitiveness, and the track record of recent years evidently convinced them that foreign penetration would remain within acceptable levels with or without a more liberal banking law.

As things turned out, the national treatment provisions, the reciprocity requirement for entry, and the liberal tone of the new Banking Law served Japanese interests well, at least for a time. National treatment after entry allowed the government to provide an ostensibly fair standard for foreign bank regulation without compromising the fundamental segmentation of the domestic market. The reciprocity test passively facilitated the overseas expansion plans of the major indigenous banks. The liberal tone underpinned a continuing measured liberalization of the domestic market, aimed simultaneously at improving internal efficiency and deflecting foreign criticism.[43] In fact, no foreign governments expressed dissatisfaction with the new law and many applauded it as a step toward a more open and "transparent" system.[44] After passage, ministry officials congratulated themselves on extricating banking issues from ongoing trade controversies.

## Foreign Banks after the Banking Law

Even as the Banking Law was being enacted, many foreign bankers were coming to see the technical legal framework for their operations as less important than the actual response of the Japanese market to their presence. Certainly they welcomed the liberalization measures codified in the Banking Law, but in their daily activities governmental controls remained evident. The administrative burden of detailed reporting to the Ministry of Finance and the close monitoring of the money market by the Bank of Japan reminded them constantly that banking in Japan was different. Still, talk of discrimination subsided noticeably, perhaps owing as much to an increase in market activity as to the process of regulatory change. Profitability actually improved in 1980, and in 1981 foreign loan portfolios registered a 17 percent increase on an aggregate basis. This uptick, in turn, encouraged new entrants. Between 1980 and 1982 17 new foreign branches and 29 representative offices opened, bringing to 104 the number of foreign banks operating in Japan. By the end of 1982, the 71 foreign banks maintaining full branches shared 3.6 percent of the domestic market for loans and 1 percent of the deposit base.[45]

At the same time, the expansion of Japanese banks abroad continued. By 1982 international operations accounted for 30 percent of the total assets of the city banks, an eightfold increase over the course of a decade. In all, 24 banks now maintained 154 branches, 40 affiliates, and 222 representative offices off shore. How this affected their profitability was difficult to determine because of the relatively low capitalization of Japanese banks and weak disclosure requirements. Overall, profit margins (loan yields minus deposit costs) for the city banks fell almost continuously throughout the 1970s from 1 percent at the start of the decade to below zero percent in 1980 before recovering to approximately 0.2 percent in 1982. At that point, international operations contributed over 10 percent to aggregate total income.[46] In particular markets, moreover, these operations were becoming very consequential. By 1983, for example, Japanese banks accounted for 11 percent of total lending to British residents; by 1984 they held 31 percent of the foreign currency assets booked in London.[47] In the United States, where 60 percent of their foreign business was generated, the Japanese banks accounted for 40 percent of all foreign bank activity by 1983; in comparison with the $22 billion in assets held by 21 American banks in Japan that year, 24 Japanese banks in the United States controlled $126 billion.[48]

Behind this rapid expansion overseas lay a complex of motivations related to declining profitability at home, to the internationalization of domestic corporations, and to accommodating signals from the Ministry of Finance. Once initiated, of course, their growth was also driven by intense competition among the Japanese banks, a competition based more on business volumes and market share than on short-term profitability.[49] Although this spectacular growth abroad perplexed foreign bankers frustrated by their own performances in Japan, of more immediate consequence was the transformation taking place in their relationships with Japanese banks in Tokyo. The cooperative partners of the past had, with the loosening of exchange controls and other liberalization moves, become direct rivals. At this point, a regulatory regime based on national treatment appeared to some foreign bankers not to be enough. Something else had to be accounting for their lack of success in Japan. A renewed deterioration in profitability after the brief respite in 1980 made the task of identifying that something else an urgent one.

Informal discussions within the foreign banking community now began to focus on broader notions of reciprocity as well as on apparent inequalities inherent in the structure of the Japanese market itself. Could foreign banks really diversify successfully into the highly competitive retail banking sector even if it was now technically easier to open branches? Could they actually acquire smaller domestic banks even if no regulations now forbade such moves?[50] Could they really move into the market for small- and medium-sized business when the rules of financial disclosure made accurate credit assessments extremely problematic? Could they ever effectively penetrate long-standing relationships such as those existing between companies and banks affiliated in close corporate formations? Could they make money in an environment where creditworthy clients were reducing their overall dependence on banks and where remaining borrowers could easily obtain very competitively priced loans from domestic banks? In the absence of a strong retail base and fully unhindered money markets, could they ever reduce their marginal funding costs to those of their domestic competitors?[51] At the start of a new decade, optimistic answers to these questions were rarely heard. Instead, some foreign bankers talked more openly about the need for continuing governmental discussions to go beyond issues of regulatory treatment to deeper issues of domestic structural transformation. Questions of market access came to be associated with such notions as equality of opportunity and effective reciprocity between foreign banks in Japan and Japanese banks overseas.

As usual, there was little unity among foreign bankers as to how reciprocity could effectively be encouraged. Some suggested holding up approval of acquisitions by Japanese banks abroad until equivalent opportunities were provided in Japan. But what test would determine equivalence? And how would the specific foreign banks to benefit from such tactics be selected? Others contended that governmental efforts should concentrate on breaking down the barriers to freer competition within Japan, thus accelerating the movement toward one set of regulatory structures and market practices in all the major financial markets of the world. As a step toward that goal, some advocated creation of an offshore banking market in Tokyo where tax and regulatory concessions would provide foreign banks with opportunities to help build the city into the future financial center of Asia. More modestly, perhaps the majority favored continued movement, with or without foreign governmental involvement, in the direction already suggested by the events of 1978–81: increased ceilings and extended terms for CDs, expanded swap limits, broadened access to central bank facilities, loosened controls over interbank markets, and reduced administrative burdens. Even with continued reform, however, few foreign bankers expected that their troubles would soon be over.

Despite the general lack of optimism, significant differences persisted in the relative performance of individual foreign banks. Creative management could, albeit with difficulty, identify and exploit distinctive market niches.[52] During the five turbulent years following 1978, for example, the earnings records of Morgan Guaranty, Manufacturers Hanover, Citibank, and Deutsche Bank stood out. The rarity of good performances, however, slowly fostered efforts among foreign bankers to cooperate in the search for general solutions. A core group of American bankers, for example, met monthly for informal luncheons where common problems were discussed, sometimes in the presence of U.S. government officials. The Financial Affairs Committee of the American Chamber of Commerce in Japan, a similar committee within the British Chamber of Commerce, and a small advisory group to the EEC office in Japan increasingly served similar purposes. Despite such efforts, however, no consensus regarding diagnosis or prescription emerged.

To the chagrin of Ministry of Finance officials pleased with their just-completed work on the Banking Law, early in 1982 foreign governments themselves raised the stakes once again. The United States Trade Representative (USTR) prepared a special report responding to continued congressional concern over a worsening bilateral trade imbalance.[53] Symbolizing the renewed urgency of the problem were tough reciprocity bills introduced in the Senate by Senators Danforth and Heinz.[54] The USTR report called for more sustained effort from the government to promote the export of American services and specifically cited Japan as a country where subtle forms of discrimination blocked market access for American firms, including banks.[55]

Within the Ministry of Finance, where memories of the Jones Report were still fresh, officials were bewildered by the new analysis. Even continuing high-level consultations with the U.S. Treasury had left ministry officials unprepared for the shocking setback. They firmly believed that the regulatory framework for foreign banking in Japan was now essentially identical to that prevailing in the United States. Foreign banks were not discriminated against; flexible policy interpretations actually favored foreigners in certain respects, and ongoing liberalization would in time provide more opportunities for profitable business.[56] Alarmed by renewed pressures from abroad, senior ministry officials assembled a team of bureaucrats and prominent domestic bankers and sent them to the United States and Europe for a two-week "explanation tour."[57] Back home, confusion came to be mixed with resentment. A new generation of policy makers was learning the lesson of its predecessors. The more you gave the foreigners, the more they wanted. Deregulation was proceeding with its own internal logic, and the ministry had legitimate aspirations in the maintenance of domestic stability. The foreigners would simply have to be patient.

In the United States, the USTR report came at a sensitive time. Within the next year pressure intensified inside both the administration and Congress to do something about the bilateral trade deficit. From the private sector, pressure came mainly from manufacturing industries.[58] Whether correct or not, a diagnosis of the problem centering on the artificially low value of the yen garnered wide support. Cognizant of a coming presidential reelection campaign and eager to forestall ill-conceived congressional action, the Reagan administration decided by the fall of 1983 to press for a new round of high-profile bilateral negotiations with Japan aimed at raising the value of the yen. The initial thesis of the American negotiators denied that the government of Japan overtly depressed the yen in order to stimulate export industries. Instead, it was held, the government accomplished the same end by implicitly refusing to satisfy existing international demand for yen-denominated assets. The value of the yen would fall to its appropriate level, therefore, only when the government allowed the yen to circulate more widely off shore and when it had truly liberalized its domestic financial market.

*85*

During the summer of 1983 an agenda for the proposed negotiations took shape under the reasserted leadership of the Treasury. Measures to dismantle Japanese barriers to the inward and outward flow of capital and to internationalize the yen led the list. To these core demands two others, decidedly of secondary importance during the early stages of discussion, were grafted: insistence on deregulation of Japan's domestic interest rates and a call for more favorable treatment of American banks, insurance companies, and securities companies. The addition of the latter item reflected lobbying by several financial institutions whose leaders saw an opportunity for assistance with their problems in Tokyo.[59] There still existed no consensus among American banks on the proposition that a new round of official negotiations would be helpful, and those who attempted to exploit this latest round of trade tensions did so with specific objectives in mind.[60] The most obvious came into public view in June 1983 when Morgan Guaranty and Nomura Securities requested ministry approval for the establishment of a joint venture trust banking company, an area traditionally closed to securities companies as well as to domestic and foreign commercial banks.

The ground had been prepared for a formal American request for talks during regular consultations between the Treasury and the ministry. The ministry initially resisted, but fearing that negotiations might take place under the auspices of the U.S. Department of State and the Ministry of Foreign Affairs, it eventually agreed. The real spark on the Japanese side, however, appeared to come from political leaders who saw the same possibilities in the talks that the American administration did: financial diplomacy promised to provide a relatively manageable mechanism for cooling trade tensions during a difficult period. Significantly, in this light, a final decision came during the November 1983 summit between President Reagan and Prime Minister Nakasone.[61] Under the bright lights of media coverage of the summit, the treasury secretary and the finance minister agreed to establish an ad hoc group to negotiate various yen/dollar exchange rate issues.[62] Between then and the following May, six meetings took place; with each one the American position became more detailed and focused. This was particularly evident on the trust banking issue, the one institutional issue most relevant to the foreign banks in Tokyo.

*The Trust Banking Episode*

Seeking new revenue sources in the difficult Japanese market, Morgan Guaranty officers had long been attracted to trust banking, an activity they engaged in successfully at home and one with a promising future in Japan.[63] Nomura Securities had similar aspirations. Despite the evident barrier represented by Japan's system of financial segmentation, the two institutions began talking in 1982. Using a loophole in existing regulations, they finally put their proposal before a very reluctant Ministry of Finance. When word of the proposal leaked, the responses of competitors were immediate. Citibank, Chemical Bank, and Bank of America rushed to put their own ventures together with other securities companies; the city banks asked the ministry for permission to set up subsidiaries to compete with the proposed new trust banks; and the existing trust banks screamed. The foreign protagonists quickly found themselves in the middle of a territorial struggle that had been going on behind closed doors since the process of deregulation began.

When it was first broached, the ministry informally turned down the Morgan-Nomura proposal. Ministry officials saw the trust banking sector as too weak to sustain increased competition and feared adverse effects on market stability. More fundamentally, they realized that the move threatened to intensify pressure on remaining interest rate controls. The decision drove the American banks to Washington, where, in the yen/dollar context, they found governmental allies.[64] Even though the ministry advised the city banks not to engage in trust banking in the United States out of deference to their regulatory environment at home, American bankers argued, Japanese banks did under U.S. law have the right to engage in trust banking. Should not U.S. banks have the same right in Japan? The logic sounded impeccable to Treasury officials, and the proposal seemed a very convenient symbol of what they were trying to achieve in the bilateral negotiations. It was promptly put on the yen/dollar agenda.

Prime Minister Nakasone undoubtedly saw the same symbolic value in the issue when he publicly declared his support for licensing the proposed joint ventures.[65] Two weeks later, perturbed ministry officials presented him with the view that two or three years would be necessary to study the proposal in order to avoid potentially catastrophic market disruption.[66] Behind the scenes, the ministry was encountering heavy resistance from the existing trust banks as well as from the city banks. The principal fear of the trust banks was that through the proposed partially opened door would later come the city banks. The city banks worried conversely that the door would remain only partially opened, their chief domestic rivals, the securities companies, thus stealing a march.[67] In normal times, this might have ended the matter. But with highly publicized financial negotiations underway, these were not normal times.

This latest American diplomatic initiative exemplified a decidedly new approach in the specificity of its aims, the bluntness of its expression, and the clarity of its mandate, despite assertions from the Federal Reserve and other domestic critics that its fundamental thesis was flawed. On the trust banking question in particular, it was also unusual that top-level political decision makers on both sides needed the same symbolic victory, albeit for their own reasons. As economic forces within Japan were working in the same direction by putting pressure on dated functional constraints within the financial system as a whole, all that appeared to be required was a judicious compromise between Japanese vested interests that would mitigate adjustment costs. The American initiative served as the catalyst.

Once begun, the intensity and public prominence of the new negotiations increased quickly. At their mid-point the American treasury secretary came to Tokyo and launched a shrill attack on the pace of change within the Japanese system. He wanted action on the various issues under discussion, especially those contributing directly to the yen's internationalization, and he was "through with patience." Only quick results would allow President Reagan to keep Democratic protectionists at bay and prevent "serious consequences" for Japan's economy.[68] Less publicly, the American negotiating team intentionally couched its positions in terms of the benefits liberalization would bring to Japan and of Japan's new place as an equal partner in the management of the international economy.[69] All of this served to heighten a sense of inevitability within the Ministry of Finance, a sense very helpful in attempts to convince reluctant domestic institutions and bureaucrats to go along.

Seeking a compromise on trust banking, ministry officials met continually with the interested parties during the spring of 1984. Three factors assisted their efforts: (1) the existence of a convenient scapegoat (the United States) on which to pin the blame for choices no one enjoyed making, (2) the feared possibility that, as had happened during debate on domestic jurisdictional matters in the context of the Banking Law, politicians could soon become more deeply involved, and (3) the belief that under proposed conditions foreign banks would have great difficulty penetrating the trust banking market.[70] More quickly than many thought possible, therefore, agreement was reached. The ministry would license a very limited number of foreign banks to operate on their own in the trust market; it would look favorably on the international expansion of trust banks; the prohibition on city banks undertaking trust business off shore would be lifted; finally, securities companies and city banks would be given greater latitude to provide investment advisory services on shore, but would not be permitted to set up full trust banks either directly or through offshore subsidiaries.[71] When the formal yen/dollar talks culminated in a bilateral understanding in May 1984, the ministry announced its intention to provide "qualified foreign banks" with trust banking licenses.[72] Specific criteria came later in the year, and the initial number of new licenses was to be limited to eight.[73] By the March 1985 deadline, nine foreign banks (six American, two Swiss, one British) had applied. To avoid an embarrassing protest and "considering Japanese banks' activities abroad," the finance minister announced in July that all nine would receive licenses.[74]

## Further Bilateral Interaction

The ad hoc committee also made progress on several other matters of direct or indirect importance to foreign banks in Japan. Under the rubric of national treatment, strongly reaffirmed by both sides, the Ministry of Finance agreed to eliminate swap limits altogether, to continue liberalizing CD limits, to expand the scope for foreign bank dealing in government bonds, to create a yen-denominated bankers acceptance market, to enhance the transparency of bank regulations, and to promote greater flexibility in interbank, foreign exchange, and Euroyen markets.[75] In a subsequent report to Congress, the Treasury congratulated Japan for making "substantial progress toward national treatment."[76]

Despite these encouraging results, it was apparent that the Treasury had encountered very strong resistance on matters touching the core mechanisms of domestic financial regulation. Suggestions, for example, that financial openness would be enhanced by completely deregulating domestic interest rates or abolishing funding restrictions in the segmented domestic market were rebuffed completely. Where truly powerful vested interests opposed change, the Americans risked provoking serious resentment and were at most able to persuade the Ministry of Finance to undertake further study. Further deregulation in Japan would have to await the outcome of ongoing domestic struggle.

At times this struggle could be marginally affected by foreign financial institutions, more by their actual activity in the marketplace than by their political involvements. This was especially evident in the securities market, where increasing competition among commercial banks, investment houses, and aggressive foreign institutions chipped away at the margins of traditional regulation. This competition intensified considerably after Citibank in November 1983 agreed to purchase a stake in a London stock brokerage firm that would effectively give it control over the firm's Tokyo branch. Although the transaction clearly violated Article 65 of the Japanese Securities and Exchange Act, which forbade bank involvement in the securities market, the Ministry of Finance approved the deal on an "exceptional basis" after three months of internal argument.[77] Needless to say, this mobilized Citibank's competitors, among them other foreign banks in Tokyo that were also quickly coming to the conclusion that their future lay not in traditional banking activities but in investment management and related areas.

This widely discussed shift in strategies seemed a natural development in a highly liquid market, a development slowed only by remaining functional distinctions between Japanese financial institutions. Citibank's initiative, not official U.S. demands, initially put significant pressure on the ministry. But during bilateral consultations that followed-up the ad hoc committee's report, treasury officials increased this pressure by pushing for expanded access for American securities companies. They were restrained initially, however, from pushing explicitly for similar access for American banks because their own domestic regulatory policies enforced identical functional distinctions in the United States. Not so constrained were officials from countries whose financial regulations made no such distinction between investment banking and commercial banking.

European governments followed the ad hoc committee talks closely. As they expected, the concessions won by the Americans were extended to them under an implicit most-favored-nation formula. This would not prove to be enough, however, for countries such as Britain, Germany, and Switzerland, whose banks still did not have the same flexibility in Japan that Japanese banks potentially enjoyed in their European operations. European dissatisfaction became patent in February 1984 when Sumitomo Bank challenged the traditional Japanese separation between banking and securities business by seeking to purchase a small Swiss bank, Banca del Gottardo. In the course of an aggressive international expansion program, Sumitomo had been attracted by the bank's universal banking capabilities and had seen the acquisition as an indirect route into European securities markets. Despite strong reservations, and indicative of changing power relationships in Japan as deregulation continued, the Ministry of Finance acquiesced.[78] Swiss and German banks in Japan subsequently requested reciprocal access to Japan's securities market but were again rebuffed in line with Article 65 prohibitions. They then pressed their home governments to take action on their behalf.[79]

Later in 1984 four Japanese securities companies, with the support of the ministry's Securities Bureau, applied to British authorities for permission to engage in banking in London. The request was initially rejected on prudential grounds because the securities companies had no clear access to the lender-of-last-resort facilities of the Bank of Japan. Although denied, an undertone of concern for reciprocity seemed apparent.[80] In response to the British decision, the ministry put a moratorium on licensing British securities companies seeking to enter Japan. Shortly thereafter, Germany responded to pressure from its own banks by making a distinction between Japanese institutions and others when it liberalized rules pertaining to its bond market. Following the change, foreign-owned banks were permitted for the first time to lead Eurodeutschemark bond issues; Japanese banks, however, were explicitly excepted, a move deliberately aimed at improving the reciprocal access of German banks in Japan. The Swiss threatened similar restraints on Japanese activities in Switzerland.[81]

In light of these controversies, a series of bilateral talks ensued between the Ministry of Finance and banking officials from Germany and Britain during 1985.[82] The key conclusion of these negotiations was a ministry decision to permit certain foreign banks from these countries to open securities offices in Japan indirectly through overseas affiliates. Together with a clarification of the prudential status of Japanese securities companies and an attendant expansion of the supervisory authority of the ministry's Banking Bureau, this concession cleared the way for an expansion of the business of foreign institutions in Japan and of their Japanese counterparts in Europe.[83] Subsequently many foreign securities companies and banks set up securities branches in Japan, several of which became members of the Tokyo Stock Exchange under unusually streamlined conditions. Japanese securities companies were enabled to continue their rapid expansion in major European banking and securities markets.[84] Within Japan there followed the predictable effort by the city banks, unhappy about the new freedom of foreign banks in Japan, to repeal Article 65 of the Securities and Exchange Law in the interest of equity. Their dissatisfaction was partly assuaged by the scale and pace of their growth overseas. By 1986, Japanese banks as a group had far outstripped their peer groups from other countries in aggregate international business volumes.[85]

What all of this would finally mean for foreign banks in Japan remained in question.[86] By 1986 some 79 foreign banks operated 115 branches, and over the previous twenty-year period aggregate foreign loan portfolios had grown by an average of 15 percent per year. Market penetration and profitability levels, however, were abysmal. Midway through the 1980s many foreign banks operated at a loss, and aggregate market share hovered between 2 and 3 percent.[87] Competitive conditions and a new phenomenon of the 1980s — loan losses — affected their positions adversely. At least so far, as some had feared, liberalization had not been the blessing many had been hoping for in the late 1970s. It had, however, greatly benefited strong domestic institutions both at home and in their burgeoning international operations. Yet there were no areas where the foreign banks were subject to regulatory constraints different from those facing their domestic competitors.[88] In fact, the number of areas where they were provided with exceptionally favorable treatment had multiplied. Some saw hope for the future in the securities field as Japan became the world's major capital exporter. But even here, the expansion of foreigners in Japan failed to match the growth of Japanese institutions abroad.[89] Nevertheless, perhaps ironically, both the Ministry of Finance and an array of foreign bankers believed that the solution to the problems of foreign institutions lay in further liberalization. On the basis of recent history, however, some bankers were beginning to express doubts.

During 1984, in the midst of its campaign for a trust banking license in Japan, Morgan Guaranty noted in its monthly journal, "If it is true that Japan enjoys an enduring comparative advantage in manufacturing, it follows that others have a comparative advantage in the field of financial and other services."[90] Tacitly accepting the logic of this assumption, foreign governments pressed for economic openness and institutional change within Japan. As they succeeded, the fundamental premise upon which their strategies were based began to look doubtful. What if the logic of Ricardo did not apply to the service sector in Japan? What if the structural arrangement of human resources in the country, the coordinating function of effective state institutions, the nature of competition in its dense and complex society, and the deepening capital intensity of its economy served to create for Japan a competitive advantage in financial services?[91] If the doubts were well founded, the fundamental problem for harmonious international relations in this sector became one of striking a stable balance between competitive efficiency, national control, and implicit obligations of fairness, a balance that could be struck only by government and not by an ideal, unfettered market.

Evolving understandings between governments and the consequently increasing specificity of tacit rules of reciprocal interaction in the banking sector represented attempts to strike such a balance. In the Japanese case, the technical complexity of the bilateral agreements reached after 1979 indicated the difficulty of squaring the standard of reciprocal national treatment with notions of control, efficiency, and fairness. Yet all of the major banking nations espoused the standard during their negotiations with Japan. They did come to insist, however, that nondiscrimination be interpreted pragmatically to balance institutional advantages. This called for ad hoc adjustments to take account of domestic structural differences and to ensure that institutional competition occurred in a manner perceived to be fair.[92] In addition to the trust banking licenses, notable examples of such adjustments came in the wake of continued intergovernmental negotiations: the granting of exceptional securities licenses to foreign banks in Tokyo in return for a lifting of restraints on Japanese institutions in foreign markets, increases in the capitalization requirements of Japanese banks, and the granting of banking licenses to select foreign securities companies in Tokyo.[93]

Within Japan, pressures associated with increasing financial interdependence and with the increasingly clear expectations of other states raised fundamental questions about the ability of government to maintain distinctive national structures at acceptable political cost. The same pressures, of course, faced other OECD countries. But in Japan's case, the dilemma was particularly acute because longstanding rigidities had bred very strong vested interests. Direct political interventions from abroad continued to provide Japanese officials with a useful tool for dealing with those interests. These officials remained hopeful that in the long term, gradual liberalization would appease everyone; in the short term, they believed that ad hoc adjustments would do the same. In such a context, they sought to preserve domestic financial and political stability, to balance competing domestic interests, and to sustain the growth of Japanese institutions at home and abroad.[94]

CHAPTER FIVE

# Canada

Nationalism has rarely been absent from debates on economic policy in Canada. With regard to the regulation of banks, it has traditionally been a central influence. The protection of domestic banks from foreign competition within the Canadian market long remained an explicit or implicit priority for both liberal and conservative governments—which makes all the more remarkable the shift in Canada's market access policy since the late 1960s. Despite nationalist opposition, during the next two decades the market was decisively opened up to foreign banks, and the country moved toward a regulatory standard of reciprocal nondiscrimination.

## THE POLICY DEBATE: RECALIBRATING MARKET STRUCTURES IN A CONFEDERAL SYSTEM

Before World War II, only three foreign banks had operated in the domestic Canadian market. Two of them—British banks that predated confederation—were absorbed by indigenous institutions early in the twentieth century. The third, Barclays Bank of England, received a charter from Parliament in 1928 but before long merged with the local Imperial Bank, which was itself later folded into the Canadian Imperial Bank of Commerce. In 1953 the National Handelsbank of the Netherlands was chartered on an exceptional basis with the proviso that it concentrate its limited operations on trade financing. The Dutch owners established the Mercantile Bank and carried on business for nine years. In 1962 Rotterdamsche Bank acquired Handelsbank and endeavored to sell its Canadian subsidi-

94

ary. The interested potential purchaser was the First National City Bank of New York (later renamed Citibank).

The roots of the subsequent political imbroglio can be traced to the year 1957.[1] The publication then of a royal commission study on the Canadian economy signaled the end of an era of unquestioned support for the free inflow of foreign investment.[2] The Gordon Report, named for the commission's chairman, Walter Gordon, documented the vast stake foreign interests had amassed in the Canadian economy and questioned whether the resulting costs in national political autonomy and long-term economic development had not exceeded associated benefits. Although its recommendations were cautious and generally downplayed at the time, the Gordon Report raised public awareness of the potential threat of foreign domination and articulated ideas that would shape the thinking of a generation of Canadian academics and policy makers. Of more immediate importance, it would crystallize the worldview of Walter Gordon himself, who when the Liberals returned to power in 1963 under Lester Pearson became minister of finance.[3]

Whether Citibank intentionally avoided contacting Walter Gordon during the initial stages of discussions with the Dutch owners of the Mercantile is still a matter of conjecture. Although they did advise the Bank of Canada of their plans, and were apparently advised to see Gordon, they in fact waited until after an agreement to purchase had been signed. At that point (July 18, 1963), Citibank's president, James Rockefeller, met with Gordon only to be told that the government of Canada would not look with favor on the bank's initiative.[4] There being no direct legal impediment to the purchase, Citibank nevertheless proceeded to close the deal. In September it acquired the controlling share of the Mercantile. In subsequent months David Rockefeller, president of Citibank's chief rival, Chase Manhattan, came to Canada to explore the possibility of acquiring the Toronto-Dominion Bank and approached Gordon in that regard. Aroused by Citibank's defiance, the finance minister quickly precluded that option by announcing that the upcoming Bank Act revision would incorporate a strict limitation on nonresident ownership of Canadian bank shares.[5]

Revision of the Bank Act began in 1964 when the government received the recommendations of the Porter Report on the financial system.[6] The report focused on the need to liberalize the Canadian financial market in order to spur competition, but agreed with the earlier Gordon Report on the question of maintaining dominant domestic control of the banking industry. To reconcile the two imperatives, it made its recommendation that foreign banks be permitted to establish a strictly limited presence in the market by way of agencies. Such entities were to have restricted powers, notably on the deposit-taking side, which would limit their penetration without obviating the potential benefits flowing from their competition in such areas as commercial lending, trade financing, and foreign exchange.

Although the Porter Report never specifically addressed the issues raised by the Mercantile situation, the subsequent draft legislation showed the direct influence of Gordon on the matter and demonstrated the sympathy his position had aroused in the mainstream of his party. Specifically, no provision was proposed for the entry of foreign bank agencies, and maximum bank ownership restrictions (10 percent for any individual person or corporation; 25 percent for any group of nonresidents) were introduced. Furthermore, because these latter restrictions could not apply to the Mercantile without blatantly violating the principle of nonretroactivity, Mercantile was directly, though anonymously, targeted in a proposal that any existing bank having nonresident ownership in excess of 25 percent— there was only one—could not possess assets totaling more than twenty times its authorized capital. Insofar as leverage is the key to bank profitability, this proposal threatened to stunt Mercantile's growth and render it uncompetitive in a marketplace where indigenous institutions commonly maintained gearing ratios of 40:1 or 50:1. The alternative was for Citibank to reduce its ownership.[7] After these proposals were presented in 1965, the U.S. State Department informally expressed its concern to the Canadian government over their apparently discriminatory and effectively retroactive character.[8]

Parliamentary consideration of the proposed Bank Act began in 1966 after a new federal election returned the Liberals to power again in a tacit coalition with the nationalist and left-leaning New Democrats. Although Gordon had by then resigned his ministry, his foreign bank proposals went to committee without major change. But prior to the November hearings of the Commons Committee on Finance, Trade, and Economic Affairs, a number of pointed exchanges took place between Canada and the United States.

In April the U.S. State Department followed up its previous informal communications with an official diplomatic note. The note objected to the discriminatory character of the nonresident control proposals and reminded the Canadian government of the "substantial benefits derived by Canadian banks from operations in the United States."[9] The Canadian Department of External Affairs replied with a lengthy explanation of the special national interest considerations behind the proposals, including the need to maintain monetary control, and contrasted Canada's eight banks with America's fourteen thousand. Extremely concerned by the broader implications of the Canadian reasoning for other types of investment in other countries, the Americans responded with a blistering telex. The message bluntly rejected the Canadian rationale and highlighted the American preference for handling investment issues on a nondiscriminatory, national treatment basis, rather than on the basis of strict reciprocity. However, the telex concluded:

> USA Govt. continues to hold the view that it is not reasonable to expect the privileged position now enjoyed by Cdn. banks in USA would continue unimpaired if only USA-owned bank in Cda. is subjected to retroactive and discriminatory treatment. In this connection, Govt. of Cda. will be aware of legislation which has been introduced before USA Congress which would provide means of giving effect to principle of reciprocity through federal control of foreign owned banks. In addition, since action contemplated by Cdn. Govt. will not only adversely affect Mercantile Bank but will also undermine ground rules on which all American-owned firms operating in Cda. must rely, USA Govt. has under exam. a number of other courses of action consistent with very serious view it takes of issue.[10]

This American reaction confirmed the worst fears of the more internationally oriented Canadian banks. During 1965 several bank chairmen, speaking for their own institutions and not collectively had made representations to the prime minister regarding the seriousness of possible retaliation and the need to establish the principle of reciprocity at home so that they could proceed with their own expansions abroad.[11] The premiers of two provinces later supplemented this more positive view of foreign banks by publicly praising Mercantile for injecting a new competitive spirit into the banking system.

Committee hearings began in November 1966. Two domestic bank chairmen, from the Bank of Montreal and the Royal Bank of Canada, testified in support of Mercantile and strongly in favor of licensing foreign bank agencies. Significantly, the Canadian Bankers Association (CBA) did not submit a brief on this particular issue, for a clear consensus could not be reached among its membership.[12] In January 1967 James Rockefeller, together with several executives from Mercantile, testified before the parliamentary committee. Commentators generally acknowledged at the time that the bankers made a poor impression and showed little understanding or sympathy for Canadian sensitivities in this area. A number of Rockefeller's comments, particularly his denial that Citibank had enlisted the support of the State Department, were received with great skepticism. Meanwhile, the heavy-handedness of U.S. communications, which had in general substance by now become publicly known, were having the opposite effect to that intended. Mitchell Sharp, Gordon's successor as finance minister, found it necessary to state in the Commons that he would not bend to external pressure on the foreign banking matter. Nevertheless, in view of the comments of interested Canadian parties, he later agreed to take a second look at the matter of foreign agencies and at possible modifications in the effective date by which Citibank would have to divest or scale down Mercantile's leverage to 20:1.

After Gordon's reinstatement to the cabinet in early 1967, even such a tentative move toward reconsideration prompted a split in the government. In part, this reflected an unusual welling-up of public support for the nationalist position. The net result of internal cabinet debates included a reaffirmation of the foreign bank proposals, no new proposal for licensing agencies, but an extension of the date for Citibank's compliance from 1967 to 1972 with the proviso that the cabinet could shorten this extension at any time if it considered such action to be in the national interest. In this form the portions of the Bank Act related to foreign banks were enacted when legislation cleared Parliament in March 1967. The U.S. State Department issued a press release branding the legislation retroactive and discriminatory but specifying no retaliatory action. None was forthcoming. Citibank reduced the assets of Mercantile to comply with the new gearing requirement but steadfastly refused to divest.

The set of circumstances surrounding the 1967 revision of the Bank Act may have been unusual, at least with respect to the stridency with which relatively extreme positions were put forward and with which aggrieved external actors attempted to reverse the course of a domestic debate. To be sure, there were moderates in the cabinet and in Parliament capable of designing a compromise solution. In the end, they were undercut by the completely counterproductive pressure coming from the U.S. government. In the face of this pressure, a balanced assessment of the costs and benefits of institutional openness in the Canadian banking sector had become impossible. In retrospect, it is possible to conclude that the Mercantile Bank affair provided a striking example of politics dominating markets and of domestic politics overriding an international normative standard explicitly promoted by the United States. Despite the economic benefits anticipated by the Porter Commission, despite the potential costs of retaliation and the concerns expressed by leading domestic bankers and despite the country's dependence on trade and invest-

ment with the United States, Canada's bank regulatory policy in 1967
reflected the views of an aggressively nationalist group considered on
the fringe of domestic political life ten years earlier. This victory,
however, would seem Pyrrhic only five years hence.

*Institutional Reform in the 1970s*

Foreign banking receded from the headlines after passage of the
1967 Bank Act, and foreign bankers shifted their sights from the
political arena back to the marketplace. In spite of its political idiosyncracies, Canada remained attractive. The country possessed vast
natural resource supplies and required significant capital imports if
those supplies were to be exploited. Its domestic economy boasted a
fair level of industrial development, and its polity, notwithstanding
occasional bursts of nationalistic enthusiasm, was stable. In an era
of rapid international expansion, Canada became an obvious target
on the strategic planning maps of the world's major banks. The continued, if limited, operation of Citibank within the country provided those banks with added competitive incentive.

The opportunity to respond to this incentive came with the redis-
covery that banking had never been explicitly defined in the British
North America Act and that the confederal nature of the Canadian
state provided an opening in the intended protective wall surrounding the domestic market. International banks could incorporate as
near-banks in Canada under provincial laws as long as they did not
accept deposits or call themselves banks. Owing to a serious difference of views between the federal and provincial governments over
the benefits of the entry of near-banks, therefore, foreign banks
indirectly began coming into Canada almost immediately after the
new Bank Act was passed.[13] Between 1968 and 1974 at least sixty
foreign institutions established small finance companies, leasing
companies, and other lending vehicles, funded primarily by means
of short-term money market instruments, usually bearing parent
guarantees.[14] Simultaneously, unimpeded by federal or provincial
restrictions, many also set up unincorporated representative offices
whose principal mandates were to solicit business for booking off
shore. As the business of the near-banks expanded and the domestic
banks began to complain, the federal government became ever more
concerned.

The CBA began studying the matter in earnest when the total
business volume of the near-banks exceeded C$1 billion in 1974.
Throughout the year, the Big Five banks sought the consensus that
had eluded them in 1966. In principle, they agreed that the near-

banks had to be brought under control. Their ability to elude the federal bank regulatory framework left them with anomalous and artificial competitive advantages, which partly accounted for the rapidity of their growth. They faced, for example, no reserve requirements on their deposits, and some of their effective business powers exceeded those of chartered banks themselves. The resulting situation was untenable. But, as in 1966, agreement ended there.

In large part, disagreements among the major domestic banks reflected differing market strategies during a period of rapid expansion and diversification both in Canada and abroad. From the end of World War II until 1970, the growth of the chartered banks in absolute terms roughly mirrored the overall expansion of the Canadian economy. But during the 1970s, their growth rates exploded; their deposits, for example, rose at an average annual rate of 18 percent.[15] A significant part of this growth was from international operations.[16]

Of course the Canadian banks had long been important players in international markets, particularly in Central and South America where historical trade patterns spawned extensive retail banking networks. Trading links also led Canadian banks to establish agencies in New York as early as the 1890s. The internationalization of the 1970s, however, was part of a broader global phenomenon of a qualitatively and quantitatively different character. The biggest growth was on the wholesale side of the business, lending and deposit taking involving governments, major corporations, and other banks. In the whirlwind of resulting cross-border competition, the Canadian banks moved decisively to match the strategic thrusts of aggressive American, Japanese, and European rivals. In absolute terms, the physical expansion of the Big Five was dramatic.[17] But just as this outward-directed growth and diversification was occurring among the Canadian banks, foreign banks sought to accomplish the same for themselves in the domestic Canadian market.

In April 1974, cognizant of this threat, the Bank of Nova Scotia (BNS) took the lead in a new attempt to build a common position by circulating an analysis of the subject to the other banks and to the minister of finance, John Turner. BNS contended that legislative prohibitions against foreign bank entry and the effective presence of those institutions in the guise of near-banks had created the worst of all worlds—unrestrained foreign competition, which hindered monetary control and weakened domestic banks, and a lack of reciprocity in law, which constrained the expansion of domestic banks abroad. To remedy this circumstance, BNS recommended that near-banks be immediately brought under the purview of the federal

Bank Act or a new foreign bank act. To the anticipated objection that such a course was effectively blocked by the division of powers spelled out in the British North America Act, BNS proposed that the federal government innovatively make use of its statutory powers under the constitution to control the entry of aliens into Canada.[18] Finally, BNS suggested that foreign banks be subject to annual licensing reviews (as opposed to the effectively ten-year review for domestic banks under the auspices of Bank Act revision), that they be restricted to two or three offices in major centers, that they be exempted from the nonresident ownership provisions of the Bank Act, but that in all other respects they be treated in a manner identical with the domestic banks.

Discussion among the Big Five continued for several months along the general lines of the BNS proposal. Although disagreements remained about the details, such as whether near-banks should be able to convert to branches of their parents, four of the banks—BNS, the Royal Bank of Canada (RBC), the Bank of Montreal (BMO), and the Canadian Imperial Bank of Commerce (CIBC)—agreed that the need for control was urgent and that some sort of reciprocity criterion should quickly be embodied in legislation.[19]

A strongly divergent view, however, came from the Toronto-Dominion Bank (TD). Bank leaders argued that Canada's situation was unique among developed countries in the vulnerability of its economy to foreign control and that this necessarily justified strict limitations on foreign bank entry.[20] Furthermore, they contended that a lack of formal reciprocity had not hindered Canadian bank expansion in the most important markets abroad and that true reciprocity would prove impossible to administer in the Canadian national market. Finally, they insisted that the growth of foreign banks threatened Canada first with a weakening of the efficiency of monetary policy—particularly because foreigners would not likely respond to moral suasion from the central bank—and ultimately with an irreversible transfer of full economic control to the United States.

This divergence of views among the banks gave the government an excuse to delay action. Further study was evidently preferred to initiatives that would in any case require review when the current Bank Act expired. Underneath this preference, however, was a more fundamental reluctance on the part of federal leaders to risk offending the provinces by moving quickly to extend federal jurisdiction in a disputed policy arena.[21] In the meantime, the growth of the foreign near-banks continued.

Governmental reluctance dissipated, however, as the statutory deadline for revision of the Bank Act approached. The issue of the near-banks would have to be dealt with in the context of a public review of the act, for domestic bankers could be counted on to press the matter vigorously. Even without their prodding, the rapid expansion of the near-banks had by the late 1970s reached a point where in federal policy-making circles the fear of an irremediable loss of financial control began overriding willingness to continue deferring to the provinces.[22] Such concerns were apparent in an influential study put out by the Economic Council of Canada in 1976. The study pointed out the unavoidable conflict between the two motive forces propelling existing federal trade and investment policies, namely, the will to reap the economic benefits of a liberal trading and investing environment and the desire to foster domestic ownership and control. It continued, "This same conflict is apparent in the field of banking. Over the last decade, world capital markets have become increasingly integrated, and banking has become an international activity, a process in which Canadian banks have participated actively, bringing tangible benefits to Canada. However, there is some uneasiness that the deposit-taking industry in Canada may be dominated by foreign, especially U.S., banks."[23] The council concluded that the latter risk was manageable and that the benefits resulting from increased foreign competition were significant. It therefore recommended that a "foreign-owned banks act" be passed in conjunction with the next Bank Act. The new act would stipulate a staged entry procedure for foreign firms, legalizing but restricting their direct banking operations in the domestic market for ten years or so and then gradually lifting constraints as growth allowed them to sell off a substantial share of their equity to Canadian residents. After the transitional period, the council recommended, regulatory policy should embody the principle of nondiscrimination.

The Economic Council's study was timed to have an impact on federal legislative proposals then being drafted in anticipation of the June 30, 1977, expiry of the Bank Act. Preparatory work had in fact been underway in the Department of Finance since September 1974 when the minister had called for submissions from any interested parties. In August 1976 a set of policy prescriptions in the form of a white paper came out of the department for public consideration and comment. Foreign banking was only one of the issues dealt with, but was surely the most significant.[24]

The white paper noted the increasing international activity of Canadian banks (258 branches, 11 agencies, 48 controlled subsidiaries, and 50 representative offices in over 60 countries) and the reciprocal effective expansion of foreign banks in Canada (over 60 banks through 120 affiliated corporations and 40 representative offices, approximately half American and slightly less than half European). Although it then emphasized the need to bring these latter institutions under an orderly federal regulatory framework, the paper went on in a tone markedly changed from governmental views put forward in the 1960s.

> Foreign banks are to be encouraged because of the additional competitive and innovative forces that they can bring to bear in the relatively highly concentrated Canadian banking system. They are to be encouraged too because of the additional financial support which they, with their world-wide connections, can bring to the development of our resources, industries and trade. There is also the further consideration that if we provide a basis in law for the operation of foreign banks in Canada, we can expect our own banks to obtain reciprocal recognition in other countries which is necessary if they are to extend their participation in international markets as we would like.[25]

On this basis, the paper proposed that the new Bank Act include the following provisions. (1) Foreign banks would be "encouraged and expected" to incorporate under federal jurisdiction in the form of subsidiaries; the branch or agency form of initial establishment would be prohibited, and representative offices would be required to register with the Inspector General of Banks.[26] (2) Affiliates of foreign banks choosing to remain outside federal control would be forbidden to raise funds in Canadian money markets under the guarantee of their parents.[27] (3) The boards of directors of foreign bank subsidiaries were to be at least half composed of Canadian citizens. (4) Although Bank Act ownership restrictions would be waived for foreign bank subsidiaries, their leverage would be restricted to 20 times their authorized (by the federal government) capital unless parent banks reduced their holdings below 25 percent. Through the mechanism of authorized capital allocations, individual banks could grow to C$500 million in assets and aggregate foreign bank operations would be limited to 15 percent of total commercial lending activity in Canada. (5) Foreign banks would be limited initially to one office, but could later be permitted to open a maximum of five branches. (6) Foreign banks would be required to maintain assets in Canada at least equal to their Canadian liabilities and to keep all relevant records within Canada.[28] (7) A foreign bank subsidiary would normally be allowed to incorporate only if "treatment as

favorable" for Canadian banks is available in its parent's home jurisdiction.[29] (8) The Foreign Investment Review Agency (established in
1973 to screen incoming direct investment) would have no jurisdiction over bank entry. Instead, applications would be made to the
inspector general of banks, acting for the minister of finance, who
would assess the potential contributions of individual applicants to
the healthy competitive development of Canadian banking before
granting licenses.[30]

These proposals were presented when difficulties were mounting
in the economy as a whole. Gross fixed capital formation, an indicator of general economic health, consistently rose in real terms during the early 1970s but peaked in 1976 and fell in 1977 and 1978.[31]
The country's balance on its external account fell from a surplus of
C$916 million in 1970 to a deficit of C$4.7 billion in 1976 and C$5.4
billion in 1979.[32] In a similar fashion, the federal budget went from
a surplus in the early 1970s to a consistently deepening deficit in the
four years following 1976. In tandem, gross external debt rose
sharply. The reversal of the government's stand of a decade earlier,
even if still somewhat tentative, reflected the changing economic
context. Although the temptation was still to err on the side of caution, the efficiency gains promised in such assessments of foreign
banking as that of the Economic Council were now taken seriously.

## The Bank Act of 1980

Publication of the white paper served as the signal for serious policy debate to begin. Reaction came swiftly. The provinces, especially
Ontario, were predictably unhappy about the prospect of losing
jurisdiction over the foreign near-banks. They were even more
incensed, however, by separate proposals to force domestic near-
banks to hold reserves at the Bank of Canada and to join a new
national payments system. Provincial governments perceived a subtle but dangerous federal assault on their financial regulatory powers, and they quickly attempted to counter it. As a result, following
a meeting of provincial and federal finance ministers in December
1976, the federal government agreed to drop the domestic near-bank
proposals. In return, the provinces acceded to federal demands on
foreign banking.

Through the CBA, the domestic banks put forward a consensus
view on most of the issues raised in the white paper but pointedly
noted their inability to reach a joint position regarding foreign
banking.[33] It was instead left for each bank to comment separately.
For the most part, the separate positions remained what they had

been in 1974 and 1975. Once again, the most atypical view came from TD. In an official submission to the government, TD held that the white paper flatly contradicted the government's objective of reducing the vulnerability of Canada's "branch plant" economy and grossly underestimated the existing competitive vigor of Canadian banking. It pointed out again that reciprocity constraints posed no impediment to chartered bank growth overseas, except in Switzerland and Japan, and that true reciprocity would not be in Canada's broader interests. "The concern of the Toronto-Dominion Bank," the submission concluded, "is not that the foreign banks will affect our earnings adversely. Rather we cannot see what advantages Canada would gain from a significant penetration of the market by foreign banks; we believe that their operations should be curtailed."[34]

Most of the foreign institutions operating in Canada as near-banks realized that their legal status was problematic; at this point they therefore chose to keep a fairly low profile in the domestic debate.[35] Quietly, the largest near-banks made private representations to policy makers in which they generally contended that the proposed regulatory treatment was unnecessarily restrictive and discriminatory. Concerned that policy makers might insist on the proposed approach, however, several lobbyists pleaded for a few changes in detail that would make a difference to their operations without contradicting the central intent of the bill. In truth, in the run-up to the new Bank Act the local representatives of the foreign banks found they lacked serious political clout partly because of their questionable legal status and partly because they lacked cohesiveness as a group.

In the head offices of the foreign banks, the subtleties of the white paper, which did after all represent a more palatable federal policy than the one proposed ten years earlier, failed to galvanize either coherent opposition or support.[36] Most banks simply prepared for the seemingly inevitable, principally by aggressively expanding their Canadian business while legislative discussions continued.[37] For their part, foreign governments adopted a judicious wait-and-see posture.[38]

During 1977 and 1978 a vigorous public debate took place in Canada on various banking issues, including the foreign bank question. The intensity of the debate was such that the Commons Standing Committee on Finance, Trade, and Economic Affairs felt compelled to postpone hearings on a new Bank Act until late in 1978.[39] Over the course of those two years the pages of the *Toronto Star,* in particular, were filled with commentary on the foreign bank matter.[40] In addition, press attention was given to discussions in the United

States over the shaping of its own foreign banking legislation and to the negative reactions generated by a spate of foreign takeovers of American banks. The echoes of earlier controversy were still heard. Walter Gordon, now in private life, took up the old struggle against the foreign banks and called unequivocally for their expulsion from Canada. "Surely," he publicly stated, "we are beginning to understand that if we continue to give up control over our economy—of our own basic industries—we shall, sooner or later, lose control of our political independence as well."[41]

When committee hearings finally began in the Commons and the Senate in 1978, the foreign bank proposals contained in the 1976 white paper remained virtually unchanged; opposition to them appeared fragmentary, and there was by then a general consensus in Ottawa on the need to control the growing foreign presence. Nevertheless, the failure of the nationalist position to arouse widespread support, in contrast to 1966, was notable. Broader economic difficulties, the existing presence of foreign banks through affiliated companies, rising doubts about the efficacy of general foreign investment controls (stimulated especially by growing troubles in the natural resource sector), and the general absence of blatant foreign governmental interference appeared to reduce the appetites of policy makers for more extreme alternatives. Majority support gradually consolidated around proposals put forward in the 1976 white paper that seemed well designed both to stimulate direct competition in domestic banking and to maintain a sufficient degree of national control. Divergent views, however, came out during the hearings.

In testimony before the committees, foreign bank spokesmen, usually local officers but occasionally visiting representatives of European and American banking federations, acceded to most of the proposed changes but expressed misgivings, especially about growth restraints in the process for allocating authorized capital and about the 15 percent market share ceiling. They argued generally that any politically determined size restrictions would only serve to undercut the government's stated goal of enhancing competition.[42] Opposing views also came from the domestic banking community, which remained, however, unable to shape a consensus position. BNS, for example, labeled the draft legislation protectionist and warned that it risked provoking retaliation. RBC opposed all statutory restrictions and favored discretionary regulation of individual foreign banks on the basis of reciprocity. BMO and CIBC generally supported the proposed legislation with minor reservations. TD, on the other hand, remained adamantly opposed and called again for heightened restrictions.[43]

Objections to the foreign bank proposals based on fears of a loss of monetary control were contradicted in the testimony of the governor of the Bank of Canada. Although the governor favored a gradual approach to foreign entry in order to mitigate uncertainties, he contended that moral suasion was no longer a key instrument of monetary policy and that other monetary control instruments were unaffected by the nationality of parent banks.[44] In light of such testimony, and in the absence of any widely supported alternative, expeditious passage of a new Bank Act basically consonant with the ideas of the 1976 white paper appeared certain. But then a larger domestic political agenda intervened.

The year 1979 was one of political turbulence within Canada.[45] Over a ten-month period the long-standing federal Liberal government fell, a minority Conservative one ruled for a short time, and the Liberals regained power with a clear majority (146 of 281 seats). The country witnessed the political death and resurrection of Prime Minister Pierre Trudeau and a perceptible shift of his Liberal party to the left.[46] A renewed sense of nationalism was apparent in reaction to an active separatist movement in Quebec and in the strong negative response engendered by Conservative proposals to reprivatize a recently nationalized oil company. Although some foreign bankers feared that this new electoral mood might lead to a stiffening of the long-delayed Bank Act, the proposed legislation retained the bipartisan support it had gathered before the elections. Proponents of the new act had been able to assuage nationalist concerns in part by pointing to the controls on foreign banking embedded in its provisions.

The delay gave valuable time to those still interested in modifying the proposed act. Although it is difficult to determine the full extent of these efforts, one study, based on a wide range of participant interviews, concluded that most related lobbying took place then at the level of ministers and senior bureaucrats to the relative neglect of members of parliament. Foreign bankers in particular lobbied as individuals or in small groups, both because their common interest was unclear and because most believed that the impression of a united front would not be well received by Canadian policy makers.[47] Even so, this lobbying apparently contributed to several minor changes in the bill before a new Parliament elected in February 1980 convened.[48]

Although the two major parties now favored the proposed bill, it still took Parliament ten months to finish dealing with it. Significantly contributing to the delay were the obstructionist tactics of the New Democrats who retained thirty-two seats in the new Commons. Most of the NDP opposition related to strictly domestic issues, but a strain of nationalistic defensiveness on the foreign banking question ran through the party's interventions in final hearings and debates.[49] Nevertheless, on November 26, 1980, a new Bank Act, fundamentally consistent with the 1976 white paper, finally became law.[50]

## THE POLICY OUTCOME: CAUTIOUS LIBERALISM

The 1980 Bank Act created two classes of banks: those listed in its Schedule A, existing or new banks whose shares were widely held and at least 75 percent owned by Canadians, and those covered by Schedule B, mainly wholly-owned subsidiaries of foreign banks. Unique conditions were placed on the licenses of the so-called Schedule B's, most importantly the requirement that individual banks could grow to a maximum asset size of 20 times their "deemed authorized capital," as determined by the inspector general.[51] When multiplied by twenty, this pool of fictitious "allocable capital" would always equal 8 percent of the domestic assets of the Schedule A banks. The growth of the Schedule B's therefore became a function of growth among the Schedule A banks. In addition to several other conditions originally proposed in the white paper, significant discretionary authority was delegated to the inspector general, acting with the consent of the finance minister.[52]

Whether at bottom the provisions of the Bank Act were intended to protect the domestic banking market or to open it up, their actual effect changed the market dramatically and quickly.[53] Anticipating adoption of legislation consistent with the 1976 white paper, individual foreign near-banks acted rationally by rapidly building up their business volumes in order better to position themselves for the capital allocations that would obviously become a scarce resource after enactment. Such strategies were assisted by overall growth in the Canadian market during this period. Their aggregate assets thus grew from C$2.4 billion in 1976 to C$9.7 billion by the end of 1980.

Once the act passed, applications for Schedule B licenses began pouring into the inspector general's newly expanded office. Licenses were subsequently granted after evaluations based on competition, safety, reciprocity, and geographic balance considerations.[54] This action followed a round of bilateral negotiations, most importantly with Japan, where the major domestic banks sought permission to open full branches. By May 1982, fifty-seven new banks (almost all

*Table 10.* Original distribution of Schedule B bank assets (C$ millions)

| Country of parent | December 1983 | June 1984 | % of total |
|---|---|---|---|
| United States total | 9,319 | 10,101 | 45.3 |
| Citibank | (2,737) | – | – |
| Chemical | (1,300) | – | – |
| Bank of America | (1,282) | – | – |
| United Kingdom total | 3,116 | 3,274 | 14.7 |
| Barclays | (1,254) | – | – |
| France | 2,638 | 2,843 | 12.7 |
| Other European | 2,263 | 2,844 | 12.7 |
| Japan | 1,468 | 2,139 | 9.6 |
| Other | 1,054 | 1,114 | 5.0 |
| Total | 19,858 | 22,315 | 100.0 |

SOURCE: Compiled from CBA, "Schedule B Statistics," Toronto, January and June 1984. The Citibank figure does not include Mercantile; by 1983 the bank retained only a 25 percent stake and would soon sell out completely because it no longer required an indirect vehicle into the market.

foreign owned) were chartered, including thirty-one that converted from near-bank status and twenty-six that established de novo.[55] Asset size varied markedly, and deemed capital was allocated on a generally proportional basis. The distribution pattern by country is suggested in Table 10. Ten of the original Schedule B's had assets in excess of C$500 million. Within three years of the Bank Act, aggregate employment among them totaled almost thirty-five hundred, of which 95 percent were Canadian citizens. The banks were permitted to open almost two hundred branches across the country in their first years of operation, although over 60 percent of their business was concentrated in the Toronto area.[56]

After much debate about the advisability of starting their own trade association, the foreign banks decided to join the CBA.[57] In general, the foreign banks welcomed the new legitimacy the Bank Act had given to their presence in Canada and quickly adapted their operations to the new regulatory environment. Early on, however, they began bridling at the more significant restrictions therein imposed, particularly the statutory 8-percent ceiling and two subsequent discretionary limitations: a 50-percent limit on offshore funding and a maximum lending limit on loans to any one client of 50 percent of a bank's capital base (excluding the capital of the parent).[58] The 8-percent ceiling subsequently became the political rallying point for the foreign banks.

The Schedule B's were a disparate group in terms of both management approach and market strategy. Although most initially went after major corporate business, some concentrated on lending to medium-sized companies, foreign exchange, or selective (mainly ethnic) retail business. But the issue of the 8-percent ceiling brought them together as both competitors and collaborators. On a competitive level, the ceiling became a target for the group as a whole, since the logical goal of each bank was to expand as quickly as possible in order to grab a maximal market share.[59] Their aggregate assets therefore grew much more quickly than the regulators had originally expected. In addition, a major recession in 1980 slowed the growth of domestic bank assets, thus fixing the maximum volume of business open to the new entrants. On a collaborative level, the ill-conceived control mechanism gave the foreign banks common cause and a clear focus for cooperation. The net result was unexpectedly rapid development of market and political pressure on the 8-percent ceiling. The issue had, in fact, become an obsession with many foreign bankers long before their aggregate market share reached 8 percent.

As early as 1981, when they were just receiving their operating licenses, presidents of Schedule B's appeared regularly in the local business press and complained vigorously about the ceiling.[60] The American presidents also seem to have initiated contacts in Washington at this time.[61] Early in 1982 the foreign banks proposed within the CBA a formal resolution calling on the minister of finance to review the situation with a view toward removal of the ceiling. The association's executive council, however, called the resolution premature and turned it down. In connection with studies going on in Washington, an American bank executive in Toronto then requested explicit statements of position from all of the major Canadian banks; none was forthcoming. Shortly thereafter, the American Bankers' Association submitted a bluntly worded briefing paper to U.S. governmental study groups, which concluded, "We must convince the Canadians that they have no legitimate need to protect their healthy banking industry from foreign competition."[62]

By the middle of 1982 leading foreign banks had agreed on a concerted strategy aimed at redressing their grievances. First, having made little progress in moving the CBA as a whole, they decided to coordinate efforts through their own subcommittee, dubbed the Schedule B Foreign Banks Executive Committee. Second, they concentrated attention on the 8-percent ceiling and postponed consideration of other restrictive measures. Third, in order to minimize the direct involvement of their parents, they decided to manage the lobbying effort both in Canada and in their home countries themselves. On this basis, the executive committee initiated a formal campaign against the ceiling by forwarding to the finance minister, Allan MacEachen, a unanimous resolution of the foreign banking community stating that the restrictive ceiling was not in accord with true reciprocity, especially in view of the continuing growth of major Canadian banks abroad, and requesting its removal at the first available opportunity. The minister responded that because the ceiling had not yet been reached, the request was too early.[63]

Around this time a consensus emerged among the foreign bankers to tone down the rhetoric and attempt gradually to persuade relevant policy makers with arguments stressing the benefits of their presence in Canada. Although the group was led principally by American bankers, it was decided that a more prominent role would be given to non-American spokesmen in order to deemphasize the bilateral aspects of the issue.[64] Key foreign bankers had previously argued both publicly and privately that Canada's Bank Act was not in conformity with the country's standing as a summit country or with its moral obligations as a liberal trading nation; henceforth the argument would be put chiefly in terms of Canada's national interest by a decidedly pro-Canadian group.[65] This approach did not preclude subtle references to the possibility of future retaliatory responses in other countries, but it did represent a marked change in the tone of the foreign banks' campaign within Canada.

Late in 1982 articles started turning up in the Canadian press about the positive contributions made by foreign banks in Canada.[66] Increasing press coverage was also given to the ceiling issue as foreign bank asset volumes continued to soar. In October the inspector general made an important concession to the Schedule B's on the question of lending limits to individual corporate names; individual loans could now be up to 100 percent of their actual capital. Another concession five months later made it easier for foreign banks to raise funding in the New York money markets. Despite these welcome changes, pressure on the 8-percent ceiling continued to mount.

By the beginning of 1983 the major foreign banks had presented their cases to their home governments and had requested that the issue be raised in official bilateral and multilateral forums.[67] Four American bank executives, for example, journeyed to Washington in February to urge federal officials to "communicate the urgency of their concerns to their counterparts in Canada."[68] Schedule B executives also stepped up their calls on officials in Ottawa, especially on the finance minister, the inspector general, the governor of the Bank of Canada, the chairman of the Commons Finance Committee, and various finance department officers. Showing considerable foresight, they also spent a great deal of time canvassing the country in an effort to build up grass roots support from, for example, businessmen who were benefiting from lower borrowing rates as a result

of foreign bank competition.[69] Finally, members of the Executive
Committee sought to strengthen their relationships with the chairmen of the Big Five in the hopes of neutralizing their opposition, if
not gaining their support.

Foreign bankers were convinced that any one of the major banks
could prevent their success in Ottawa. Inside the Big Five, the calculation of interests was complicated. On the one hand, Schedule B
competition was definitely hurting, especially in the corporate market, where many of the foreigners appeared to be willing to lend at
a loss in order to establish an initial market share. On the other
hand, the Schedule B's themselves could be valuable correspondent
banking customers. Strategic planners within the domestic banks
were also increasingly mindful of the needs of their international
divisions. By mid-1983, the postures of the Big Five on the foreign
bank request for removal of the ceiling appeared as follows: RBC
strongly supported, BNS and BMO supported, a crisis-ridden CIBC
was neutral but leaning away from support, and TD was neutral but
not opposing. The shift of the latter bank was notable. It was widely
believed that the bank's previous position had deeply offended
incoming foreigners and cost it considerable correspondent business. Furthermore, far from weakening in the wake of the 1980 act,
TD's selective approach in external markets was paying off hand-
somely in the recession then underway. TD could therefore afford to
be less recalcitrant, even if it could not be enthusiastic.[70]

Foreign bank lobbying during this period appears to have accen-
tuated strains developing within the federal government over the
appropriate degree of openness in Canadian investment and capital
markets. The domestic economy remained in severe recession and
the Canadian/U.S. exchange rate was falling.[71] Despite climbing
unemployment and inflation, the Bank of Canada, with the grudg-
ing support of the cabinet, was forced by the threat of capital flight
to keep Canadian interest rates relatively high. In such an environment, and with the gross external debt of the country rising rapidly,
reactions to foreign investment appeared to be shifting within the
government and in the country at large.[72] In the perennial domestic
debate between free marketeers and interventionists, the latter were
in retreat even before the Liberals fell in 1984.

At the bureaucratic level, this shift was well exemplified by an
increasingly spirited internal debate over Canada's refusal to accede
to the OECD capital movements code.[73] Officials within the External Affairs Department, which represented Canada at the OECD,
began pushing hard for accession in 1981. It was simply embarrassing, they argued, to endure the persistent criticism in Paris about

various restrictions on foreign investment and about the Bank Act. Furthermore, a degree of flexibility could in any case be maintained by acceding to the code with whatever reservations seemed particularly important, as other countries had done. Despite such arguments, a powerful group of policy planners within the Finance Department, which effectively had the last word before any recommendation would be submitted to the cabinet, remained opposed to accession because of its possible impact on the autonomy of domestic policy. In the event that perceptions of the national interest shifted again, the code would be yet another complicating element to be taken into consideration if investment restrictions became an attractive policy option. For a long time, the policy planners in the Finance Department had their way. These were the same officials who were being actively courted by the foreign bankers in their quest for abolition of the 8-percent ceiling.[74]

By March 1983 a number of foreign banks were approaching their individual growth limits and, owing to recession-induced stagnation among the Schedule A banks, it began to look as if the inspector general would run out of allocable capital within the year. During a meeting with foreign bank representatives that month, the finance minister, Marc Lalonde, agreed finally to review the matter and allow the Commons Finance Committee to make a formal recommendation. In May the inspector general's office forwarded a report on the ceiling to the committee without submitting any policy advice.[75] The committee subsequently agreed to hold hearings and at the same time commissioned a study on the general grievances of the foreign banks to compare and contrast Canada's approach with those of its OECD partners.[76]

In anticipation of the hearings, the Executive Committee of the foreign banks commissioned a Gallup poll of the chief financial officers of three hundred large Canadian corporations, a sample drawn from the largest one thousand. The poll revealed that 57 percent were using a foreign bank to complement their domestic banking relationships and that a majority favored fewer restrictions on foreign bank activity.[77] Also prior to the hearings, a very small number of individuals and organizations submitted supportive statements of position, the most significant of which came from RBC, the foreign bank Executive Committee, and the Trust Companies Association.[78] Finally, a letter arrived from the chairman of BMO supporting an increase in the ceiling but opposing the principle of opening the Bank Act for review between its formal decennial renewals.[79] In the background, the chairman of the U.S. Senate Banking Committee announced early in September of 1983 that he was concerned about

a lack of reciprocity for American banks abroad and was consider-
ing an appropriate amendment to the International Banking Act.[80]
Consistent with this concern, the Canadian hearings began with a
U.S. Treasury official in attendance.

As the hearings opened late in September, the committee chairman, a Liberal, noted that he was "very amenable" to arguments in
favor of lifting the ceiling; the senior Conservative member agreed
that some changes appeared to be required; and the senior New
Democratic party member called the ceiling "peculiar" but declared
himself not yet sure about supporting its abolition.[81] Very quickly
during the course of testimony, it became clear that little opposition
actually existed. Moreover, when the Executive Committee of the
foreign banks testified, with a French banker as spokesman and Japanese, British, and American bankers in supporting roles, the overall tone of the hearing was quite positive.[82] A number of
parliamentarians, however, did make the point that the Schedule B's
should do more to spread the benefits of their competitive endeavors
to small- and medium-sized customers. Few were astonished then,
when the committee's unanimous final report recommended complete removal of a numerical ceiling on the Schedule B's and reliance on discretionary supervision that would not inhibit the growth
of foreign banks, subject to continuing administrative evaluations of
reciprocity, contributions to competitive banking in Canada, parent
bank solvency, and loan portfolio diversity.

Considering the extent of press coverage and the spirited public
debate on the same issue in 1967 and late 1970, reaction in 1983 was
surprisingly limited. The nationalist *Toronto Star* carried editorials
opposing any change in the ceiling, and an influential columnist for
*Maclean's,* the leading Canadian weekly, wrote a piece that harked
back to 1967 concerns about national financial autonomy. But most
other coverage was favorable. Even the *Star* had to admit that the
debate over lifting the ceiling was "like the sound of one hand
clapping."[83]

Finance Minister Lalonde received the committee's report and
agreed to give the matter "very careful consideration" in cabinet.[84]
Privately, the minister let foreign bankers know that he supported
amending legislation as long as domestic consensus reigned and the
government did not have to expend any political capital, a resource
rapidly dwindling at the time. Success seemed at hand, until several
complications arose. The first came when the Bank of Montreal
decided publicly to oppose opening the Bank Act between scheduled
reviews. To foreign bankers this was outrageous, especially in view of
the fact that BMO announced around the same time its agreement

to purchase Harris Bankcorp of Chicago, then the thirty-third largest bank in the United States. The acquisition, however, had to be approved in Washington. Following discussions between American Schedule B executives and U.S. regulators, BMO discovered that its position on the ceiling in Canada was not seen in Washington as consistent with its desires for expansion in the United States. BMO subsequently made it known in Ottawa that its views had changed; it now saw no reason not to amend the Bank Act.[85]

The second complication came in November when the Bank of Nova Scotia became enmeshed in an American court case that raised sensitive questions about the extraterritorial application of U.S. laws, a long-standing irritant in Canada's bilateral relations with the United States.[86] A loud diplomatic row ensued, and the chairman of BNS called several foreign bank executives to announce his intention to oppose removal of the ceiling until his American problem was resolved.[87] Several American bankers and their head offices quickly moved to smooth the way for official Canadian representations in Washington. Eventually, an intergovernmental commission was established to examine the BNS case in its broader context. BNS then reversed its position on the ceiling issue.

In April 1984, despite political uncertainties caused by the impending resignation of Prime Minister Trudeau, the government introduced Bill C-30, a simple amendment to the Bank Act raising the foreign bank ceiling from 8 percent to 16 percent. The change from the prior recommendation of the Standing Committee came from inside the cabinet, where a consensus against complete removal of the ceiling emerged. In light of continued concerns about Canadian predominance in the banking system, the cabinet decided that abolition should wait upon more detailed consideration during a formal Bank Act revision. Moreover, retention of an explicit limit at this point was believed necessary to defuse residual nationalist opposition. Foreign bankers were not displeased with the resulting bill, although they would have preferred complete removal. What little general reaction there was from other quarters, considering the bill's apparently technical nature, was positive.[88]

That the government was willing to move the bill during the closing weeks of a very busy parliamentary session reflected a number of considerations. First, all-party agreement was expected and there would therefore be no risk of the bill becoming an issue in the election campaign many saw on the horizon. Second, the U.S. Treasury was about to publish a new study for the Congress on the treatment of U.S. banks abroad; the Canadian ceiling would surely be discussed, and few in the Finance Department now saw any point in reawakening American passions when opposition within Canada was so limited.[89] Third, the finance minister evidently perceived an opportunity to make a favorable impression on an international business community alienated by past economic policies in Canada.[90]

To the surprise of all concerned, unanimous agreement on Bill C-30 evaporated on May 9 when the New Democratic party announced its opposition. Sensing a potentially useful campaign issue or, as spokesmen claimed, genuinely disappointed that the government was apparently giving a higher priority to the legislative needs of foreign banks than to those of smaller domestic institutions, the party accused the government of wasting "valuable parliamentary time with furthering the interests of foreign banks."[91] In consequence, the government immediately lowered the priority of the bill on the Commons agenda.

The mood was somber at the June 1984 annual meeting of the foreign bank section of the CBA, which followed shortly thereafter. Bill C-30 appeared dead, at least until a summer election was out of the way and a new government established. Nevertheless, the bankers decided to pursue one last round of lobbying, this time particularly targeting important constituents of the NDP. Within weeks the party shifted its stand; although it remained formally opposed, it consented to an informal agreement, mediated by foreign bank lobbyists, that would allow C-30 to move forward. At the second reading of the bill, each party made one short speech. With the NDP then abstaining from active opposition, the bill expeditiously passed second reading and was reported for third and final reading the same day. Senate approval and royal assent came the next day. For the jubilant foreign bankers, attention could then shift from the legislative arena to the regulatory arena, where further work aimed at easing residual restrictions could take place out of the public eye.

Anticipated passage of Bill C-30 and the successful financial liberalization that followed the 1980 Bank Act strengthened the position of internationalists within the federal government. At the May 1984 OECD ministerial meeting, the external affairs minister announced Canada's intention to accede to the capital movements code.[92] The decision followed a detailed comparative review of Canada's foreign investment policies and capital requirements within the Finance Department and the External Affairs Department. In view of the shift in national attitudes with respect to foreign investment, as demonstrated in the quiet debate over foreign banking, there now appeared to be little to gain from remaining outside the evolving multilateral framework embodied in the code. Moreover, to those officials who favored a more consistently liberal foreign economic

Canada

policy and sought mechanisms to constrain recurrent bouts of
nationalist passion, the code still seemed a potentially useful, if
modest, tool.[93] For its part, the Conservative government elected late
in 1984 would oversee further developments along these same lines.[94]

If the situation of foreign banks in Canada remained difficult after
passage of Bill C-30, the difficulty was now more because of the
degree of competition inherent in the Canadian market than because
of governmentally imposed restrictions. Legally the banks had more
than enough room to grow. On regulatory matters other than the
ceiling, several annoying distinctions between major domestic and
foreign banks remained, but their actual impact on performance was
questionable. Foreign banks, for example, still needed to renew their
licenses more regularly, could not set up foreign branches, and were
subjected to unique capital requirements tied partly to performance
in the so-called middle market. In actual practice, especially for the
large institutions represented in Canada, such limitations were neither particularly unusual nor painful. For Canadian regulators,
however, continuing discretionary tools, local capital requirements,
and the growth oversight process enabled them to maintain prudential stability while encouraging foreign banks to broaden the base of
their operations in Canada.[95] The amended regulatory structure as
a whole tended towards more equitable treatment between foreign
and domestic banks than had regulations prevailing in 1976 or in
1967, even if it still fell short of a fully transparent, nondiscriminatory ideal. To be sure, national dominance in the banking system
remained important, and the possibility of future conflict with other
countries remained. But the cautious shift in the locus of decision for
ensuring such dominance, from the cabinet room to the marketplace, showed that Canada now differed from its major OECD partners mainly in the explicitness with which the priority was expressed.
As in other countries, continued national control was finally seen as
compatible with gradually increasing degrees of institutional openness. Remaining pressures for the protection of sovereign prerogatives were coming into new balance with emerging pressures for
competitive efficiency.

After 1984 a turbulent economic environment and the response of
Canadian regulators to situations of financial crisis gave foreign
banks new challenges and new opportunities. Following the outright
failures of two small banks in 1985, the first in Canada since 1923,
the British Lloyd's Bank was permitted to purchase most of the assets
of the ailing Continental Bank. Similarly, Hongkong and Shanghai
Bank was vigorously encouraged to take over the struggling Bank of
British Columbia.[96] Foreign bank market share jumped rapidly from

117

around 9 percent to over 12 percent. From an historical point of view, two things were striking about these events. First, the time-honored method of allowing the Big Five to absorb problem banks failed, most plausibly because an unusual overload of bad domestic and international loans left major banks with little appetite for emergency acquisitions. Second, there was a distinct, and in retrospect surprising, absence of debate at the national level on the question of financial sovereignty. Contrary to the reaction Citibank had engendered in 1967, the policy community and the citizenry at large greeted the dramatic foreign takeovers with indifference, if not relief. Indeed, federal policy makers and the taxpayers they represent went so far as effectively to subsidize the deals through the deposit insurance system. An inverse relationship between economic distress and Canadian nationalism appeared evident.

New strategic options for foreign banks were also created when policy makers at both federal and provincial levels of government moved in 1986 to reform Canada's segmented financial structure. As regulators battled over jurisdiction, and both foreign and domestic institutions exploited consequent regulatory gaps reminiscent of the near-banking loopholes of the 1960s, formerly clear boundaries between banking, securities, insurance, and trust markets began to blur. Barriers to entry and freer competition were gradually lowered. After a policy consensus developed on opening securities markets to commercial banks, for example, the Big Five and major foreign banks moved rapidly to acquire or establish brokerage firms. Bilateral trade negotiations with the United States in 1987 reinforced this general policy trajectory; the text of the draft agreement promised national treatment, including exemption from the asset ceiling and other strictures, for American banks. At the federal level, regulatory reform and trade liberalization clearly reflected the ideological commitments of the Conservative government that had come to power late in 1984. At the provincial level, competition for the jobs and other perceived benefits of an active financial sector tended to move policy in the same direction. Policy makers at both levels came generally to support the argument long made by foreign bankers that the competitiveness of Canadian institutions and markets had to be enhanced if they were not to fall behind world standards. To a considerable extent, this goal entailed a further movement away from the closure and rigidly controlled openness of the past. Only concerns over effective reciprocity acted at times to temper attendant policies.

CHAPTER SIX

# Australia

On February 27, 1985, the Commonwealth government of Australia invited sixteen of the world's largest commercial banks to establish full-scale operations in its domestic market. The move complemented a decision taken five months earlier to complete the opening of the country's wholesale financial market by allowing virtually unrestricted entry to any foreign banks caring to enter. Following entry, both full banks and merchant banks were to be regulated in the same manner as their domestic peer institutions.

By the standards of many other developed countries, the policy decisions facilitating foreign entry and expansion in Australian banking markets came late and appeared cautious. But by Australia's own lights, they looked surprisingly decisive. More surprising still, the moves came as part of a broader policy to tighten the embrace between Australia and the international economy, a policy intentionally designed and implemented by a Labor government whose party had long opposed such a strategy. The history of the Australian Labor party (ALP) provides ample evidence of both a longstanding antipathy to privately owned banks in general and a deep ambivalence regarding foreign investment. In the public mind the party was identified with regulation, wealth redistribution, and the quest for national autonomy. Yet in the mid-1980s it adopted the bankers' agenda: deregulation, internationalization, and financial liberalization. And it did so willingly, under the banner of economic growth, competition, and market solutions.

THE POLICY DEBATE: COMPETITION OR CONTROL?

With only slight exaggeration, it may be said that foreign banks came to Australia with the early convict transports. Because it entered the modern era as a colony of Great Britain, British banks were able to establish direct operations early on. As indigenous banks grew and domestic banking markets deepened, however, the national identity of the original banks faded.[1] Prior to federation in 1901 several non-British foreign banks operated in the domestic market at various times. The Bank of New Zealand entered in 1872 with unrestricted business powers owing to an implicit reciprocity understanding that facilitated the expansion of Australian banks in New Zealand. In 1881 an ancestor of the Banque Nationale de Paris, attracted by an expanding wool trade, was permitted to open a branch in Melbourne under a restricted license. Also to facilitate trade, similar licenses were provided to the Yokohama Specie Bank (predecessor to the Bank of Tokyo) in 1915 and the Bank of China in 1942. The former had its license revoked in 1941 when war broke out; the latter declared its loyalty to Taiwan in 1949 and closed its doors in 1972 after Australia formally recognized the government in Peking. Finally, two American banks, National City Bank and Central Union Trust Company (now Manufacturers Hanover), opened representative offices for brief periods in the late 1920s, but both were closed with the onset of the Great Depression.

Except for temporary establishments during the war, no other foreign institutions succeeded in establishing commercial banking operations in the country until the mid-1980s. Testifying before the 1937 Royal Commission on Money and Banking, the chief manager of the National Bank of Australasia provided unusually candid insight into the difficulties encountered by any foreign bank that tried to enter:

> About thirteen years ago [in fact, 1922] the American Express Company, which is a recognized American banking concern, endeavoured to establish itself in Australia and opened an office in Sydney, but pressure was brought to bear so that the office was closed.... I could not say by whom that pressure was brought to bear, but the position was made intolerable, and the office only remained open a few months.... [In preventing the establishment of a new bank] we may have to seek government assistance. We could, of course, refuse such a bank clearing facilities.[2]

The trading banks (major domestic banks) of the pre–World War II period were few in number (five in Melbourne, two in Sydney) and effectively organized to protect market shares. Indeed, the Australian Bankers' Association (AuBA) even maintained agreed pricing lists and other market stabilizing measures until the Trade Practices Act of 1974 made such activities illegal.[3] Limited foreign entry before 1945, however, also reflected a lack of persistent interest on the part of foreign banks themselves. Before the postwar economic expansion and the marked growth of multinational corporations, for most banks the potential profits from a direct presence appeared low enough to justify continued reliance on correspondent relationships in the handling of any Australian requirements. But such perceptions began to change after the war, and the fundamentally political nature of the ban on entry became clear. In the wake of severely restrictive banking regulations promulgated by the Commonwealth government during the war years, an effective prohibition on foreign entry became accepted policy after 1945.[4] Policy makers never stated the reasons for the ban, but the secretary of the AuBA cited several post hoc justifications in 1969: "[Restrictions on entry reflected] the prospective proliferation of foreign banks in Australia unless discriminatory policies were applied; concern about the possible weakening of controls over the banking system, which could lessen the effectiveness of monetary policy; the absence of any apparent advantages for the Australian banking system and the Australian people; and the lack of justification for altering the existing banking structure when Australian banks already meet the country's needs."[5] In its 1972 study of foreign investment, the Treasury simply cited banking as one of the key sectors of the economy, a label that justified policies aimed at ensuring dominant domestic ownership and control.[6]

Despite the ban on foreign banking, an expanding Australian economy attracted foreign financial institutions; during the 1950s the more adventurous began to find ways of gaining a foothold inside it. Most often this entailed setting up a representative office or taking an equity participation in a locally incorporated nonbank financial institution (NBFI). Both of these activities skirted accepted definitions of banking, a term traditionally reserved in Australia for an institution permitted to take deposits subject to withdrawal by check, to trade in foreign exchange, to use the word *bank* in its corporate title, and to call upon the central bank for support in case of need.[7] They were able to get around these understandings principally because representative offices transacted no business directly and NBFIs were chartered under state, not federal, laws.

As in the Canadian system, the federal government under the Australian constitution has jurisdiction over banking (except for several state-owned banks). Other financial activity may, however, fall under the authority of the separate states. Merchant banks (NBFIs operating mainly in wholesale money markets) and finance companies (providing, for example, hire-purchase and leasing credit) fall within the latter category and receive their corporate charters under state-administered companies acts. The first foreign-owned merchant bank was established in Melbourne in 1949.[8] Eight years later the Bank of Tokyo opened the first modern representative office; Bank of America followed in 1964; First National City Bank, in 1965. With the onset of the mining boom in the late 1960s, the number of both types of operations increased dramatically. By 1971 approximately ninety-five foreign banks were active in Australia through either vehicle.

The NBFIs remained much smaller than the domestic banks, but their rate of growth was unmatched, partly because they were able to avoid costly federal banking controls. For example, from an asset base of A$250 million (or 0.7 percent of the domestic financial market) in 1969, merchant banks, both domestic and foreign, grew to A$2.1 billion (3.5 percent) in 1973.[9] An increasing volume of financial transactions was intermediated outside the banking system, and foreign institutions were participating in this trend. Apart from causing anxiety in the executive suites of the domestic banks, this phenomenon led to a rise in the number of calls for federal regulation, especially from the parliamentary Labor party. The calls became especially strident in 1971 after First National City Bank acquired an effective 40 percent shareholding in Australia's second largest finance company, IAC (Holdings) Ltd. Unconvinced that the costs of this capital injection exceeded its benefits and hesitant about the constitutional implications of preventing it, the Liberal/National government took no action. Later in the year, however, when overseas interests began making overtures to the small Bank of Queensland, the government moved quickly to plug the permissive loophole in the Banking Act. In October, without opposition, Parliament passed the Bank (Shareholdings) Act which put a 10 percent limit on any single shareholding in an existing bank.[10] At the same time, despite opposition demands, the government again deferred to the states and refused to move on the broader issue of foreign penetration through the establishment of NBFIs.

By the time the Bank (Shareholdings) Act was finally proclaimed in 1972, the political sensitivity of foreign investment in general was reaching a peak. When Labor came to power late in the year the government immediately began considering mechanisms for stemming the growth of foreign control in the financial sector.[11] In

August 1973 the new government announced special guidelines making federal approval necessary for future overseas investments in NBFIs; henceforth, foreign shareholdings in excess of 50 percent would be discouraged. The Financial Corporations Act of 1974 required all NBFIs to register with the Commonwealth government and to provide regular statistical information to the Reserve Bank. Part IV of the original act also empowered government to impose specific limiting controls on NBFIs, such as gearing ratios and interest rate ceilings; however, on the advice of the Treasury, and again faced with the possibility of a constitutional challenge, the Labor government decided to hold Part IV in abeyance.[12]

The difficulty of actually limiting the growth of NBFIs or restraining the foreign influx became apparent immediately. Amidst deteriorating economic conditions and a drastic downturn in domestic property markets, a number of financial institutions encountered severe solvency problems. The most prominent involved IAC (Holdings) Ltd., which was on the verge of collapse in 1974, potentially taking with it several other institutions, including a federal government struggling to maintain its credibility as an economic manager. After intensive negotiations, IAC's major shareholder, First National City Bank, agreed to a massive support operation in return for the hard-won right to purchase 51 percent of the company's equity.[13] IAC and the NBFI sector as a whole continued to grow, notwithstanding the concerns of Labor or of the conservative coalition that succeeded it in 1975. Between 1975 and 1978 the share of aggregate domestic financial assets held by finance companies and merchant banks together rose from 15.2 percent to 16.1 percent, while the share of domestic banks fell from 41.3 percent to 38.6 percent.[14]

All of this foreign activity helped encourage the domestic banks eventually to expand their own offshore operations. In addition to retail branches in neighboring Pacific islands, the Australian banks built their own networks of representative offices, agencies, subsidiaries, and wholesale branches, the most important of them in London, New York, Tokyo, Singapore, and Hong Kong. By 1975 assets of the banks' offshore offices represented 15 percent of their total assets; by 1980 that proportion would rise to 21 percent.[15] As their international aspirations developed, however, the banks increasingly came up against reciprocity requirements imposed by other governments. Because foreign banks could not operate as full banks in Australia, such requirements were difficult to meet. Interestingly, though, it would not be until 1983 that concerns on this score would have even a modest impact on the joint public position of the domestic banks. In the long debate over foreign bank entry, the domestic banks consistently supported the existing protectionist policy. Their domestic concerns clearly outweighed their international concerns throughout.

## The Campbell Inquiry

As early as 1975 the idea of convening a new panel to review the financial system was in the air. Malcolm Fraser mentioned it briefly during his election campaign that year and picked it up again, though with little enthusiasm, during his second successful campaign as Liberal leader in 1977. The principal motive for these early hints seems to have been a desire to appeal to a small business community perceived to be disgruntled by inadequate support from the banks. After each election the idea was dropped but it never quite disappeared. Aside from the absence of broad pressure from the business community, its low priority resulted principally from a deep ambivalence within the Fraser government. This ambivalence resulted in part from an ongoing ideological struggle between two distinct strands of conservatism: one identified with a kind of Tory paternalism deeply rooted in Australia's British connection and pastoral history, the other committed to the ideal of efficient markets in a mainly urban future.[16]

But problems associated with public finance, the exchange market, and the banking system had become pressing by 1978. Partly in self-defense, the seven major private banks — the targets of much associated criticism — started formulating responses early in the year when the Australia and New Zealand Bank (ANZ) drew up a discussion paper for the AuBA.[17] The paper focused on the erosion of the banks' market share and ascribed it to their inability "when operating under monetary controls, to compete effectively with certain nonbank financial institutions which do not have similar controls placed on them."[18] Two possible solutions existed: the first involved granting greater freedom to the banks, the second, which ANZ itself initially favored, involved neutralizing the discriminatory impact of controls by extending them to NBFIs.

As the members of the AuBA pondered this assessment, successive crises and a disillusionment with ad hoc temporary solutions were convincing the treasurer, John Howard, of the need for broad reform.[19] Discussions with advisers and contacts in the financial community reinforced his commitment; to a lesser extent, so too did occasional introductions to regulatory changes in other countries during periodic trips abroad. Over the objections of senior treasury officials who feared destabilizing the financial markets, Howard came to see a public inquiry, similar to the royal commission that had reviewed the financial system in 1937, as a means of coming to grips with interrelated financial difficulties and of breaking down vested interests in the regulatory structure.

A majority of the cabinet eventually went along with the treasurer's suggestion, but motives were mixed; some felt that the outcome of such an inquiry could be controlled if need be, others saw it as a politically acceptable way of postponing decisions, still others hoped it might actually reinvigorate the existing structure of regulation. More difficult to explain were cabinet decisions to appoint a committee, later known as the Campbell Committee, composed of market-oriented individuals, mainly from within the financial community, and to provide them with suggestively deregulatory and open-ended terms of reference.[20] The committee was to examine any issues it considered relevant, but was to bear in mind "the importance of the efficiency of the financial system for the government's free enterprise objectives and broad goals for national economic prosperity."[21] Again, ministers who would later oppose final recommendations of the Campbell Committee probably saw little harm in going along with a nonbinding review, the conclusions of which could be shelved if they proved distasteful. Besides, the review would likely take a long time. But the treasurer had clearer aspirations. "The objective of the Inquiry," he announced at the start, "was not more regulation by government."[22] During the coming years he would constantly return to this theme in public speeches.

Over the course of two years and ten months the Campbell Committee conducted what journalists came to describe as a national teach-in. The committee received over three hundred submissions from interested parties, commissioned several major studies, and held over one hundred public (and a number of private) hearings across the country. Although a range of financial issues was considered, the question of foreign bank entry and regulation was prominent from the beginning, and its priority rose as the review neared its concluding stage. Because the exercise forced institutions with the most to gain or lose from reform to articulate and defend explicit positions, the record of the committee contains valuable insights into the underlying politics of Australian financial regulation. Actual decisions would eventually come at a less visible layer of the policy-making process, but even those whose principal lobbying efforts remained at that level took the inquiry seriously.

## The Domestic Banks and Regulatory Reform

The overt involvement of Australian banks in party politics during the 1947 nationalization struggle has turned out to be historically unique. Certainly the banks have long been significant contributors to Liberal party coffers, and the private opinions of particular leading bankers have been taken seriously on matters most fundamental to their business. As institutions, however, the banks have often simply reacted to policy initiatives taken by the cabinet and the Treasury and informally communicated by the Reserve Bank. They were therefore initially hesitant about the public nature of the Campbell inquiry but eventually came to welcome it as an opportunity to divert criticism and focus attention on the obsolescence of traditional regulatory controls.[23]

The 1978 ANZ paper initiated a rigorous rethinking of the tacit arrangement whereby the banks accepted the controls of the postwar monetary policy framework in exchange for an assured market. The several delegates to the Special Industry Committee of the AuBA all agreed that in its present form the arrangement was no longer tenable. But beyond that they shared no immediate consensus.[24] Differing domestic business bases and divergent management strategies complicated matters, as did a fair amount of dissension within the banks themselves. For example, smaller banks with limited international aspirations, such as the Commercial Banking Company of Sydney and the Commercial Bank of Australia, found it difficult to weight reciprocity arguments very heavily. Indeed, it would take several years of rapid growth before the international divisions of the large banks would be able to push such arguments anywhere near the forefront of concern within their own institutions.

In general, the banks wanted to restore their preeminence in the domestic market but eventually abandoned hope of doing so by way of extending controls to their nonbank competitors. Such a path, they agreed after lengthy internal debate, would probably only create opportunities for new types of financial institutions. The best hope lay instead with expanded freedom to compete and thereby to win back the deposit and loan business that had shifted to the NBFIs. This change entailed the abolition of deposit and lending controls and the creation of new, market-based tools for the indirect implementation of monetary policy. But in response to the timely call of the Campbell Committee for an AuBA submission covering its broader agenda, the banks found it difficult to maintain their newfound enthusiasm across the board. Deregulation of interest rates, maturity controls, and other limitations on bank operations logically implied dismantling controls that served to protect banking markets, such as entry restraints. Deregulation without new entry would provide a patently unacceptable bonanza to the banks. In the public forum of the Campbell Committee, the need to appear logical and consistent came to have a causal significance of its own, but on the question of foreign entry the banks sought mightily to rationalize delay. As Dr. Johnson might have noted, the prospect of foreign bank entry concentrated their minds wonderfully.

The managing directors who approved the first AuBA submission to the Campbell Committee in 1979 were equivocal about deregulation. Their joint submission stressed themes of efficiency and the restoration of competitive balance when it called for the abandonment of rigid quantitative and qualitative controls and for reliance by government on broadly based and economically neutral policy tools, such as Reserve Bank open-market operations. On the question of new entry, it raised few objections to extending the logic of deregulation as long as prospective entrants were domestically owned. On the harder issue of foreign bank entry, however, the banks could only agree:

> Although Australian banks are well-equipped to meet foreign bank competition, it is only realistic to recognize that the entry of foreign banks would have major implications for the local banking system. In the event that Government policy was changed to permit the conditional entry of foreign banks in Australia, any arrangements would clearly need to be consistent with stability in the banking industry and with the needs of domestic economic and monetary policy. Any change in existing policy will therefore require very careful coordination by the monetary authorities and consultation with the existing banking industry would be critical.[25]

On related matters, the AuBA submission included a recommendation for the gradual liberalization of the foreign exchange market, a traditional preserve of the banks, but no recommendation for an increase in the number of foreign exchange trading licenses.[26]

The banks individually also submitted position papers to the committee, which tended to be more explicit on the same points. The ANZ submission, for example, argued that foreign banks would add little to the supply of loanable funds and would accelerate the closure of branches in isolated areas. At most, the bank advocated, any new foreign bank entrants should be limited to offshore transactions, such as lending to nonresidents. It conceded, however, that "at an appropriate time" controlled entry into a free Australian foreign exchange market might be advisable.[27] The Bank of New South Wales hailed the existing level of competition within the financial system and expressed skepticism about direct foreign bank entry increasing efficiency. While not opposing a "controlled opening," the bank insisted that any new entrants participate in both wholesale and less profitable retail markets and that entry be justified by economic ties between Australia and the home countries of any entrants, including reciprocal banking access.[28] The Commonwealth Bank took a similar line but looked more favorably on foreign participation in the foreign exchange market even without banking licenses. Full licenses, it held, should be given to foreign banks only after existing banks had had "reasonable time" to adjust to any new deregulated environment.[29] The only bank to give a stridently different view was the Commercial Banking Company (CBC) of Sydney. Somewhat surprisingly, given its support for the AuBA submission, the bank bluntly recommended that full banking licenses not be provided to any foreign banks and that foreigners remain excluded from the foreign exchange market.[30]

In testimony before the Campbell Committee, chief executives from the banks amplified these views and unintentionally provided a glimpse of painful internal struggles over the foreign-related issues. The head of the ANZ, for instance, felt the market would need to "settle down" following deregulation before new entrants could be introduced without disruption. Under questioning he later frankly responded, "I'm not in favor of the admission of foreign banks to our market."[31] His counterpart at the CBC of Sydney, Victor Martin, who would several years later lead another government's review of the same issues, argued more colorfully for the indefinite postponement of foreign entry. "Here are we," Martin stated, "we have been on a chain for a long time. And if you have got a dog on a chain you do not let the most savage dog in the district at him until you have let him off that chain."[32]

The joint position of the AuBA later became more specific. In supplementary submissions to the committee, the association cited the effective control by foreign banks of almost 50 percent of the assets of Australian merchant banks (in 1978) and 18 percent of the assets of finance companies, both sectors growing more rapidly than banks. This represented "sufficient" competition for the banks, but if the government insisted on more, this base and the legacy of monetary controls on the domestic banks would give foreign entrants a "competitive advantage" unless their entry was phased in gradually as direct controls were abolished.[33] For related reasons, the AuBA argued, full access to payments systems should continue to be restricted to banks.[34] In time, more by happenstance than design, the banks would get most of what they wanted. Their protestations about the adequacy of competition, however, were received skeptically during the Campbell deliberations, especially after a series of bank mergers took place.

The new merger activity began in May 1979 when the Reserve Bank engineered the takeover of a collapsing Bank of Adelaide by a reluctant ANZ.[35] The ensuing battle for competitive position led in 1981 to battles between the ANZ and the Bank of New South Wales for the Commercial Bank of Australia as well as between the ANZ and the National Bank for the CBC of Sydney. When the battles were over, only four major domestic banks were left in Australia: Westpac (formerly BNSW), ANZ, Commonwealth, and National.

The underlying motivations for the mergers varied between the banks and are still debatable, but several common factors appear preeminent. The banks were sensitive not only about their aggregate market share decline but also — and to a greater extent — about relative changes among themselves. Strong incentives therefore existed to preempt strategic expansion by rivals through takeovers. A degree of defensive planning against the possibility of future foreign entrants attempting to expand quickly through acquisitions seems also to have been involved, even though such an event would have necessitated legislative amendment. Future foreign competition of this nature would additionally have raised the price tags of potential targets; in such a light, 1981 prices appeared low. Bank executives themselves later ascribed their decisions to the need generally to prepare for foreign entry by creating institutions of appropriate scale. In retrospect, however, this explanation too conveniently aimed at deflecting criticism, especially from a political Left aghast at increased concentration in the banking system. More plausibly, bank managers sought to reduce uncertainty resulting only partly from the foreign entry question.

Somewhat more difficult to explain is the speed with which the treasurer approved the mergers, despite intense opposition from the ALP and the bank unions as well as strong reservations from his National party colleagues. At the time, Howard expressed concern about concentration in banking but claimed not to see clear grounds for a governmental veto. In light of his subsequent stands, it is more likely that he consented in order to raise pressures for foreign bank entry. Indeed, this turned out to be the ultimate effect of the mergers. Ironically, the domestic banks had undercut their own arguments for delay and arguably accelerated the process of policy change. For the members of the Campbell Committee the mergers increased the urgency of the foreign entry question.

## The Foreign Banks and the Merchant Banks

Curiously, the foreign banks themselves had a limited impact on the Campbell deliberations. Although they were invited to make their case for entry and equal treatment, most seem to have missed the opportunity. Their submissions were few; they formed no united front despite broadly common orientations to the major issues at hand; and their arguments lacked depth. Several factors appear to account for this poor showing. Many foreign banks discounted the value of public statements and were uncomfortable about taking a prominent role in the proceedings. Though they followed the hearings closely, and some even brought in senior head office executives for presentations, those actively lobbying for change kept their focus squarely on key decision makers in Canberra. Although many were anxious outside the public limelight to entertain committee members and provide support as requested, few believed that the committee's recommendations would necessarily be decisive. In addition, the foreign banks were unable to coordinate specific positions as a group. Unlike the situation, for example, in Canada, foreign bankers on the scene generally concluded that if any entry into banking was eventually permitted, it would be limited in scope. Banking licenses would initially be scarce. Competitive impulses therefore outweighed incentives to collaborate. Disagreements on tactics, as well as splits between head office and local representatives, reinforced such calculations.

In all, twelve foreign banks made formal presentations. Virtually all stressed the theme that foreign banks permitted to operate as full banks would bring benefits to Australia far surpassing any actual or imagined costs. When they bothered to spell these benefits out, the presentations did so at a high level of generality. Foreign banks would facilitate inward and outward capital flows, thereby enhancing economic efficiency. They would add depth to the foreign exchange market. They would increase employment in the financial sector and accelerate the process of innovation. They would increase the availability of trade financing and assist Australian exports. Little empirical evidence was provided, however, to support these claims. An ideological commitment to competitive markets lay at the core of their assertions, and, fortuitously, they struck a sympathetic chord with committee members. None of these claims, however, assisted in the effort to sell the same commitment to an ambivalent government.

Aside from stressing nebulous benefits, a few banks did softly point out a more specific cost of continued protectionism — retaliatory moves by foreign governments against Australian bank operations overseas. Such warnings were always couched in diplomatic musings and were never expressed by official spokesmen of foreign governments; they did, however, come at the same time that the U.S. Treasury published its first study on the treatment of American banks overseas. The Australian section of that study pointed out that although twenty-one U.S. bank subsidiaries with U.S.$700 million in assets in 1973 had grown to twenty-eight controlling U.S.$2.9 billion by 1978, restrictions imposed by the Australian government denied "equal competitive opportunity."[36] This theme came up repeatedly when foreign bankers testified before the Campbell Committee. On especially problematic matters, such as whether any new foreign entrants should be required to take on local partners, the bankers frequently contended that treatment different from that imposed on their domestic rivals would hamper their ability to compete effectively. Equal competitive conditions, they implied, were more a right than a privilege. Most went to great lengths, nevertheless, to appear flexible on the details.[37]

Some of the foreign banks already participating in Australian nonbanking ventures received further representation before the committee through their affiliates or through the Australian Merchant Banking Association (AMBA). Four merchant banks, all predominantly owned by American banks, gave formal presentations, and the AMBA made two separate submissions.[38] Understandably, inasmuch as it represented institutions owned by both domestic and foreign parents, the AMBA encountered great difficulty in reaching consensus on the key issues before the committee. Notwithstanding the disparate aims of their ultimate owners, merchant bankers wanted to preserve a distinct institutional role for themselves in changing markets. Consistent with the position of many foreign banks therefore, the AMBA gradually came to adopt a position opposing the status quo. AMBA submissions argued, for example, for a new tiered banking system that would provide limited licenses to merchant banks enabling them to deal in foreign exchange and giving them some access to Reserve Bank lender-of-last-resort facilities.

*Other Views*

Despite explicit appeals for submissions from groups of all political persuasions, the Campbell Committee received very few opinions from the Left. Significantly, the ALP and its principal constituent organization, the Australian Council of Trades Unions (ACTU), declined to make submissions. But two unions unaffiliated with the ALP, the Australian Bank Employees' Union (ABEU) and the Commonwealth Bank Officers' Association (CBOA), did make submissions and testify before the committee. The tone of their presentations helps explain the apparent apathy of the Left as a whole.[39]

The unions attacked both the government and the committee itself for failure to ensure the representation of nonfinancial interests in their deliberations. They disagreed with the deregulatory trajectory set out in the committee's terms of reference, especially with regard to foreign banks. The expansion of foreign institutions in the banking system, union spokesmen contended, threatened to weaken the ability of the Australian government to protect the interests of its own citizens and to ensure that the benefits of economic development flowed through to them. Furthermore, the actual operations of foreign banks could upset the balance within the domestic banks between retail and corporate banking, to the detriment of bank workers and the users of small branches. Rapid introduction of new technology by foreign banks and failure to respect the mores of industrial relations in the country could exacerbate such a trend. As the struggle over foreign bank entry intensified in coming years, the unions would elaborate on these themes.

For similar reasons, and preferring the additional licensing of purely domestic institutions, the Australian Federation of Credit Union Leagues opposed foreign bank entry. The domestic institutions likely to be in the best position actually to start up a new banking operation, the life insurance companies, came to the opposite view.[40] Also notable was the support given to both deregulation and foreign entry by the National Farmers' Federation, a new peak association established in July 1979. Although its rural membership had traditionally been associated with the National/Country party and with that party's long-standing support for broad economic controls, things had begun to change in the late 1970s when a core group of market-oriented strategists gradually led the principal farm organizations to see a freer system, including more flexible exchange rates and a more competitive banking system, as beneficial for farming interests.

Industrial and small business groups contributed little to committee consideration of the foreign-related issues. The few submissions of business lobbies rarely touched on the issue of foreign entry. Only two individual corporate submissions mentioned the subject, and both concluded that the gains from foreign entry would be small.[41] This comparative lack of attention is difficult to read, especially because the financial institutions pushing the liberalization line often did so in the name of the consumer of financial services. The potential benefits of foreign bank competition were apparently perceived to be too minor or too intangible for consumer groups to mobilize in support.

In partial compensation for the dearth of views from users of financial services, the committee commissioned an economic analysis of the foreign entry issue. After demonstrating that Australian banks were conducting relatively high-cost operations in comparison with other OECD countries, the resulting study advocated a mixed policy package of deregulation and increased competition. The study estimated that net benefits to Australia would accrue from foreign bank entry in the areas of foreign exchange, trade financing, and wholesale financial intermediation; few benefits, however, were seen as coming from foreign participation in retail activities. Moreover, allowing domestic banks to retain their privileged position in retail markets, the study argued, would offset the adjustment costs resulting from increased competition in other areas. The study therefore concluded with the recommendations that a limited number of licenses be made available to foreign banks, that the banks be allowed to set up either branches or wholly owned subsidiaries, and that they be restricted to undertaking wholesale business.[42]

No one testifying before the Campbell Committee attempted to place the foreign bank issue in the context of broad international efforts to sustain free markets. The commitments of international organizations like the OECD to the liberalization of capital flows and the opening of financial markets were never mentioned. No one argued that Australia had obligations to support openness in an increasingly integrated global economy. Occasional indirect suggestions concerning the appropriateness of reciprocity were all that committee members heard about the wider environment of foreign bank issues. In retrospect, this gap in the record of the inquiry would surprise participants who later became involved in broader international liberalization programs.[43]

## The Campbell Synthesis

Over the long course of their deliberations, the members of the Campbell Committee became unreservedly committed to deregulation as the solution to the interrelated problems besetting the financial system. They also came to agree on a fairly polemical approach in the presentation of a rigorously consistent set of recommendations to government. By stressing concepts of efficiency, competition, and flexibility, they sought to drive home the salutary implications of a broader reliance by government on market forces.

On the question of foreign bank entry, the committee favored a "carefully managed" opening of domestic markets in the name of increased efficiency. As a first step, they suggested that an initially limited, but not small, number of foreign banks be licensed in order to avoid a "socially unacceptable loss of resident ownership and control." Deliberately rejecting a Canadian-style market share ceiling for foreign banks, they argued that restricting only the number of licenses would prove more effective, would be simpler to manage, and would not nullify the benefits sought from broadened competition. Further, in line with the overriding theme that governments should seek to ensure competitive neutrality between participants in markets, they held that new foreign entrants should be treated in a fully nondiscriminatory manner and therefore should not be required to take on local equity partners. The committee made no mention of reciprocity either as a condition of entry or as a reason for providing nondiscriminatory regulatory treatment after entry. Finally, the committee called for immediate action, thus rejecting the AuBA's plea for a delay on foreign entry until other effects of deregulation had been assimilated.[44]

On related questions, the committee came out strongly for letting the exchange rate float and dismantling exchange controls, but with prudential considerations in mind they suggested that foreign exchange licenses continue to be restricted to banks. They also advocated creation of a limited offshore banking market, where banks could lend to nonresidents at concessionary terms. In short, on these and other issues more domestic in nature the committee fully met the deregulatory hopes of its principal political sponsors.

## Aftermath of the Campbell Report

Reaction to the Campbell recommendations came swiftly; indeed, anticipating its deregulatory thrust, opponents and supporters began preparing responses even before their release. Foreign banks widely expected some form of limited entry to be advocated and individually had already stepped up public and private campaigns to position themselves favorably with the government. The trading banks predictably welcomed the committee's call for domestic deregulation. In the wake of the mergers and their own continued expansion overseas, their opposition to early foreign entry remained, but their public positions began to soften.[45]

Negative reaction to the report as a whole also came from predictable places. The bank unions quickly mobilized for a fight at the parliamentary level, especially on the foreign bank issue. They found ready allies in a Labor party that saw potential for the Campbell Report to develop into an election issue. Following up a public campaign against the bank mergers, ALP leaders greeted the report's recommendations with derision. Subsequently, a political strategy based on opposition to the removal of interest rate controls and to foreign bank entry rapidly took shape. A small splinter party with a foothold in the Senate, the Australian Democrats, saw the same potential and moved in the same direction. Simultaneously, splits in the government itself over the recommendations became public. National party ministers immediately let it be known that they strongly opposed floating the currency and disturbing market arrangements that aided farmers and kept small rural branches open.[46] The prime minister was widely believed to have shared this view. For different reasons, but again over the same issues, disputes emerged between the treasurer and the Treasury. The Treasury had consistently urged the Campbell Committee to approach domestic deregulation cautiously and not to recommend dismantling exchange controls or letting in foreign banks.[47] In Parliament, the treasurer bluntly dissociated himself from this view. Prior to presenting the report, however, Howard and his advisers realized that the extent of the opposition threatened to kill the deregulation agenda even before implementation plans were worked out.

Howard's strategy to save the report evidently centered around approval of the bank mergers, several seemingly innocuous anticipatory reforms at the margins of financial regulation, and a carefully crafted tabling speech.[48] None of the marginal changes directly threatened any vested interests by themselves, but the treasurer expected them together to raise pressures for further deregulation. The tabling speech stressed the theme of political realism. It promised to leaven an essentially economic document with concern for social and political sensitivities; the government itself would assess the issues, seek to balance efficiency and equity considerations, and ensure that no domestic interest groups would be made worse off by

*Table 11.* Aggregate assets of Australian banks' overseas offices,
June 1980–December 1982 (A$ billions)

| Country | June 1980 | June 1982 | December 1982 |
|---|---|---|---|
| United Kingdom | 4.2 | 6.0 | 6.6 |
| United States | 1.0 | 3.3 | 4.0 |
| Singapore & | 0.4 | 1.4 | 2.1 |
| Hong Kong | | 0.9 | 1.1 |
| New Zealand | 2.0 | 2.5 | 2.7 |
| Papua New Guinea | 0.32 | 0.34 | 0.34 |
| Other Pacific | 0.27 | 0.31 | 0.34 |
| Total | 8.19 | 14.75 | 17.18 |

SOURCE: Reserve Bank of Australia, *Bulletin* (March 1983), 599.
NOTE: Figures include interbank items.

financial reform.[49] Bankers perceived a government backing away
from the report; recalcitrant ministers and ALP leaders thought they
had killed it; and Howard hoped he had kept it alive. The report was
then commended to the public for debate and to a working party
within the Treasury for implementation proposals.[50] Considering its
venue, the working party would not have an easy time. In one of the
remarkable ironies of contemporary Australian politics, extensive
implementation, particularly of the more contentious recommendations, would have to wait until the ALP came to power.

The year 1982 was exceptionally difficult for the Liberal party.
Severe recession, widespread drought, and a wage explosion combined to exacerbate both inflation and unemployment. Economic
crisis and accusations of indecisiveness knocked the Fraser government off-balance; internal dissension, including a leadership challenge, ensured it would stay that way. Financial liberalization slipped
far down on the cabinet's list of priorities. The treasurer did continue during 1982 to make changes of ultimate significance, but the
major politicized issues, including foreign bank entry, were left
unresolved.[51]

Despite the domestic bankers' concerns about the future of deregulation, delays engendered by domestic politics worked to their benefit; 1982 turned out for them to be a productive year spent digesting
the effects of the mergers and accelerating expansion overseas. For
the four major banks this expansion concentrated principally on the
United States, Singapore, and Hong Kong. During the period June
1980 to December 1982 aggregate overseas assets more than doubled
(Table 11). In all of their most important overseas markets, however,
reciprocity problems were becoming more serious; in Japan, a market viewed as very promising, such problems completely debarred the
banks from direct participation.[52]

The reciprocity problem remained barely visible within Australia itself until late 1982. Most foreign bankers—indeed, virtually all those living in Australia and following the debate closely—considered it better to adopt a conciliatory public posture.[53] Everyone wanted a chance to win one of a probable limited number of future licenses; everyone knew that political factors would affect final choices; and no one wanted to risk offending the politicians and administrators who would make those choices—that is, no one except Citibank of New York.

During a visit in December 1982 Citibank's vice-chairman publicly criticized the government for limiting foreign entry and for considering the possibility of forcing prospective foreign entrants to bring in local shareholders. Citibank would accept a license only for a full branch or wholly owned subsidiary and only these alternatives would meet the "test of fair play and reciprocity."[54] Anything less for American banks, the senior executive added, could result in retaliation against Australian operations in the United States. The subsequent uproar in Australia apparently encouraged Citibank's local representatives to backtrack. Although they would in future continue to make clear their desire for a full branch or 100-percent-owned subsidiary, they worked hard over the next two-and-a-half years to assure all concerned that this desire was merely a strong preference and that even Citibank could be flexible. Determined to avoid repeating Citibank's faux pas, most other foreign bankers continued to stress the benefits of their entry whenever they chose to make public comments.

The foreign bank issue came before the cabinet in September 1982 when the treasury working party submitted a proposal. Its severely restrictive conditions on foreign entry proved unacceptable to the treasurer, and it was sent back for revision.[55] Throughout this period the parliamentary opposition, apart from engaging in its own internal leadership struggle, attacked the government vigorously on the subject of financial deregulation. At its 1982 biennial national conference, the ALP adopted a new platform on which it expected to fight the next election. In a victory for its left wing, four key economic planks were aimed precisely at these concerns. The party pledged to "maintain and extend essential regulatory power . . . for control of interest rates and lending policies of financial corporations, retain a central role for government in the determination of the exchange rate, and implement effective controls over foreign capital inflows and the operations of transnational corporations in Australia."[56] Further, in the belief that "foreign domination of the Australian economy . . . endangers our national sovereignty," the party promised to "maintain existing restrictions on foreign entry to strategic sectors of the economy including banking, and reverse the current trend towards increased foreign domination of the Australian economy by seeking increased Australian ownership and control of resources and enterprises by carefully regulating foreign investment and short term financial flows."[57] Finally, the party committed itself to clarifying and tightening foreign investment guidelines to ensure that net economic benefits accrued to Australia and that Australian ownership and control of key sectors was maintained.

A revised treasury proposal finally came back to the cabinet in December 1982, and Howard made it known that a decision was imminent. In spite of continued hesitation in some quarters of the government, circumstances now augured well for opening the banking market. Howard was pressing the cabinet persistently on the issue, and foreign bankers were relentless in their lobbying.[58] But neither factor appeared decisive. Much more important was the changing electoral calculus in the minds of key ministers. Despite continued economic problems, on December 4 the Liberals unexpectedly won a signal federal by-election in Victoria. The earlier loss of another by-election and ominous declines in opinion polls made this success particularly heartening. Furthermore, the victory was widely attributed to the government's dramatic announcement in mid-November of a plan for a twelve-month public- and private-sector wage freeze; the popular plan aimed at stalling a bout of cost-push inflation and at reducing unemployment simultaneously by ploughing resulting public sector savings into works programs. Whether the plan would actually work or not, its immediate effect was to portray the government as finally resolute on the economy.[59] And just as the cabinet was congratulating itself on its new-found decisiveness, the treasurer charged ahead with the Treasury's reformulated foreign bank proposal and provided his colleagues with another chance to exhibit resolution. The cabinet approved the proposal as presented, and Howard announced its content on January 13, 1983.

Citing the incremental deregulatory moves that had taken place in recent years and the effects of mergers on the banking system, the treasurer announced a decision in principle to allow the initial entry of "around ten" foreign banks.[60] The new banks would operate as separately incorporated subsidiaries, would have to meet the same prudential standards as new domestic banks (whose entry was also being facilitated), and would be required to provide a "wide range of banking services and a reasonable branch network." In addition, 50-percent local equity would be encouraged, but the new policy "would allow scope for entry on the basis of less than 50-percent Australian equity when net economic benefits outweigh the general desirability of an effective partnership." In choosing among the applicants, the government would consider local equity, bank standing, scope of services to be provided, geographical balance, reciprocity, and previous associations with Australia.

Reaction from the banking community occurred along familiar lines. Foreign bankers expressed joy at the apparent flexibility of the new policy and at the number — higher than expected — of prospective entrants. They complained, however, about the local equity preference. The AuBA and domestic bank leaders came out with strongly worded statements on the "inappropriateness" of allowing foreign bank entry before full domestic deregulation had taken place.[61] On one point, however, they agreed with their foreign rivals. If foreign entry was inevitable, then it should occur without local equity involved. Usually couched in terms of prudential stability, an underlying reason for the position was surely a fear that a principal source of local equity would be local insurance companies, whose existing networks would pose an immediate threat to the branch networks of the banks. Only later would the banks also be concerned that a local equity requirement might set an undesirable precedent for other countries in the regulation of their own international operations.

Considering the possibility of a serious political reaction, the cabinet decision did take some courage, especially with election rumors in the air. Both the treasurer and the prime minister made the judgment that the issue would not become a major one in an election. They reasoned that Australians were more engaged by other issues, especially basic economic ones, and that opposition to foreign banks and foreign investment was not now deep seated in the electorate at large. Evidence of the increasing financial sophistication of the Australian public, such as favorable market responses to innovations introduced by NBFIs, confirmed them in this view.[62] Later events proved them correct; the Liberals lost the election on other issues. But at the time there remained a question as to the ultimate impact of the entry decision. When the decision was taken, Fraser was in fact about to call an election. Hoping to take advantage of disarray in the leadership of the ALP and of recent upswings in his government's popularity, Fraser finally requested a double dissolution of Parliament on February 3, 1983. March 5 would be election day, some three months before any foreign bank licenses were to be granted, and Labor's response to the bank entry decision was therefore of some moment.

At first, ALP spokesmen reacted in accordance with stated party policy. They opposed the foreign bank decision vigorously and warned that any future Labor government would review the terms of any licenses previously granted. The spokesman on economic affairs, Paul Keating, warned that his party would seek to stop any related legislation. With the votes of the Australian Democrats, the opposition did in fact have enough votes in the Senate to block any such legislation.[63] To the consternation of the opposition, however, Howard quickly announced that new bank licenses would be granted under discretionary authority.[64] This raised a good deal of ire and Labor remained opposed, but as the campaign proceeded, ambiguities began to emerge in its position. At a February press conference, the party's new leader, Robert Hawke, asserted that "certain conclusions follow" from his party's platform, and "as presently advised" they entailed a cancellation of any foreign bank invitations.[65] Shortly thereafter, however, Keating publicly stated that a Labor government would commission a new review of the financial system that could result in some foreign entry subject to very stringent controls. He reiterated this message in reassuring private conversations with individual foreign bankers.

Behind the apparent softening of Labor's stand lay intense internal debate. Clearly the left wing of the party, reinforced by increasingly vocal bank unions, remained adamantly opposed to foreign bank entry.[66] Indeed, during the election campaign the ABEU sponsored a series of national advertisements condemning the Liberals' policy and urging voters to reject "Mr. Howard's dangerous experiment."[67] But the influence of the left wing had been waning, especially on economic matters, since the fall of the previous Labor government in 1975 amidst widespread accusations of economic mismanagement. By 1983 the party's right wing had asserted itself, and its two pragmatic leaders, Hawke and Keating, had come to the fore. Over the next two years it would become evident that both men disagreed with parts of the 1982 platform but felt compelled to go along during the election campaign.[68] When their early poses of opposition to foreign bank entry failed to generate a strong reaction from the electorate, however, they felt free to downplay the issue in anticipation of a review of party policy after the election. This inclination, in turn, received important reinforcement from key state-level ALP leaders, notably the premiers of New South Wales and Victoria, who had actively begun competing with one another in urging foreign banks to consider setting up prospective headquarters in their capital cities. As it turned out, other issues dominated the campaign, and success at the polls brought the ALP to power.

This outcome effectively ended the first attempt to open up Australian banking.

## The New Priorities of Labor

A plethora of economic problems awaited the new Labor government, not the least of them a speculative currency crisis prompted by its election. Soon after taking office, the government devalued the Australian dollar to halt the capital outflow, but its leaders immediately realized that long-term stability depended upon reassuring a wary business community. After quickly mastering his new portfolio as treasurer, Keating concluded that business confidence was not necessarily antithetical to progress toward the social goals of his party. In fact, he saw both being served by an economic strategy focused on the restoration of growth and price stability. In such a context, financial deregulation promised to break an apparent roadblock to growth and appeal to business.[69] Less stringent foreign investment controls would do the same, and an incomes policy would help restrain inflation. In these views the treasurer had the support of his prime minister. At base, the new leaders of the ALP seemed comfortable with the liberal values of efficiency, competition, and open markets, at least in the financial sector. They were, nevertheless, clever enough not to appear ideologically committed. Labor's traditional equity concerns remained, but social experimentation would have to wait on sustained economic growth and the extended term in office that such growth should allow. In the middle-class country Australia had become, this outcome could best be assured by working with markets, not against them. A shift in the mood of the party, the leaders hoped, would allow them to begin putting this pragmatic vision into practice. The party's platform, however, remained an impediment.

The effort to amend stated party policy began shortly after the election when Keating confirmed that financial regulatory changes made by the previous government would not be rolled back. He soon followed up with the appointment of a small committee under the now-retired banker, Victor Martin, to review the Campbell Report in light of "the government's social and economic objectives."[70] Around the same time he initiated a review of foreign investment policy within the Treasury. Left-wing party members were skeptical about the intent of both reviews, but they took some comfort from the strongly antiforeign bank stance previously taken by Martin and from several tough decisions recently made by the government on specific foreign investment proposals, including its denial of permission for Citibank to acquire a 100-percent shareholding in an already foreign-controlled merchant bank.[71] The ABEU nevertheless remained very concerned about the intentions of the government and launched another media campaign specifically aimed at bolstering opposition to any weakening of Labor's antiforeign bank policy stance.[72]

## The Martin Report

From the start of their deliberations, the members of the Martin Group realized that theirs was a political task. Especially on important but sensitive issues, the Campbell Report had failed to provide sufficient guidance to government as to implementation. The group readily agreed on the general deregulatory trajectory of the earlier report; even Martin had apparently softened his previous views with the passage of time. Implementation, they concluded, meant selling the idea to the rank and file of the ALP.

In its review the group relied heavily on the record of the Campbell Committee and did not solicit new submissions or hold hearings, although it did accept unsolicited position papers. The most important of these came once again from the domestic banks. An AuBA paper concentrated almost entirely on the onerous burden of remaining controls on lending rates, deposit maturities, and bank liquidity. On foreign bank entry, the association's position had barely changed. No entry should be allowed until the remaining controls were abolished and a transition period had passed. The AuBA recommended that when the time for some foreign entry came, no local equity should be required, existing banks should be protected from takeovers, and reciprocity should be taken into account. The association also suggested as an interim alternative to full foreign entry the legalization of offshore banking, including the lending of foreign currencies to residents.[73] Individual banks complemented the AuBA submission with their own. On foreign banking, the most interesting addition came from Westpac, which argued, "In the event that some foreign banks are admitted, Westpac strongly believes that the Australian Government should involve itself in negotiations for reciprocal access in those cases where this appears to protect the interests of Australian banks, e.g. Japan, South Korea, and Taiwan."[74] Such involvement would constitute a new departure for a government traditionally reluctant to intervene in commercial transactions.

The Martin Group's final report, completed in December 1983 but released to the public on February 22, 1984, recommended continued but gradual deregulation in order to increase competition and efficiency in financial markets. Unlike the Campbell Report, it concentrated almost exclusively on institutional issues, specifically the most contentious issues related to the banking system, such as foreign entry, access of the domestic payments system, prudential regulation, and the role of NBFIs.[75] Many of its recommendations affected the existing and future operations of foreign banks. In arriving at them, the group claimed to have looked closely at trends in the structure of financial intermediation within Australia, including especially the continued rapid growth of merchant banks.[76]

The group saw no objection to opening the banking market to foreign interests in a limited fashion without waiting for further deregulation. "Limited" to the group meant four to six new banks with foreign shareholdings of less than 50 percent, but with a maximum of 50 percent permitted when net economic benefits were deemed sufficient by the government. The group further suggested several entry criteria broadly similar to those listed by the previous government; curiously, however, they did not list reciprocity as one of them. They also dismissed offshore banking as an alternative for foreign banks because they doubted that the positive effects on the domestic economy justified necessary tax concessions. They recommended consideration of licensing qualified NBFIs to deal in foreign exchange without full bank licenses. Finally, recognizing the need for some ownership rationalization in the merchant banking sector (especially if full deregulation permitted domestic banks to win back market share by eroding the short-term funding bases of merchant banks), the group promoted the idea of a short moratorium on foreign investment guidelines to allow, for example, foreign (as well as domestic) banks to own up to 100 percent of individual merchant banks.[77]

The chief general manager of Westpac greeted the Martin Report with the words, "I couldn't have written it better myself."[78] In contrast, Labor's left wing was not so delighted. One prominent left-wing backbencher wrote a stinging critique for his party colleagues reminding them that they had "unequivocally" rejected similar recommendations from the Campbell Committee and arguing that there was "no reason whatsoever to believe that allowing the entry of large oligopolistic foreign banks will necessarily increase competition."[79] For decidedly different reasons, objections also came from foreign banks and academic economists who saw the report as a retreat from the progressive thinking of the Campbell Committee. Beneath these reactions were doubts about the true intentions of the Labor government and therefore about the use to which the Martin

Report would be put. Indications of those intentions came even before the report was released.

In July 1983, two months after the Martin Group had begun its work, the government announced a new agreement with the state premiers that would increase the flexibility and autonomy of certain local borrowing authorities; the method of government financing had taken another step toward free markets. More fundamentally, the floating of the dollar in December 1983, against the continuing advice of the treasury secretary, if not all of his colleagues, showed a government willing to bear potentially high political costs for the sake of "rationalist" goals. But the government's real designs became much more apparent in a decision quietly tacked on to the more spectacular decision to float: the abolition of the bulk of the apparatus of exchange control. This move would entail no simple effort. The extensive bureaucracy built up since the war was now to be dismantled. The difficulty of reestablishing such an apparatus in the absence of grave economic crisis implied a fundamental commitment by the government to market solutions and increased openness. The foreign bank question tested that commitment.

By the beginning of 1984 serious opposition to the controlled entry of foreign banks was essentially reduced to the left wing of the ALP and the bank unions. Within the government, opponents were quickly losing their influence. The other antagonistic group, the domestic banks, was by now convinced that entry was imminent and its pro forma public stance on the issue was patently shallow. As a lever to accelerate the pace of domestic deregulation, the banks' position was increasingly compromised by their own expansions abroad. A prime instance of their consequent dilemma was occurring in the United States where their dramatic growth left them mired in a high-profile dispute with the state of Illinois over reciprocity.[80] Stepped up congressional scrutiny, reinforced by a degree of lobbying in Washington by American banks, added to their discomfort.[81]

Despite having weakened in the decade since the fall of the Whitlam government, the Left still constituted the single largest faction within the ALP and could carry the party when aligned with a group of centrists. In 1984, therefore, the prime minister and the treasurer could not afford completely to ignore the Left, especially on so symbolic an issue as foreign bank entry. Although not quite as sensitive as the question of abolishing remaining interest rate controls, the very words *foreign banks* conjured up two of the party's historical bogeys. In their attempt to win over the soul of the party and reconcile it to their new economic strategy, its pragmatic leaders thus decided to try gradually to convince their opponents, or at least to let the Left talk itself out. Because resolution did not seem urgent, they could afford to take time. Such an approach was evident even before release of the Martin Report when Keating leaked the group's recommendations on foreign banks and expressed his support. The next day Hawke declared the intention of his government to foster greater competition in the banking sector and sounded a theme to which he and Keating returned constantly over the coming months. In view of their involvement in the fall of previous Labor governments, Hawke argued, the party owed nothing to the domestic banks and should not seek to protect them. The message had a visceral appeal, but the Left responded that it was up to a full party conference to change such important policy positions.

The Martin Report itself represented a key step in the leaders' strategy. Upon making it public, Keating endorsed its conclusion that "many of the current official constraints on the financial system operate to limit desirable competition and developments in the community's interests without significantly contributing to the Government's economic and social objectives."[82] The next step was to convince the parliamentary caucus of the ALP that specific policy responses followed from this conclusion, including expanding the number of foreign exchange dealers, scrapping deposit maturity controls, and licensing foreign banks.

The treasurer, his staff, and Martin Group members worked diligently to explain and defend their position within the caucus. After they had convinced a group of centrists, the leadership controlled the numbers needed to push through a broad reform package. They decided nevertheless to postpone a final decision on foreign entry until after the next national conference, now scheduled for July. Partly to maintain momentum, however, the treasurer acceded in March to pressure from state premiers and business lobbyists to establish a working party that would draft possible legislation on offshore banking. The next month the cabinet announced simultaneous decisions to abolish remaining deposit-taking restrictions on domestic banks, effective August 1, and to license without numerical restriction qualifying NBFIs as foreign exchange dealers.[83] With deregulation thus innocuously progressing, the leaders then sought to isolate stalwart opponents who might never fully be reconciled to it. In May they reached a tacit agreement with the trade union federation (ACTU); in return for muted opposition to foreign bank entry, they gave a commitment not to abolish interest rate controls on housing loans.[84] A disappointed ABEU remained adamantly and actively opposed.

In the period leading up to the July conference, the treasurer in particular spent considerable time with Labor groups across the country arguing the merits of foreign bank entry. He also gave a great deal of attention to the work of the party's Economic Policy Committee, the body responsible for drafting relevant planks for a new platform. Left-wing delegates on the committee attempted strenuously to have the 1982 planks reaffirmed. Delegates supporting the treasurer eventually rejected this position, but the refusal of the Left to concede prevented the emergence of a consensus. Although no formal vote was taken, the treasurer's apparent strength on the issue enabled him to place his own planks before the conference. These generally endorsed the principle of controlled foreign bank entry in order to stimulate competition and economic growth. The planks remained intentionally vague, however, on specific plans for implementation.

Immediately before the conference began, Keating's planks ran into difficulties when centrist delegates sought to strike a middle position between the Left and the leadership by specifying strict numerical limits on prospective new banks and tight entry criteria, including a minimum Australian equity participation of 50 percent, forced unionization, and a requirement for union consultation before the introduction of new banking technology. With the centrists holding the balance, the treasurer agreed to a carefully worded compromise.[85] The conference finally debated the issue on July 9, 1984. During that debate a series of unconvincing speeches from the Left decried the government's willingness to subvert Australia's national sovereignty and called for the extension of direct controls over domestic financial institutions.[86] As a practical alternative to the proposed planks, the Left pressed for granting bank licenses to domestic building societies and credit unions and proposed a two-year delay on foreign licensing to permit an assessment of the need for further competition. To the contrary, stressing disapproval of de facto protection for the domestic banks and a perceived need for increased competition, the premiers of Victoria, South Australia, and Western Australia, the prime minister, and the treasurer spoke strongly in favor of the planks.[87] After several hours of debate the conference rejected the Left's proposals by a vote of fifty-six to forty-one and subsequently endorsed the treasurer's planks as amended in his discussions with the centrists.

The successful planks focused on some traditional and some new themes for Labor: the need to promote an "environment conducive to high levels of economic growth," the identification of unemployment as the most serious economic and social problem faced by Australia, the necessity of a long-term "national strategy" to compensate for market failures, the importance of corporatist machinery for reaching consensus between major economic groups, and the need to improve overall economic performance by stimulating competition in the banking sector. To accomplish the latter, the government was authorized to license new domestic banks and to offer a "very limited number" of licenses to foreign banks on the condition that "every effort is made to achieve a minimum of 50-percent Australian equity in each new banking venture." Other conditions included: full unionization of the new banks, consultation with unions on technological change, subsidiary rather than branch structures for new entrants to insulate Australia from the international debt crisis, arrangements to ensure that the majority of Australians had access to the new banks' services, and periodic review of the performance of the new entrants to monitor "their contribution to the economic and social performance of the Australian economy."[88] As the future would show, this judicious wording left the government with all the flexibility it needed to open the banking markets as it deemed appropriate.

## The Policy Outcome: Reconciling Competition, Control, and History

Labor's policy turnaround was greeted with enthusiasm by the foreign banking community, condemned by the ABEU and the Australian Democrats, and hailed by the Liberals and the new leaders of the National party.[89] The domestic banks, though not fully reconciled to the impending entry of new competition, seemed resigned to the inevitable. Partly in anticipation, their strategic expansions continued apace.[90] The position of the Treasury had also shifted on the issue, a change underlined by the resignation of the treasury secretary one month after the Labor conference.[91]

The treasurer and his staff spent the month following the conference thrashing out detailed entry criteria for the new banks now certain to arrive. At the same time they reconsidered problems experienced in the merchant banking sector as a result of complicated ownership structures and the newly invigorated competitiveness of the domestic banks. Foreign bank lobbying on this score had intensified during the past year, and the AMBA had publicly called for a six-month moratorium on foreign investment guidelines to allow a restructuring to occur among the merchant banks. With an eye on potential reciprocity-related problems resulting from the anticipated limited opening of the banking markets, the treasurer had already decided to accede to the proposal, over the objections of some in the Treasury who warned that it would lead to the unrestricted entry of a large number of new foreign banks in the wholesale market. Once again, however, in order to counter critical reaction, the treasurer chose to delay this decision until the foreign bank announcement was ready. By so doing, he was also able to bury a potentially more far-reaching policy change beneath a more politically sensational one.

On September 10, 1984, shortly before traveling to Washington to attend the annual meeting of the IMF, the treasurer announced the new policies of the government. Applications were to be accepted from foreign and domestic parties for a limited number of new banking licenses. The actual number would "depend on the number of worthwhile applications received." Stressing the paramount need for increased competition and innovation, the government would "seek to achieve a minimum of 50-percent Australian equity in new banking ventures [but would] be prepared to consider" proposals with less than 50 percent in cases promising "significant benefits to Australia." Further, applicants "should seek to provide a wide range of banking services, though they may wish to emphasize certain areas of business in which they have special expertise." They should also "give full recognition to the interests of people employed in the banking industry." Finally, mindful of reciprocity concerns, a wide geographical spread would be sought among countries with which Australia had significant economic relationships. At the same time, the treasurer announced a twelve-month moratorium on ownership restrictions in the merchant banking sector to allow it to adjust to new competitive circumstances.[92]

After two long years of agonizing internal deliberation, the Labor government had not just taken Australian policy back to where the Liberals had left it but had gone much farther. That it was able to do so reflected the absence by the fall of 1984 of any effective opposition.[93] Paul Keating personally had done more than any other proponent of increased financial openness to ensure this outcome.

Keating's ideas and tactics had to a certain extent been shaped by his previous contacts outside Australia. During the term of the previous Labor government and in opposition, for example, Keating had special responsibility for the minerals sector and had been deeply impressed by the innovativeness of certain foreign lenders. Continued contact with premier international banks in the ensuing years had reinforced this impression. At the 1984 annual meeting of the IMF in Washington, those same banks welcomed him like a conquering hero. Here was the man who had brought a formerly retrograde Australia to the forefront of deregulation among the advanced industrial countries. Prominent financial magazines named him Finance Minister of the Year. The American Federal Reserve Board chairman congratulated him, and private bankers courted his favor. In turn, Keating used the opportunity to promote increased foreign investment in his country.[94] His indeed was a new Labor party.

Major international banks competed strenuously with one another to strengthen individual claims for full banking licenses. Many did so by committing significant resources to the preparation of formal applications and by actively recruiting local financial talent, notably from the junior ranks of the Treasury and Reserve Bank.[95] Others sought out helpful alliances with local institutions, especially insurance companies and state government agencies. Still others determined that their present and future interests in Australia were best served by taking up the option of full ownership in the merchant banking sector.[96] In the end, all of this strategic planning led to forty-two applications from nineteen countries for full banking licenses and over one hundred decisions to set up new or reconstituted merchant banks.[97]

Another federal election in late 1984 set the stage for final action. Once again, the foreign bank issue failed to emerge as a key issue in the campaign, despite the vigorous efforts of the now-isolated Australian Democrats. Although Labor won reelection, its majority was reduced. This partial rebuke by the electorate left the Hawke administration in a position similar to that of the last Fraser government. If it was to restore its political momentum and achieve its economic goals, it once again needed to demonstrate resolution and decisiveness. The final foreign banking decision represented a convenient opportunity for doing just that.

At the end of February 1985, after a day-long cabinet meeting during which a package presented by the treasurer was debated exhaustively and ultimately agreed upon in full, the treasurer announced that sixteen foreign banks were being invited to establish operations in Australia. "In selecting the sixteen," he stated, "the Government has been influenced by the fact that half of the 42 applications received clearly met the requirements set. . . . [Therefore] to maximize the benefits to Australia from the very high quality response . . . we have decided that a greater rather than a smaller number should be approved."[98] The list included five American banks, three British, three Japanese, and one each from Canada, Germany, New Zealand, Hong Kong, and Singapore. Citibank, Morgan Guaranty, Bankers Trust, National Westminster, Barclays,

National Bank of New Zealand, Bank of Tokyo, Deutsche Bank, and Overseas Chinese Bank were all permitted to open wholly owned subsidiaries. The others were to come in under joint ventures with Australian institutions, including three with state-government-affiliated groups.[99]

Aside from the political predilections of the leadership, there existed compelling new reasons for the large number of new licenses.[100] Most importantly, reciprocity considerations had now become significant. In October 1984 the Japanese Ministry of Finance initiated discussions with the Australian Treasury aimed at ensuring equitable treatment for Japanese banks. If four Australian banks wanted to come to Tokyo, at least four Japanese banks would have to be let into Australia, preferably without restrictions. At the urging of the domestic banks and out of consideration for geographical balance, the government sought to hold the number of incoming Japanese entrants below four. Australian negotiators argued that strict reciprocity was unnecessary, especially in view of the merchant banking moratorium, which allowed unrestricted entry to any Japanese banks interested solely in wholesale business. Japan remained adamant, and Australia raised the stakes by freezing all Japanese merchant banking applications; Japan, in turn, threatened to close down the Tokyo branch of Grindlay's Bank, which had recently been acquired by ANZ. Only after the government had let it be known that it was about to announce the successful applicants without any Japanese representation did Japan finally concede.

Reciprocity and/or trade considerations also directly entered into decisions on entrants from New Zealand, Hong Kong, and Singapore.[101] Although no formal representations took place with respect to other countries, the government was certainly aware of the reciprocal expectations of the United States and Britain; in view of the Japanese negotiations and the traditional importance of economic and other linkages with these countries, it was apparent that no purpose would be served by allowing in fewer than three banks from each. Regarding the United States, the government also wanted to demonstrate a continued commitment to close relations, especially in the wake of mounting tensions on bilateral defense matters. A larger number and a mixed local equity picture allowed the government to obfuscate concessions granted to certain banks in return for particular expected benefits.[102]

Within Australia reaction to the opening of the domestic banking markets was unsurprising. As the treasurer expected, public attention concentrated on the limited opening of the retail market represented by the entry of the sixteen and not on the more fundamental change in the institutional structure of the wholesale market.[103] Among politicians, the Australian Democrats stood alone in opposition. Holding their fire for another day and a more promising issue, the Labor Left scarcely reacted at all. Even the ABEU now downplayed its previous philosophical opposition and promised cooperation as long as the new entrants "presented themselves as good employers and corporate citizens."[104] The most noteworthy negative responses came from domestic banks surprised by the large number and from certain successful foreign banks surprised by the greater success of their colleagues on the local equity matter.[105]

Australia's new commitment to financial openness became more apparent in the aftermath of the entry decision when the locus of associated regulatory policy shifted from the more overtly politicized cabinet room to the murkier recesses of the Reserve Bank. The Labor government had made it clear to the Bank that regulation of the new entrants was to be nondiscriminatory; like institutions were to be treated in like manner, regardless of the nationality of their shareholders. Despite the Reserve Bank's subsequent cautious approach during the start-up phase of the foreign entrants, it was in fact fully committed to the Campbell principle of competitive neutrality. Australia's market access policy therefore came close to the standard other countries described as equal competitive opportunity and national treatment.[106]

A further indication of Australia's new commitment to financial openness was shown in moves to follow up the deregulation of currency and banking markets by officially embracing liberalization as a normative concept. In the wake of policy change, the Treasury initiated a major strategic review of the country's posture with respect to various international economic agreements. For example, early in 1985 officials debated the wisdom of removing reservations attached to Australia's 1971 acceptance of the OECD Code of Liberalization of Capital Movements. In June discussions began between Australia and the OECD committee responsible for the code. Some within the Treasury initially argued against lifting the reservations in order to keep options open should policy adjustments be deemed necessary in the future. Others countered that to move back to exchange controls or a closed banking market would cause such severe disruptions in the domestic economy as to be politically unthinkable except in the face of a major crisis. In that unlikely event, they contended, no international code or treaty would stop any country from doing what it judged essential. Little was to be lost then by bringing Australia's reservations into line with the new reality of its markets—but something was to be gained. In essence, Australia's new posture toward the code would be one further element to be taken into account by future policy makers and, at the margin, might make the difference between defending open markets or sliding incrementally away from them. The prospect of possible censure from partners in the OECD would help stiffen backbones. Furthermore, because Australia was now relatively open to international capital movements and its more outward-looking business institutions were in a position to benefit from such an environment, there was something to be gained by using the code to encourage openness in other countries still relatively closed. Such a view eventually won out. In the middle of 1985 the treasurer, on the advice of his officials, signed instructions to Australia's OECD delegation allowing them to release seven reservations to the liberalization code.[107] A broader reassessment of these issues, informed by new ideological commitments, subsequently continued within the government. As Australia reconsidered trade issues, foreign investment guidelines, and continued financial liberalization, an awareness of the wider normative aspect of its policy trajectory finally became evident.[108]

# CHAPTER SEVEN

# Converging Policies and Developing Norms

## DOMESTIC POLICY CONVERGENCE

In recent years the United States, Japan, Canada, and Australia reassessed the institutional linkages between their domestic banking markets and those of other states. Central to consequent policy reform was the question of the proper place of foreign banks. All four countries addressed this question in regulatory environments that reflected economic change, technological innovation, rising inward and outward investment flows, and volatile exchange rates. Regulatory policies themselves, however, came under pressure only when such developments were politically internalized. Policies regulating the access of foreign banks were reformulated only after the political interests of domestic banks shifted, after key governmental actors rearticulated public interests and crafted sustainable political compromises, after foreign banks individually or collectively pursued new markets aggressively, and after foreign governments became advocates for reciprocal openness. Market access policies changed only when those actors most directly affected by them mobilized politically in domestic contexts.

By the middle of the 1980s the interaction of those actors in each case fostered the adoption of generally liberal policies. Across the four countries, although perfectly free markets had not been created, the trajectories of policy development over several decades converged toward increased openness, expanded competition, and nondiscriminatory regulation. Indeed, only when the foreign banking issue became embroiled in more broadly politicized debates—for example, in Canada in 1967 and in Australia several years later—did temporary moves away from such goals occur.

Although the four processes of regulatory reform shared basic similarities, each demonstrated how important political idiosyncracies shaped unique policy outcomes. Of the four countries, Japan and Australia had the most centralized public sectors with respect to financial regulation. Governmental influences therefore predominated in debates over reform. Conversely, with their more porous decision-making structures and deep jurisdictional tensions, the central governments of the United States and Canada had relatively less cohesive regulatory authority over their banking markets. The role of private sector actors was accordingly more prominent in each case. In this sector, the relative strength of state institutions helps explain particular policy outcomes, especially if the concept of strength embraces not only the ability to impose central direction by fiat, but also the capacity of official institutions to retain control over an agenda by adeptly encouraging compromises among powerful vested interests. By such a measure, for example, the Japanese state, even if weakening within Japan as private sector actors strengthened, continued to appear stronger than an American state unable to fill an anomalous regulatory void until private sector interests reached their own internal consensus. Similarly, the Australian state appeared relatively stronger than a Canadian state subtly and effectively, over time, penetrated by organized private foreign interests.

Looked at another way, Japan and Canada were relatively more vulnerable to external pressures. In Japan, a dependence on export markets and resulting political sensitivities gave foreign governments a distinctive influence on internal bank regulatory debates. In Canada, historically deep linkages with American markets created important opportunities in particular for the influence of American banks. On the other hand, Australia and the United States, because of geographical distance in the former case and absolute size in the latter, appeared relatively more impervious to outside influences. Their respective debates on foreign bank access were therefore more obviously dominated by domestic interests.

Viewed comparatively, then, a particular set of political actors played an especially catalytic role in each of the four countries. Although policies converged in a common direction, important differences remained. Borders around national banking markets became more porous, but they did not disappear. No state was required to admit or legitimate the direct presence of foreign banks. No agency forced any of them to move against their will toward more equitable regulatory treatment. Idiosyncratic domestic structures mediated between common pressures and changing national policies. The four case studies demonstrate that those domestic structures were fundamentally political and conditioned by unique historical relationships between governments and markets. Tables 12 through 15, with summary reviews, recapitulate the manner in which market access policy developed in the four countries.

## United States

The essential catalyst to policy development in the U.S. case originated in the private sector. Federal authorities, most notably the Federal Reserve and various legislators in both houses of Congress, were unable to move proposals for control over an expanding foreign banking presence until the domestic banks most affected reached the level of consensus necessary to sustain an extension of federal jurisdiction. A strategy of delay was associated closely with the interests of money-center banks. But neither they nor the more numerous regional banks dictated policy. National policy makers were explicitly concerned with balancing competing domestic interests and with providing a basis for fair competition from foreign institutions. Any enduring policy initiative, however, had to take the core interests of the range of domestic banks fully into account. Very little room for maneuver existed as long as the banks themselves perceived those interests to be opposed.

Most immediately affected by the relatively uncontrolled growth of foreign banks, especially during the 1970s, were the numerous regional and smaller domestic banking institutions unable themselves to expand across state lines or to compensate abroad for market share losses at home. In the Bankers' Association for Foreign Trade these banks found their voice, and early in the decade they constituted the interest group most receptive to the control proposals of the Fed. Their desires were long blocked, however, by major money-center banks ostensibly concerned about the possibility of retaliation abroad against their extensive and growing international operations. Less obviously, these same institutions subtly sought to use the nascent interstate operations of the foreigners to advance their own more fundamental domestic political agenda, the removal of geographic restrictions on their activities within the United States. In the end, a tacit consensus between regional and money-center banks emerged when foreign bank operations, especially those involving acquisitions, reached a point where market share losses became intolerable for both sets of domestic institutions.

The original initiative for the new federal policy came during the 1960s from individual legislators concerned by one or another aspect of foreign participation in the U.S. banking market. More signifi-

*Table 12.* Development of foreign bank access policy in the United States, 1967–87

|  | 1967–73 | 1974–77 | 1978–87 |
|---|---|---|---|
| Domestic bank assessments of protection, reciprocity | No consensus, most favor protection | Developing consensus | Tacit consensus on appropriate balance |
| Foreign bank presence | Rising | Accelerating | Rising |
| Foreign bank political activity | Low | High | Lower |
| Domestic government assessments of competition, control | Federal policy vacuum and state autonomy favor rising competition | Control issues rise | Stable balance with increasing centralization |
| Foreign government pressure | Low | Rising | Receding |

cantly, it was soon picked up by a Federal Reserve Board worried about the efficacy of monetary policy tools and increasingly concerned about the possible international consequences of congressional nativism in this sector. The Fed proposed to extend its authority to cover foreign banking and began working assiduously to secure the necessary mandate. Opposing the Fed were other parts of the federal bureaucracy and, more importantly, state regulators jealous of their prerogatives in the complex dual banking system. Paradoxically, the tenacity of the states' opposition provided foreign banks with an extended opportunity to expand so broadly within the domestic market that the foreign presence eventually reached the point where states' rights arguments began to pale and the case for an extension of federal authority became compelling. At base, therefore, the policy debate on foreign banking was as much about the distribution of regulatory power within the U.S. system as about providing a political foundation for fair competition in the banking market.

As a consequence of the impasse between federal and state claims in the early 1970s, the competitiveness of foreign banks was enhanced by default. A policy void at the federal level favored their rapid growth. But by 1977 that growth itself was posing a now-obvious threat to overall monetary control and to continuation of the traditional ban on interstate banking. Within the federal government, assessments of the value of extending control over foreign banking rose and assessments of the value of foreign-induced competition became much more measured. The opportunity to act on these assessments came when domestic banks reached their own agreement on the need for action. Even then, however, state regulators as a group did not acquiesce; they simply lacked the power to stop the federal incursion, especially after splits developed between states over such issues as allowing foreign, as opposed to out-of-state, takeovers of failing institutions.

By late 1977, recognizing the new consensus in the domestic banking community and facing the possibility that restrictionist pressures could become unmanageable if the foreign banking issue became intertwined with more contentious and broadly politicized issues, procompetitive federal legislators finally decided to seize the moment. Despite continued opposition from state regulators, the resulting International Banking Act legitimated the foreign operations already established under state laws, brought future foreign activities under expanded federal control, provided a mechanism for advancing the interests of domestic banks abroad, and codified subtle measures for the gradual extension of domestic and foreign interstate banking networks.

The final policy rested fundamentally on a deft compromise between conflicting private interests. Smaller domestic banks succeeded in stopping the uncontrolled expansion of their foreign competitors, while larger banks managed to prevent adoption of onerous restraints, which potentially threatened their own domestic and international strategies. For their part, the political activity of foreign institutions, as distinct from their market activity, played a subsidiary role in shaping policy. In essence, their influence was effective only as long as their interests coincided with those of their major domestic bank allies. The full grandfathering of foreign operations in existence before 1978 resulted directly from this alliance of interests. In a basic sense, this significant concession represented part of the price paid by domestic competitors for the control measures ultimately put into place. The final compromise proved bearable to all interested parties; it therefore proved sustainable.

Despite the control orientation of the International Banking Act and of subsequent federal policy development in the wake of the act, the ultimate effect of new federal policy was a liberalizing one. By the late 1970s the United States had passed the point where a federal policy vacuum—an anomaly that implicitly subsidized the foreign competitors of indigenous banks—could unquestionably endure. A new layer of federal governmental involvement in the national banking market resulted. The effects of that new involvement, however, turned out not to be illiberal or anticompetitive. On the one hand, a range of institutions came under federal monetary control for the first time; on the other, their existence and future expansion was thereby unambiguously rendered legitimate. Similarly, although the ability of state authorities to stimulate competition by allowing unimpeded cross-state foreign banking was curtailed, their ability to limit entirely the entry of foreign-owned operations was also restrained. In addition, states lost their ability to insist that all types of foreign entry meet strict reciprocity tests. The complete grandfathering of existing foreign establishments, the creation of a federally authorized branching option, the amendment of Edge Act restrictions on both foreign and domestic banks, and the continued flexibility provided to nonbanking affiliates and foreign representative offices all proved conducive to broader openness and competition. National policy moved from de facto void to de jure equal treatment. Its trajectory was toward nondiscrimination. The continued entry and expansion of foreign banks after 1978, especially in submarkets traditionally restricted, testified to its essentially liberal character.

Similarly, the absence of retaliatory actions abroad following the passage of the International Banking Act make it plausible to conclude that foreign governments did not interpret the new law as restrictionist. Most central banks saw the extension of federal monetary controls as reasonable, if not belated, and most finance ministries were pleased with the generous grandfathering provisions finally enacted. Periodic complaints about perceived competitive inequalities after 1978, from both foreign and domestic banks, appeared transient and mainly reflected the unavoidable consequences of an increasing interpenetration of national financial markets themselves still fundamentally conditioned by different political, legal, and economic structures.

Notwithstanding the fact that domestic political factors proved most consequential in the development of the new federal policy on foreign banking, from 1973 onward key policy makers in fact remained sensitive to the international dimension. Pressure from foreign governments, at times directly expressed but most often implied in the increasingly cohesive lobbying of foreign bankers, constituted an evident, if subsidiary, element in the long debate preceding adoption of the International Banking Act. More importantly, policy makers themselves, notably in the Federal Reserve, Treasury, and Senate, were increasingly aware that their discussions were taking place within a larger arena. By 1978 the dominant consensus explicitly supported the twin aims of enhancing the position of U.S. banks abroad and reciprocally granting fair access to foreign banks in the United States. The national treatment concept ideally suited federal desires to preserve basic market structures while progressively expanding market openness both at home and abroad. The decisions fully to legitimate the existing privileged networks of foreign banks in the domestic market, as well as to mandate administrative efforts to discourage protectionism abroad, became elements in general U.S. foreign investment policy.

Tensions did not altogether disappear after 1978, especially those related to international reciprocity, additional foreign acquisitions, and the sometimes contentious effects of identical regulations on structurally diverse institutions. But in retrospect the International Banking Act did provide a stable and fair political framework capable of accommodating persistent pressures for internationalization and federalization within a complex domestic banking system. And after the heyday of U.S. financial hegemony had passed, the act established a firm basis for increasingly active U.S. diplomatic efforts aimed at the reciprocal opening of markets abroad.

## Japan

Before the late 1960s the few foreign banks operating directly in Japan played a limited but important role in the economic reconstruction of the country. Governmentally imposed restrictions were tolerated by the banks themselves, and the closure of the market to new entrants was acquiesced in by their home governments. Foreign pressure to reopen the market became evident only in the late 1960s and initially came from banks, not from governments preoccupied with other aspects of bilateral relations. This early limited pressure coincided with cautious moves of domestic banks into overseas markets. Although the door to the market came slightly ajar, protectionist constraints limited the activities of the expanding foreign sector. Satisfied with their profitability and lacking any alternative strategies, foreign banks quietly consented.

The crucial period of change began around 1976. A rapid expansion in the number of foreign banks coincided with a sharp decline in profitability. Similar profitability pressures contributed to a simultaneous explosion in the offshore growth of Japanese banks. In response, partly because of organizational problems, partly because they lacked domestic political allies, and partly because Japanese governmental oversight was so centralized and difficult to penetrate, increasing numbers of foreign banks called upon their governments to intervene. The timing of such requests appears fortuitous in retrospect.

*Table 13.* Development of foreign bank access policy in Japan, 1950–87

|  | 1950–68 | 1969–75 | 1976–82 | 1983–87 |
|---|---|---|---|---|
| Foreign government pressure | Low | Rising | High | High |
| Foreign bank presence | Restricted | Increasing | Increasing rapidly | Increasing slowly |
| Foreign bank political activity | Low | Low | Low in Japan. Increasing with own governments | Rising in Japan. High with own governments |
| Domestic government assessments of competition, control | Direct control | Control recedes | Competition rising | Competition, indirect control |
| Domestic bank assessments of protection, reciprocity | Protection dominant | Protection dominant | Reciprocity rising | Reciprocity rising |

Although governments may have acted in any case, their inclination to initiate discussions in the complex area of Japanese financial regulation received a boost from burgeoning domestic political pressures on the trade front. For the United States, such an inclination was reinforced by a new proactive stance in the Treasury Department following passage of the International Banking Act. On the Japanese side, the subsequent politicization of banking-related issues unleashed a number of forces. Political leaders sought quick solutions in a sector seen as relatively more manageable than others. The Ministry of Finance sought the same in order to reduce the chance of direct intervention by politicians. The most important vested interests, whether articulate or not, had something to gain off shore from concessions made on shore; some also stood to gain domestically if foreign pressure helped accelerate the overall process of financial deregulation. Around this time, governmental priorities were in any case shifting cautiously away from the direct control objectives of the early postwar period toward liberalization, albeit liberalization with overall stability preserved. Administrative change ensued. Operational privileges for foreign banks were extended — but at the cost of terminating an important but declining monopoly over foreign currency lending. At the end of this first round of reform, legislative change codified Japan's new policy approach and brought it explicitly into conformity with earlier bilateral and multilateral commitments.

A very similar cycle of policy change began again in 1983. Once more, an expanding foreign presence compounded structural profitability problems. Mobilized by continuing trade worries, governments, especially that of the United States, intervened and helped bring financial liberalization issues to the top of the economic agenda. In such an environment, arguments based on reciprocity, about which the Japanese preferred to be relatively more explicit, were often well received. In general, where powerful interests within Japan were pushing in a similar direction, catalytic external pressure and ensuing bilateral negotiations achieved substantial progress. By the end of this second phase, foreign banking institutions had few complaints about their formal access to the domestic market in Japan. As far as regulatory policy was concerned, Japan appeared nearly as liberal as any other OECD country. Indeed, the degree to which Japan's foreign bank regulatory policy had converged with those of other major banking countries provided a striking contrast to the lack of convergence apparent in other economic arenas.

To be sure, problems remained but few foreign bankers believed that solutions were clear-cut or readily designed. The bankers now had the right to compete without official discrimination. But as Japan became the world's largest exporter of capital in the mid-1980s, many foreign bankers continued to find their growth constrained in a desperately competitive domestic market where custom, functional segmentation, and an upswing in securities activities (as opposed to traditional bank lending) worked against them. Continuing liberalization of the Japanese system was held out by the Ministry of Finance as a solution. But perceptions of fairness were increasingly shaped by disputes over comparative market shares of foreign banks in Japan and of Japanese banks abroad. Having under pressure given up the tools to distribute market shares within Japan in the manner of the immediate postwar years and having predictably over time lost power relative to a resurgent private sector, the government of Japan found itself treading a difficult path between foreign expectations and requirements for domestic political stability. To satisfy persistent critics in foreign governments, throughout the 1980s it attempted to recognize more explicitly the reciprocal understanding behind the standard of national treatment. In one case after another, it made ad hoc adjustments in specific regulatory policies aimed at assuaging foreign concerns while gradually overseeing structural reform in its own market. Foreign pressure undoubtedly often proved useful in Japanese governmental attempts to break persistent logjams created by opposing domestic interests, but it proved much less successful when no obvious domestic constituency, in either the public or the private sector, was present to support requested changes. By the late 1980s foreign banks and their governments remained perplexed by continued competitive problems within Japan, while at the same time the regulatory standards that they had helped strengthen were undoubtedly benefiting vigorous Japanese institutions both at home and abroad. The future of those standards depended very much on how that perplexity would be dispelled. In that regard, Japanese policy makers now had a principal responsibility.

## Canada

Foreign bankers themselves had a critical impact on policy development in Canada. When Citibank's acquisition of Mercantile Bank represented a unique case in 1967, both governmental and public concerns had a clear target. The stakes involved in Citibank's continued presence, even if overstated or misunderstood, were apparent at the time. The bank's lack of sensitivity to Canadian fears, compounded by ham-handed U.S. government intervention, gave ammunition to a determined group of economic nationalists. The consequent attempt to close the domestic banking market was assured when moderate policy makers were left with no room to maneuver. But, although harsh federal legislation aimed at closure was adopted in 1967, contrary provincial policies created a loophole. The entry of provincially licensed foreign quasi-banking operations, innocuous at first, gradually reached a level that obfuscated perceptions of the national interest and made decisive movement toward closure more difficult. Competitive pressures unleashed by the unanticipated failure to expel Citibank and by the division of jurisdiction over financial regulation in the confederal Canadian state had opened the way for this expansion. As a result, the national government's most advantageous policy option was to extend its jurisdiction in order to maintain control over the domestic banking system while legitimating the expanding foreign presence.

This option was effectively articulated in the 1980 Bank Act, which reversed the policy established in 1967. The effectiveness of foreign bank lobbying after passage of the 1980 act facilitated the enactment of a later bill that doubled foreign banks' allowable market share. An 8-percent ceiling legislated in 1980, and the market activity it stimulated, gave the banks a common cause; a conscious shift in political tactics by key U.S. bankers gave them the effective

*Table 14.* Development of foreign bank access policy in Canada, 1965–87

|  | 1965–67 | 1976–80 | 1982–87 |
|---|---|---|---|
| Foreign bank presence | Minimal | Rising sharply | Rising gradually |
| Foreign bank political activity | Low | Rising | Rising sharply |
| Domestic bank assessments of protection, reciprocity | Protection dominant | Reciprocity rising | Reciprocity tacitly accepted |
| Domestic government assessments of competition, control | Direct control dominant | Competition rising | Indirect control, competition favored |
| Foreign government pressure | High, overt | Lower | Stable, subtle |

leadership lacking in previous years. The new approach was more subtle than in 1967, and external governmental pressure, a counterproductive factor in the earlier period, was now managed in a manner calculated to influence but not offend Canadian sensibilities. In Washington, the banks were aided by an official strategy more enlightened than the one evident in the 1960s. Within Canada, rising economic troubles, which tended to cool nationalist passions and shift policy-making priorities, assisted their cause.

In 1984 a firm consensus among the foreign banks on goal and method guided a relentless lobbying campaign, the legitimacy of which was never questioned in Canada because the lobbyists were now clearly operating from within the system. Foreign bank efforts to line up support complemented their activities in the marketplace, and the number of provinces and domestic businesses benefiting from their capital imports, job creation, and competitiveness rose. Without that successful campaign of alliance building, legislative and subsequent administrative actions to expand openness would not have come as quickly as they did.

The decisions to move toward a controlled openness and gradually to accept related multilateral obligations were hastened by the recognition of reciprocity as an important policy goal. Changing strategic assessments by leading domestic banks provided the backdrop for policy reconsideration. In the 1960s a stable level of domestic bank involvement overseas allowed reciprocity to remain low in the policy hierarchy, and overt external threats to sovereign prerogatives kept it low. By the late 1970s, although still ranking below considerations of national predominance in the domestic market, reciprocity had become a more prominent value as the internationalization of the domestic banks continued apace. At this point, an observer might have expected a rising internationalist consensus among the domestic banks, driven by the need for reciprocity, to accelerate policy movement. Instead, the inability of the Big Five to reach a consensus unintentionally facilitated the de facto expansion of the foreign near-banks by providing little coherent guidance to policy makers. Conversely, an observer might have expected that the increased effective competition thereby engendered would consolidate the position of the domestic banks in a protectionist direction. But such consolidation in fact never developed. The banks' eventual willingness to go along with the legislation of 1980 and 1984 indicated acquiescence more than positive acceptance of the value of reciprocity. Nevertheless, the ambiguity of the banks' positions did help make it possible for the national government to respond positively in the mid-1980s to the calls of foreign banks for more equitable treatment.

In the two decades following 1967 federal policy makers' tolerance for the competitive impulse of the foreign banks rose significantly. The political will behind Canada's move toward openness was increasingly influenced by perceptions within the national government that the existing level of competition within the banking system was inadequate. And foreign bankers themselves eventually learned to exploit this changing mood very effectively. Rapidly rising interest rates and expanding profitability among domestic banks in the late 1970s made it easier for officials to justify concessions to foreigners promising to lower costs for consumers of banking services. Foreign banks made a persuasive case in this respect, one that would come back to haunt them when expanded market access was later conditioned on broadening the base of consumers so benefiting. Domestic economic traumas in the late 1970s and early 1980s also encouraged strategic rethinking as policy makers sought mechanisms for renewing domestic economic growth. The important point here, however, is that by the mid-1980s Canadian policy makers and foreign bankers shared increasingly similar ideological commitments to the ideals of more open and freer competition. These commitments were demonstrated in subsequent years as Canadian policy makers permitted foreigners to take advantage of continuing financial deregulation within the country, albeit on the increasingly clear assumption that reciprocation in terms of equivalent access would be forthcoming. Both the character of their home market and the opportunities of their institutions abroad were thereby intentionally reshaped.

164

The new tolerance did not imply, however, an abandonment of the policy goals of maintaining prudential stability and ensuring national predominance in a sensitive sector of the domestic economy. The traditional goals were reflected in the caution with which policy change was undertaken and the safeguards that were retained. The policy outcome nevertheless demonstrated a heavier weighting of the value of competition and a new balance between it and traditional control values. Market access policy moved away from closure by political fiat to a controlled openness that allowed increasing scope for market forces to determine the level of foreign involvement in the changing Canadian financial system.

*Australia*

In line with its historical economic development, Australia was a net capital importer during the period of recovery and growth following World War II. Its need for capital, in particular to underwrite major natural resource projects, attracted expanding foreign financial institutions. A selective definition of banking in federal law and, as in the U.S. and Canadian cases, a jurisdictional split affecting financial regulation, provided foreign institutions with initial opportunities to engage in limited quasi-banking operations in local submarkets, despite the traditional antipathy of oligopolistic domestic banks and powerful administrative arms of the central government. The consequent foreign advance remained restricted but was stimulated by general economic growth and by the erosion of a peculiar system of direct monetary policy implementation. By their presence in the marketplace, foreign nonbank financial institutions and representative offices both benefited from and contributed to this erosion in a way that traditional foreign portfolio investors could not. In time the NBFIs expanded into all activities not expressly forbidden.

During the 1970s, in the midst of a great national debate over the implications of foreign investment, foreign banks began to Australianize themselves by taking on local equity, local management, and local staff. Their activities accelerated the development of domestic money markets, while the day-to-day decisions of corporate treasurers ratified their local presence. In addition, their institutional forms gradually rendered legitimate their participation in the political arena, where they could press for greater regulatory flexibility and take part in the public debate about their future. Eventually their growth was perceived as a serious problem for the existing system of financial regulation, but their presence had given them a cer-

Table 15. Development of foreign bank access policy in Australia, 1965-87

| | 1965-70 | 1972-75 | 1979-82 | 1982-87 |
|---|---|---|---|---|
| Domestic government assessments of competition, control | Direct control favored | Direct control favored | Increased competition favored, direct control recedes | Increased competition, indirect control strongly favored |
| Foreign bank presence | Increasing rapidly | Increasing rapidly | Increasing more slowly | Stable |
| Foreign bank political activity | Low | Low | Increasing | Active |
| Domestic bank assessments of protection, reciprocity | Protection preferred | Protection preferred | Reciprocity concerns rising | Reciprocity concerns now evident |
| Foreign government pressure | Low | Low | Rising | Rising |

tain claim for inclusion in any reformed financial system. Of course, their interests had a lower priority than those of local banks and still lower than those of the state. Although the foreigners were able over time to build important political alliances, unlike in the Canadian case, their effectiveness in mobilizing domestic interests benefiting from their presence was reduced by the competitiveness that characterized their relationships with one another. The nature of policy change in Australia and the likely trajectory of reform worked to discourage any broad collaboration. The direct influence of the foreigners as a group was therefore limited.

Throughout the early 1970s a high degree of sensitivity marked Australian policy makers' responses to the presence of foreign institutions. Foreign investment had become a salient political issue, and foreign banks were a potent symbol of the perceived problem. In 1972 a Liberal government quickly passed legislation to prevent foreign takeovers in the banking sector. Two years later, in a highly charged atmosphere, a Labor government passed the Financial Corporations Act, which aimed at restoring directly the viability of the the postwar system of monetary control. But here again federalism and the technical complexity of changing markets came into account; the operative section of the act was never proclaimed, although it remained as a residual threat and reminder of where ultimate regulatory power resided.

In subsequent years domestic economic difficulties simultaneously raised the cost of moving back to the directly controlled system of the 1940s and lowered the political sensitivity of foreign involvement in domestic finance. The consciousness-raising exercise of the Campbell Committee worked in the same direction; so too did the realization that no important domestic interest groups would unambiguously be hurt by opening the banking markets. Despite the emotional fears of the bank unions and the self-serving protests of domestic banks, it became evident that the formal entry of foreign banks would force no particular group to bear unacceptable economic costs. By the early 1980s a cautious Liberal government perceived that the reduced sensitivity of the issue provided the scope necessary to improve the efficiency of domestic banking markets by opening them to direct, if still limited, foreign participation. After two years of internal debate, a Labor government came to an even more procompetitive conclusion. Nevertheless, under both governments, the preservation of national predominance in the domestic markets remained important. As in other countries, liberalization had its limits. The surprising thing in the Australian case is that these limits receded fairly rapidly. In 1982, few observers would have predicted as extensive an opening as in fact occurred in both wholesale and retail domestic markets over the next three years.

Somewhat misleadingly, this change was often perceived as deregulatory. In reality, throughout the long debate over alternative courses, government remained the most important actor in the system and the ultimately crucial catalyst to policy change. Final decision came only after assessments of the appropriate balance between control and competition in the banking system had shifted inside the central government. For the relevant parts of a relatively cohesive Australian state, the question was not really about getting out of markets in deference to the private sector but about adapting regulatory structures to changing markets so that an appropriate level of control could be assured. The postwar relationship between state and market was no longer working. Monetary policy implemented by way of direct controls was becoming ineffective. In like manner, a system of financial regulation relying on direct intervention and informal guidance by the state was breaking down. The expansion of financial intermediation outside the banking system provided the clearest evidence of the problem. Thus, the movement to open the banking markets to foreign competition took place as part of a larger process in which the mechanisms of state authority shifted from the direct and informal to the indirect and increasingly formalized, and from the local level to the national.

Market forces had greater scope within the new structure; a more effective and indirectly implemented monetary policy depended on efficient markets. At the same time, a larger share of market activity came under the watchful, if more distant, eye of the central government. A system of direct control gradually gave way to one that served the dual objectives of competition-induced efficiency and indirect control. In concrete terms, regulatory power shifted from the Treasury to the Reserve Bank and the role of the cabinet moved away from detailed decision making to more general oversight, although both the cabinet and the Treasury retained significant discretionary authority. The debate over foreign banking thus took place in a context biased toward expanded competition. Although governmental perceptions of the need for greater competition reflected an historically deep and complex relationship between the state and domestic banks, the process of policy change itself provides evidence of the continued authority of relatively strong and independent state institutions. Opening the banking markets required no significant legislative change and no effective consensus among domestic banks. Especially in comparison with the U.S. and Canadian cases, the autonomy of central decision makers is striking. Political leaders often were able to push ahead with strong ideological commitments despite the existence of significant opposition.

The efforts of private sector actors became more obvious as the policy process advanced, but the public sector maintained its ability to define a fairly coherent conception of a national interest that corresponded completely to no particular private interests. Increasing concentration within the banking system provided a background condition for this conception; so too did the deterioration of the aggregate market share of the domestic banks and their accelerating internationalization. But the actual political interests of the banks were far from determinative. The banks benefited more from their historically conditioned positions in domestic markets than from their ability to insist that national policy conform to their needs. Their general interests were in fact increasingly ambiguous. Even when their specific interests appeared fairly clear, such as their interest in continued protection in the retail market, it was not evident that the banks were able to prevent adoption of contradictory policy. In the past the banks could limit direct foreign entry because foreign banks did not have sufficient economic incentive to push aggressively, and because institutions of the state fully agreed that the national interest coincided with their own. In the contemporary period this situation changed. The state came to see an overriding need for increased competition, provided that competition took place under a more effective regulatory structure. The fact that direct foreign entry was delayed was not the result of bank demands but of a coincidence of these demands and the political preoccupations first of Tory paternalists then of Left nationalists. The two groups were unlikely political allies, who never really mastered the technical details of an arcane subject matter, and neither had any fondness for the banks.

Insofar as the banks sought to maintain protected domestic markets, their own strategic moves to concentrate domestically and expand internationally undercut their capacity to adopt logically justified postures in the public debate. Unlike in the U.S. and Canadian cases, however, these strategic decisions did not initially push the more internationally oriented of the banks to favor market opening as a tool to serve their own interests. Domestic considerations outweighed concern for reciprocity until late in the day. By virtue of their position in the markets and the fact that reintermediation served the state's control objective, the banks effectively, and luckily, adapted to policy change; they did not initiate it and they did not direct it. The state did both. There is little doubt, however, that a subtle shift in the orientation of the leading banks toward international markets did make it easier for the government to open the domestic market by the mid-1980s. Despite their recalcitrant public postures, the banks' rapid strategic moves abroad occurred with the prospect of domestic changes clearly in mind. As events played themselves out, the banks were given time to adjust their strategic plans away from reliance on a high degree of protection at home. The lack of explicit reciprocity within Australia eventually threatened to become a serious problem for Australian banks in certain markets, especially in Japan, Southeast Asia, and, to a lesser extent, in certain regions of the United States. Although the persistence of domestic priorities in the minds of senior Australian bank executives kept such problems in the background for a number of years, by 1985 their stake in reciprocally open markets was evident to all.

Foreign governmental pressure had only a limited impact on the Australian policy process until the trajectory of policy development became clear. For many of its trading partners, Australia remained a distant land, and the development of its banking system attracted little interest, especially because the low level of Australian bank involvement abroad kept reciprocity considerations to a minimum. Japan's interest in Australia long remained centered around natural resource issues; that of the United States continued to focus on defense matters. The government in Canberra could therefore design a coherent foreign bank access policy with few direct external constraints. It could not, however, cut itself off from the indirect effects of economic interdependence. Questions of the overall international competitiveness of Australia's economy provided an important background condition with which the government had to deal in its consideration of the most appropriate banking system for the future.

The interest of foreign governments in the Australian case was piqued in the early 1980s as changes affecting their national banks seemed imminent. The expected liberal direction of those changes, however, prevented them from becoming blatantly involved in pushing their own agendas. Indeed, few foreign banks were requesting their own governments to do so. Concerns about reciprocity began to rise, however, as leading Australian banks started taking advantage of open doors elsewhere. When the final direction of Australian policy became evident, foreign governments mobilized to ensure equitable treatment for their own institutions. In the implementation of that decision, reciprocity and other international considerations began to figure prominently. In difficult negotiations, especially with Japan and several European states, the costs and the benefits of increased openness came home to Australian policy makers. By the mid-1980s, the policy makers and the domestic banks they regulated finally grasped the possibilities and the obligations inherent in opening banking markets. The role of financial diplomacy and reciprocal understandings subsequently became more prominent in Australian foreign policy making. The eventual ideologically informed embrace of greater openness and the extension of increasingly equitable treatment to foreign banks in Australia testified to a new awareness of the benefits of increased competition in the domestic markets and of the options now available to Australian institutions abroad. The costs of reversing course were significantly higher than they had been even a decade earlier.

## FOREIGN BANKING IN EUROPE

A brief overview of comparable policy development in Europe suggests that the phenomenon of opening banking markets goes beyond the four cases examined here, and that the analytical categories illustrated have wider applicability.

National banks have long intermediated transborder flows within Europe, mainly at the wholesale level, and have often done so through institutional offshoots abroad. Italian and Dutch banks active in the fourteenth and fifteenth centuries were in this respect recognizable precursors of the multinational corporations of today.[1] Nevertheless, owing to explicit or implicit governmental policies, tacit gentlemen's agreements between major national banks, and apparent lack of strategic motivation on the part of European banks, the physical interpenetration of European national markets remained very limited until late in the twentieth century. In the late 1950s U.S. banks began following their corporate clients and increasingly took advantage of accommodating legal environments in Britain, France, and Germany. Before World War II, six American banks maintained full branches in London, four in Paris. By 1971 thirty American banks had offshoots in Europe, mainly in Britain, France, Germany, and Switzerland. Of course, European banks would have liked to protect their home markets from the U.S. forays, but their actual long-term response was a competitive one. The initiation of the European Economic Community at precisely the time of this early American expansion helped shape this response as well as the response of member governments.

Since the late 1950s (the early 1970s in the case of Britain), the major states of Europe have reformed their foreign bank regulatory policies in the context of developing the European Common Market.[2] From the beginning, one of the goals of the community has been to create a single European market for financial services. In the banking sector, this aspiration has always included two aspects: the harmonization and liberalization of member state policies regarding the treatment of banks from other member states and the formation of a common external policy toward banks from third countries. The first aspect implied the adoption of liberal policies by individual member countries, providing, for instance, clear rights of establishment to nonindigenous banks, the acceptance of parallel rights of community banks to deliver services transnationally without the necessity of physical establishment, and the adoption of uniform prudential standards for cooperating home country supervisors.[3] The reality of the mid-1980s remained far from such ideals, but some noteworthy progress had been made, especially in creating a common external policy.

Article 57 of the Treaty of Rome explicitly called for the coordination across the community of national legislation respecting banking in order to enable the creation of a truly common market in this sector. The commission of the nascent European Economic Community began working to make this declaration of intent effective in the early 1960s as part of efforts to harmonize national economic laws covering a range of sectors. Because the issues affected the jealously guarded autonomy of monetary policy, early attempts to harmonize banking laws foundered. Britain's entry into the community in 1973 created additional complications, but the early efforts did at least lead in that year to a broadly stated directive formally guaranteeing the abolition of restrictions on freedom of establishment and freedom to provide services in the banking sector. In essence, member states agreed unanimously to endow banks from other member states with "the same rights as nationals" and to abolish practices "which result in treatment . . . that is discriminatory by comparison with that applied to nationals."[4]

The same rights were automatically extended to existing and future operations of banks from nonmember countries that established in a member state in subsidiary form. That is, institutions separately (from their parent organizations) licensed and capitalized and maintaining corporate offices within the community were viewed as full participants in community markets. Attendant rights were extended without regard to reciprocity from the home states of parent organizations.[5] Not so easy to reach agreement on, however, were detailed measures to make such rights fully operative through harmonizing diverse national regulatory laws and practices, some of which tended to have more onerous and effectively discriminatory consequences for foreign banks even when they were ostensibly applied in a nationality-blind manner. For example, the treatment of foreign bank subsidiaries (or branches, for that matter) as independent entities unable to call on the capital resources of their parents could lead to overly conservative capitalization requirements and lending limits, both of which could render the subsidiaries uncompetitive with major local institutions. Fully harmonized national prudential standards promised to mitigate such effects, but they long remained elusive.

In 1969 a working group of the EEC Commission began planning for the detailed harmonization of national banking laws. Three years later they issued a draft directive on coordination, a document of such precision that its adoption would have been tantamount to the creation in one leap of a communitywide banking law. The proposal unleashed a deluge of criticism and was effectively spurned after the entry of Britain, which had a very significant and flexibly managed banking sector and no formal banking law. In addition to expressing concerns over monetary policy, Britain objected strongly to the adoption of key measures whose short-run effects might actually have restricted activities in the City. The commission decided that the long-range goal of a common banking market would best be advanced by incremental steps. "Gradual alignment" of discrete national laws and policies became the new watchwords within the Brussels bureaucracy, and the 1972 draft directive was shelved.[6]

Other disagreements persisted. Ireland, Italy, and later France and Denmark, for example, insisted on maintaining a criterion of economic need in their procedures for reviewing all or some types of bank licensing applications, a criterion that potentially could serve to protect local markets even if it ostensibly aimed merely at preventing overbanking. Extended debate over such matters and over a broader communitywide policy that would deal fairly with existing institutions as well as aspiring entrants encouraged distinct groups of banks, such as U.S. banks in London, to establish joint lobbying associations to promote their interests within community institutions and in the national capitals of Europe. In 1974 this debate became intertwined with early moves by U.S. regulators to rationalize parallel policy in the United States. Central to ensuing trans-Atlantic diplomacy were vague notions of reciprocity. A common position of European bankers and their governments was that if new U.S. initiatives extended geographic restrictions to foreign banking operations in the United States, it might no longer be appropriate to allow U.S. subsidiaries in Europe to branch throughout the EEC, an option they, more than any other national group, had exploited in the period before 1974.[7] The vigor with which this position was put forward, as well as the resulting concerns of the more internationally oriented U.S. banks, contributed to an eventual compromise whereby established foreign banking entities in the United States were exempted from new restrictions and new entrants were provided with several options for future growth.

Within Europe, the same diplomatic interplay helped focus attention on the need for a common approach, at least with respect to the question of treatment of banks from non-EEC countries. Here a consensus eventually formed around three key principles originally put forward in the ill-fated 1972 draft directive: national treatment, most-favored-nation status, and reciprocity. In December 1977 the Council of Ministers agreed to the so-called First Coordination Directive, which included a general statement of policy based on these principles.[8] The directive essentially reiterated the existing policy of national treatment for parent banks or subsidiaries established in a member state and made explicit a new joint policy on the treatment of foreign bank branches. Henceforth, members agreed not to provide more favorable regulatory treatment than that accorded to branches of banks from other members; they also assigned to community authorities the right to negotiate on the basis of reciprocity agreements with third countries guaranteeing identical treatment throughout the community to branches of banks from those countries. The directive did not, however, spell out the scope of regulations to be covered by such agreements or define the levels of equivalence that would constitute reciprocity. This lack of specificity was partly attributable to differences of view among the nine member states and partly to difficulties posed by structural distinctions between various national banking markets. Britain was known to prefer a flexible approach capable of deepening perceived benefits of competition and innovation by extending openness throughout the community as a whole. Conversely, France and Italy appeared much more conscious of the costs of openness.[9] The directive finally adopted was a compromise between the two positions. The foreign banking sections of the directive, however, did constitute the embryo of a more detailed approach that would evolve over time in a decidedly liberal direction. As implemented, the directive proved generally acceptable to other major banking countries. Indeed, the new joint policy framework reinforced the opening of banking markets that would continue during the next decade.

The 1977 coordination directive represented a significant, if still limited, step toward broader community goals. Besides codifying a common approach to banking establishments from third countries, it facilitated the adoption and/or reform of national banking legislation in several important areas, especially ones relating to the authorization of banking ventures. It also encouraged for the first time official collaboration between national supervisory agencies. Finally, it initiated an effort to reach agreement on precise prudential standards to be applied across the community, a development that promised to enhance market stability and to render cross-border competition fairer.[10] In most member states, national regulations were readily brought into conformity.[11]

By the early 1980s overt forms of discrimination against nonindigenous banks were almost completely abolished within the community. Although more subtle discrimination remained a possibility in particular states, surveys taken after adoption of the coordination directive indicated very few complaints, none serious, among practicing bankers or foreign regulators. Nevertheless, the community as a whole was still far from its ultimate goal of creating a common banking market. Even in 1977 it was already obvious that core impediments to realizing that goal related to basic restrictions on capital movements, the stuff of which banking transactions (and monetary disturbances) were made. A persistent contradiction between integrative goals and national autonomy remained undeniable. To the proponents of expanded freedom in the banking sector, the way forward necessitated resolving the contradiction. Thoroughgoing financial integration appeared to be a prerequisite for further progress. The essential question then focused on whether such an integration was possible in the absence of deeper political integration. Despite the daunting agenda, the European Commission did not abandon incremental functional efforts to encourage further liberalization. The ideal of completely harmonized policies remained, but energies concentrated on reaching basic prudential standards, common and simplified reporting requirements, and parallel licensing conditions. Even in such delimited areas, however, the complications posed by fundamental differences between national banking structures encouraged a continual reassessment of the most appropriate methods for achieving such common standards.[12]

The long-standing debate about integration and liberalization within the European Community should not obscure the fact that national policies on the regulation of foreign banks have been converging. The general understanding between members may lack the specificity of hard law, but it is embedded in convergent national laws and practices. By the late-1980s, a stable balance was emerging between values assigned by member states to increasing competition and maintaining control. Community members have gone at least as far as any other OECD countries in opening their national markets to expanded foreign competition, in internalizing a right of establishment in the banking sector, and in adopting a common regulatory norm of mutual nondiscrimination.[13] In the 1980s the reciprocal element implicit in that norm became more precise, especially in reaction to the remarkably rapid growth of Japanese banks inside the community.[14] Liberal treatment was gradually tied more directly to specific expectations about reciprocity of competitive opportunities and not just to formal legal equivalence. In the course of the bilateral and multilateral discussions which continued through the 1980s, however, the results of this explicitness tended in the direction of a more open Japan, not a more generally closed Europe.

Both inside and outside the community, a broader trend toward financial liberalization facilitated the expansion of foreign banks across Europe throughout the contemporary period. The existence and growth of Eurocurrency lending and bond markets and the erosion of exchange control arrangements accelerated the pace of change in interdependent national markets. Nevertheless, structural distinctions, varying state preferences, and discrete domestic economic policies maintained some evident institutional borders around those markets. Within individual states, intentional reform of the principles and techniques for regulating foreign participants formed a part of changing policy frameworks that accommodated, encouraged, and sought to control the effects of liberalization.

Competition for the jobs, prestige, and other perceived advantages associated with Euromarket activity contributed to an easing of regulatory burdens on foreign banks in many countries, most prominently Britain, Belgium, Luxembourg, and the Netherlands.[15] In the latter country regulatory reforms in 1984 and 1985 abolished residual limits on the business powers of foreign banks; by the end of 1985 nearly half of the existing ninety banking entities in Holland, controlling a third of the country's deposit base, were foreign owned. Competition for banking assets with the major Dutch banks was especially intense, and although local institutions continued to dominate the national market, accommodating government policy aimed partly at restraining an increasing tendency toward concentration. Similarly, federal and cantonal policy facilitated the rapid expansion of foreign banks in Switzerland, including growth in the lucrative private banking market. In turn, seeking to attract some of the business traditionally flowing to Switzerland, Austria progressively made it easier for foreign banks to operate in its market.

The growth of foreign banking in Scandinavia occurred relatively late, and the policy changes associated with the opening of domestic banking markets in the 1980s had obvious similarities to developments in Canada and Australia. In Denmark, the market leader in this respect because of its membership in the EEC, foreign bankers were given access privileges in 1975. Finland opened its doors in 1982, Norway followed early in 1985, and Sweden, very cautiously, joined the movement several months later. The Swedish case, in particular, sheds light on the political dynamics of such regulatory change.

Traditionally hostile to foreign bank entry, Sweden long permitted only foreign bank representative offices inside its borders and applied very strict conditions to their activities. The idiosyncracies of debt and monetary management in Sweden's unique political economy, and the centrality of major domestic banks therein, help explain a long-standing sensitivity to foreign penetration. Despite the technological and economic change sweeping the European banking scene during the 1970s and 1980s, Sweden demonstrated that it was possible for a relatively small country to resist exogenous pressures for liberalization. When such pressures became internalized, however, they were not easy to ignore. This internalization occurred through a number of avenues. The monetary effects of a persistent deficit in the current account of its balance of payments, problems in public debt management, the expansion abroad of Swedish corporations, a rapid rise in corporate liquidity during a period of high interest rates, a profitability squeeze in a highly concentrated banking sector, and the persistent encouragement of foreign bank representatives interested in expanding their involvement in the Swedish market all contributed to a reevaluation of policy. After some of the same factors stimulated the strategic redirection of Swedish banks toward overseas markets, the elements were in place for a decisive opening of the domestic banking market. An extended domestic debate on the subject in fact postponed such a development, but one significant push from outside facilitated the reconciliation of the various interests involved. The push came from neighboring Norway, which moved first toward opening its own banking market and did so explicitly on the basis of reciprocity. The final decisions to allow the limited establishment of foreign banks in Sweden subsequently came along familiar lines as assessments of the benefits of increased competition shifted. Exchange and interest rate controls were removed first. Swedish banks, now more tolerant of reciprocity arguments, were given time to adjust in anticipation of expanded competition. Finally, a cautious government invited foreign banks to apply for licenses enabling the establishment of subsidiaries.[16]

Patterns of policy making across Europe, both inside and outside the community, were thus generally consistent with those in the United States, Japan, Canada, and Australia. An uncontrolled homogenization of national banking structures decidedly did not occur, but national markets opened. Politics, especially the domestic politics associated with shifting assessments of the benefits of competition and reciprocity, remained central. Foreign bank regulatory policies evolving in national and community decision-making arenas continued to differ in subtle ways, but they generally converged in the direction of increased openness and nondiscrimination.

DEVELOPING INTERNATIONAL NORMS

Although the United States, Japan, Canada, and Australia developed access policies within unique domestic structures, the convergence of policy toward more common standards of regulatory treatment suggests an overarching process of interstate communication. The four states did not simply set ground rules for foreign banks interested in operating inside controlled markets. They communicated expectations to one another, and through their actual practices began to create an intersubjective normative framework that helped stabilize their relations in this sector.

In the American case, one of the explicit goals of several agencies within the federal government was the creation and strengthening of interstate normative standards. At the point of clearest policy articulation, in the 1978 International Banking Act, Congress adopted national treatment as the norm that would least disrupt domestic arrangements and still provide support for the operations of U.S. banks abroad. Further, by mandating a periodic review of problems faced by those banks, Congress tied that norm to a basic expectation of reciprocity. The administration interpreted this as a mandate to press vigorously for greater access for those banks to overseas markets. Broad-ranging diplomatic efforts ensued, and governmental pressure was often subtly brought to bear in various bilateral and multilateral forums. As the expectation of reciprocity underlying U.S. policy became clearer over time, these efforts became associated with expanding openness abroad and within the United States. But comparison with the other three countries indicates the limits of the American policy initiative. In no case did external governmental pressure push decision making toward openness unless powerful domestic factors were moving in the same direction. At most, it helpfully pushed against an opening door. In general, American and, at times, European diplomatic exertions to propagate normative standards in the banking sector helped define the goal, but they did not determine actual outcomes.

The United States thus played a prominent role in articulating aims, but it did not play a hegemonic one. In the Japanese, Australian, and Canadian cases, American banks and government officials exerted no preponderant influence over the course of domestic decision-making processes. Indeed, when they tried to do so overtly in Canada in 1967, the result was the opposite of that intended. Nevertheless, in each case, the United States had a unique impact. From the late 1950s onward, part of that role involved American bankers incrementally disturbing preexisting domestic market patterns, and thereby encouraging emulation among defensive, but well-positioned, local bankers. During the next two decades, American government officials with their own agendas took an increasingly prominent stance on banking issues. Having in 1978 decided on U.S. market access policy, for mainly domestic reasons, Congress became involved in promoting American norms abroad. Successive administrations, principally through the Treasury Department, took up the same cause in more cohesive, and often more subtle, diplomacy. American banks and government organs used each other to advance related goals. Government did not appear simply to be a pawn of the banks. Indeed, those banks were often divided in their evaluations of the true benefits of a laissez-faire ideal at home and abroad. Conversely, government organs, again especially the Treasury, often appeared driven by strong ideological commitments not always related to the specific interests of U.S. financial institutions. This was especially true in Japan in the late 1970s and early 1980s.

In all three of the other cases, U.S. officials attempted to promote the goal toward which they hoped access policies would converge. In every case, policy adjusted accordingly because more fundamental domestic political factors were evolving in a congenial way. Still, it would be a mistake to ignore completely the subtle effect of goal articulation by the United States. The word *hegemon* does not capture this subtlety; a better word is *bellwether*.[17] Before 1978, but certainly after, the United States did try to take the lead in encouraging other states to move toward openness in their banking systems. Often supported by like-minded European states, notably Britain and Germany, American public and private diplomacy promoted national treatment and made clearer the attendant expectation of reciprocity. Paradoxically, as that diplomacy appeared to succeed, most dramatically in Japan, the accuracy of the calculation of general American interests ostensibly underlying it came into question. The United States remained a bellwether, but as other states followed and American banks lost their preeminent position in international financial markets, the prospect arose that other states might benefit disproportionately from expanded openness. Nevertheless, despite periodic tensions usually related to foreign acquisitions of American institutions, there was little evidence by the late-1980s that the United States was moving away from openness and toward closure in the institutional structure of its own banking market. By then, despite the absence of hegemonic conditions, a normative framework intentionally embraced by similarly situated states was becoming more obvious.

The Canadian case provides a good example of how normative development and domestic political change interacted with one another. During the discussions leading up to the 1967 Bank Act, the existence of an implicit obligation to extend reciprocity to foreign banks was mooted, especially in the Porter Report. In the end, it was overridden when direct American governmental pressure exacerbated nationalist passions. During the early stages of foreign bank lobbying after 1980, international obligations were cited more forcefully, but were eventually downplayed for tactical reasons. Still, within the national government, Canada's direct stake in an open international banking system, both in absolute terms and in terms of the country's reputation, had become manifest, partly because of domestic economic troubles and partly because of persistent international criticism. Carefully communicated external expectations now reinforced the evolution of domestic financial liberalization and contributed to the government's decision cautiously to formalize its support for further multilateral normative development in the OECD.[18] Few government officials, however, saw this decision as a radical reorientation of policy. Domestic considerations could still override external obligations, for example, in the wake of any future perceived crisis related to incoming investment flows. But the threshold for such perceptions was raised after 1980. Following the articulation of a more liberal policy on foreign banking, Canadian policy makers were more aware of the external dimension of their regulatory decisions. For the first time, they also deliberately used the opening of their domestic market as a tool for furthering their own diplomatic aims abroad, such as assuring access for Canadian institutions to the Japanese banking market. Throughout the course of policy evolution in the 1980s, free-market-oriented officials within the government were strengthened as external reactions to potentially retrogressive policy movements became more salient. This new outlook was most obvious in bilateral negotiations with the United States over freer trade and investment.

In Australia obligations of reciprocal treatment barely entered a long debate on foreign bank regulation until the changing contours of domestic politics finally made compelling the case for a more open national market. Subsequently, procompetitive ideological inclinations within the central government and the gradual internationalization of domestic institutions accelerated movement along a more liberal policy trajectory. Eventually, external demands for reciprocity, especially from Asian countries, coincided with internal perceptions of the usefulness of tying domestic access rights more closely to equivalent treatment for Australian institutions abroad. Through a series of remarkable moves, Australian policy makers thereafter consciously enmeshed their country in an expanding network of reciprocal obligations.

The subtlety of these obligations comes out most clearly in the Japanese case. As in other more formalized economic regimes, the durability of emergent foreign banking norms depended upon mutual perceptions of fairness. Other states appeared willing to cooperate with Japan in setting more equivalent standards for competition as long as they remained satisfied that unique domestic arrangements within Japan were not disproportionately subsidizing

national institutions. Of course, in Japan and other advanced industrial countries domestic banks have what might be considered an
advantage by virtue of their market positions, history, and cultural
identification with indigenous clients. This advantage does not in
itself, however, constitute protectionism or imply that an insidious
nativism underpins national policies.[19] If protectionism can be con-
strued as the consequence of natural advantages, all countries of the
OECD may correctly be labeled protectionist in their banking sectors. But this judgment only obscures the nature and extent of policy
changes that have occurred in Japan and elsewhere.

At a certain point, market success has to do with competitive
advantages and not neomercantilism. In banking, the sources of
such advantages are deep and complex, and they often have to do
with culture and long-standing relationships as well as with governmentally sanctioned operating and prudential structures. If states
allow foreign banks the same business powers as domestic banks, over
time persevering institutions may be expected to develop their own
advantages, perhaps involving reductions in their cost structures at
home. If they do not develop such advantages, they will fail. But the
reason for their failure will be conditions in their home markets or
competition, not protectionism, in their host markets.

In the Japanese case, as well as others, a fundamental recalibra-
tion of the domestic regulatory balance between imperatives of competition and control took place. Neither in Japan nor in the other
countries did control disappear as a key governmental priority, and
in no country did domestic banks enthusiastically welcome any
decreases in levels of official protection. In characteristic ways within
Japan and the other cases, however, a rising official tolerance for
expanded competition on an increasingly common regulatory basis,
as well as an increasing tolerance for reciprocity among domestic
banks, fostered tendencies toward openness and away from traditional closure. It nevertheless remains true that such tendencies must
continue to be reinforced by the consonant actions of states if normative development is to persist. If, for example, the continuing liberalization of Japan's financial system fails to benefit a reasonable
cross-section of competent foreign participants or if expanding
openness abroad is perceived by others to benefit unfairly Japanese
institutions, evolving cross-national standards may erode. As foreign
institutions struggled to enhance their competence in the Japanese
market, Japanese public and private institutions had an increasingly
obvious incentive to mollify remaining perceptions of unfairness by
continuing to make judicious exceptions for foreign institutions and

by moving toward more widely accepted international prudential conventions.

Partly because the communication of more specific foreign expectations of reciprocity helped break domestic political logjams, Japan made significant progress toward financial openness in the 1980s. In Japan's case and others, evolving international normative standards began to feed back into complex and ongoing domestic processes of policy making. Should convergent domestic interests later diverge, those standards could of course be abrogated. But international normative development itself promised to reinforce convergence as it became embedded in domestic structures of political power.

When each of the four states decided for its own reasons to move toward acceptance of the legitimate participation in its national market of banks licensed elsewhere, it effectively entered into a process of communication with other states. Expectations of reciprocity lay at the base of this process. Although no advanced industrial state could claim by the late 1980s to be completely open, virtually all had moved decisively in this direction. External expectations and actual domestic policies moved toward greater conformity, and those policies were thereby endowed with an intersubjective sense of legitimacy. A customarily accepted set of coordinating norms was emerging.

Such a view of interstate normative development approximates conceptions of customary or implicit law articulated by a group of jurisprudential and anthropological theorists. Lon Fuller, applying such ideas to the relations of states, described customary rules as a "baseline for interaction."[20] As between individuals, customary rules arose "out of situations of human interaction where each participant guides himself by an anticipation of what the other will do and expect him to do. There will be involved an expression of reciprocal intentions that we may call an open-ended kind of bargaining."[21] Legal anthropologists who study dispute-settlement procedures in societies lacking centralized authority structures have shown how customary norms arising from patterned behavior allow such societies to maintain themselves by accommodating conflict.[22] In contemporary banking markets an analogous process has manifested itself. Expectations of reciprocal interaction and ideologically consonant emphases on competitive efficiency have effectively been coordinating foreign bank regulatory policies across a range of states. Parallel policy reforms have deepened unwritten ground rules for intensified competition. Because interacting states were both attracted by the spoils of growing capital markets and committed to retaining important domestic regulatory prerogatives, converging access policies have aimed at striking a balance between efficiency, control, and fairness.

The international standards that were strengthened over some thirty years of policy reform were organized around mutual establishment rights and nondiscrimination, albeit with discretionary adjustments to provide ostensibly fairer conditions of access across markets still structurally distinct.[23] States at advanced stages of economic development were expected to respond to one another in similar but not necessarily identical ways. These standards imposed no requirement to eliminate idiosyncratic national structures or methods of regulation, but they proscribed differentiating between similarly situated nationals and foreigners.[24] They implied no requirement that nonindigenous banks necessarily penetrate domestic markets to any particular level, only that political impediments to penetration up to levels determined by reasonably fair market competition be eliminated.[25]

Normative concepts suggesting this type of regulatory treatment have in fact been included in various international agreements, some of which touch on banking.[26] Many of the friendship, commerce, and navigation treaties negotiated between the United States and some forty other countries earlier in this century extended national treatment to certain types of foreign banking operations, particularly those engaged in trade financing and international lending.[27] The International Banking Act of 1978, as discussed, superseded many of these exceptions and further advanced the national treatment norm in the American case. The General Agreement on Tariffs and Trade (GATT) included similar provisions, but these have usually been interpreted to cover products, not services or the establishment of businesses. Nevertheless, within GATT, discussions began in the early 1980s on extending the agreement to cover such service industries as banking. Separate bilateral negotiations on freer trade and investment, for example between the United States and Canada, have since moved in this direction. Analogous standards have been included in two agreements negotiated under the auspices of the OECD: the Code of Liberalization of Capital Movements and the Declaration on International Investment and Multinational Enterprises. Although these instruments are not recognized to have the same force as formal treaties and both leave room for discretion, they are notable for defining establishment rights and nondiscrimination as a multilateral goal and thereby influencing the terms of continuing discussions. Moreover, the liberalization code in particular has provided an organizational mechanism for the periodic public review of exceptions insisted upon by member states. Within the European Economic Community, as we saw, a series of coordinating directives have given institutional expression to the persistent goal of fully open national markets. Finally, developing agreements between central banks on common capital adequacy and supervisory policies have promised to encourage the emergence cross-nationally of more equitable competitive conditions.

In spite of the evidence that an increasing degree of explicit multilateral coordination is possible in the banking sector, reasonable arguments can be made against efforts to codify specific market access rules in a formal and broadly based multilateral forum. As the case studies show, the state and market structures involved in the politics of banking access are exceedingly complex. Continued progress toward openness and nondiscrimination in the banking markets of OECD states, and perhaps in the markets of more advanced developing states, may depend upon minimizing the scope of detailed public negotiations and avoiding highly politicized attempts to engineer tradeoffs across other sectors. Despite the pressures of economic interdependence, states continue to exhibit unique sensitivities concerning their banking markets. During recent decades market openness has usually been extended most effectively when underlying interests could be kept within bounded policy arenas.

Tacit agreements and understandings do, however, have drawbacks, particularly when the number of states involved expands and when national structures differ dramatically. Among those states sharing essentially similar orientations to economic liberalism, it may well be possible for an implicit deepening of regulatory norms to persist in a changing banking sector. But as the Japanese case demonstrates, states with other traditions may find it difficult to deal with implicit expectations. If market openness is to broaden and the incipient normative framework for banking access is to extend beyond the OECD, therefore, the critical assumption of reciprocity defined in terms of reasonably equivalent competitive opportunities across markets may have to become somewhat more explicit.[28] Movement in this direction is already evident in the late 1980s. A lesson of the experiences examined in this book is that the success of such an approach depends very much on the existence of accommodating domestic political bases for policy reform in less open states as well as on the deft management of attendant diplomacy.

After three decades of policy development, the institutional interpenetration of national banking markets in the advanced industrial world is now well developed. Convergent domestic laws and practices are creating a basic normative foundation for necessary interstate coordination on market access issues. Increasingly accepted regulatory standards, embedded in unique domestic structures, are important elements in an evolving process through which competition in one sector of modern capitalism is broadened and equilibrated by the interaction of the states at its core.

# Glossary

Acquisition: Purchase of one institution by another. The purchaser gains a controlling interest by obtaining at least a majority of the voting shares of a firm from the owners. Governments have often established limits on the amount of voting shares in a bank that may be owned by a single individual or institutional group. Other limits may restrict the amount of shares purchasable by a foreign individual or group.

Affiliate: A company partly owned or controlled by another. A parent institution usually owns less than 50 percent of the voting shares of an affiliate. The connection between parent and affiliate is therefore not as strong as that between parent and subsidiary.

Agency: Banking office not possessing full banking powers. In the United States, for example, agencies are usually restricted in their deposit taking powers.

Antitrust policy: Governmental policy designed to discourage the formation of monopolies or business combines that threaten to restrain competition in particular industries.

Arbitrage: Buying a product, security, commodity, or currency in one market and (usually) simultaneously selling it in another. The process attempts to profit from anomalies (resulting from borders, geographic distance, imperfect knowledge, etc.) that create temporary price differentials between markets.

Assets: In a bank, primarily loans, income-producing securities, and property carried on the balance sheet.

Balance sheet: A firm's accounting statement of assets, liabilities, and capital. As a financial report, a balance sheet portrays a company's condition at a particular time.

Booking point: A branch or other office of a bank where an asset or liability is formally entered into the bank's accounts. There may be tax or other reasons for choosing one location over another.

Branch: An office of a bank usually possessing full banking powers under local law, that is, an office usually providing a range of deposit, lending, and financial service functions. A branch is an integral part of a bank and usually retains no capital base of its own unless specifically required to do so by regulatory authorities.

Branch banking: A banking system that permits banks to expand geographically through the establishment of branch offices.

Building society: A financial institution whose major activity traditionally involves financing real estate.

Capital adequacy: The amount of shareholders' capital required to satisfy regulatory authorities and others that a bank's depositors and creditors are appropriately protected. When a bank is liquidated, the shareholders have last call on its assets. Regulatory differences across nations regarding the optimal amount of capital a bank should maintain can influence bank competitiveness. Banks required to maintain less capital to support a given amount of liabilities may be able to price their assets more competitively than banks required to maintain more capital.

Certificate of deposit (CD): A bank deposit, usually of large-denomination, tradable, and bearing an interest rate set by market forces. Originally invented to circumvent governmental controls on interest rates.

Chartered bank: Any of the institutions licensed by the Canadian Parliament to engage in commercial banking.

City bank: Any of the large commercial banks of Japan.

Clearing bank: A major commercial bank in a national or regional financial center. Clearing banks serve as centers for the disbursement and collection of funds associated with checks and other interbank payments.

Commercial bank: An institution licensed by a government to provide a range of financial services usually encompassing the taking of deposits subject to immediate withdrawal (e.g., checking deposits), other payments services, and the making of loans. In many countries, commercial banks originally limited their major lending activities to companies at short term.

Commercial paper: Negotiable debt instruments, usually short term and unsecured, sold by corporations directly to investors, such as other corporations, as a means of raising funds without borrowing from banks.

Competitive neutrality: The ideal of minimal regulatory differentiation between like-situated or competitive institutions advocated in the Campbell Committee's 1981 report on the Australian financial system.

Conditional reciprocity: Policy allowing discretion in deciding whether the types of regulation encountered by a state's nationals in a foreign country are fair and roughly equivalent to regulations imposed by the state on comparable foreign institutions operating within its jurisdiction.

Cooperative society: An association that pools resources from member-owners and provides financial services on this basis.

Correspondent bank: A bank that provides financial services (such as payments clearing, foreign exchange, and trade financing) for another bank.

Deemed authorized capital: The means by which the Canadian government decided to limit the growth of foreign banks in 1980. By holding each bank to a leverage ratio (20:1) based on an amount of authorized capital allocated by the government and by holding the aggregate of those allocations in fixed relation to the assets of domestic banks, the government set a ceiling on overall foreign bank growth.

De novo operation: A start-up establishment initiated where none existed before. As a strategy for institutional expansion, a de novo operation is an alternative to acquisition.

Deposit costs: The interest, administrative, and other expenses paid by a bank on a deposit that it accepts.

Disintermediation: Movement of funds out of relatively low-yielding bank deposits to higher-yielding investments in financial markets. Disintermediation occurs when savers choose to lend their funds directly to borrowers and thereby cut out the traditional intermediary services performed by banks. Often associated with interest rate ceilings imposed by a government on the pricing of bank deposits and/or loans that restrain banks from matching the prices that a freer market would set.

Dual banking system: Regulatory structure in the United States that permits two levels of governments, the federal and the state, to maintain jurisdiction over banking activity.

Edge Act: A 1919 U.S. federal law (Section 25[a] of the Federal Reserve Act) providing an exception to interstate banking prohibitions by allowing banks to set up subsidiaries outside their home states for purposes (mainly) of providing trade financing and other internationally oriented financial services.

Equity: Capital invested in a company by its owners.

Eurocurrency: A currency deposited or lent outside its home country. Euroyen, for example, are yen held outside Japan, often on the books of a non-Japanese bank.

Federal Deposit Insurance Corporation (FDIC): Institution established by the U.S. government to insure against default deposits accepted by member banks.

Fiduciary service: Financial service provided by licensed institutions, such as trust companies, on behalf of clients. Assets may be held in trust, investments may be managed, and so forth. Some countries restrict commercial bank provision of such services.

Finance company: Any one of a wide range of companies capable of making loans and providing other kinds of financial services. Often more limited in its powers than a bank, especially in deposit gathering, a finance company may nevertheless possess certain advantages; for example, it may not be required by government to hold prudential reserves on funds received.

Functional segmentation: The splitting of a financial market by governmental regulation along lines defined by business type. In the United States, for example, the Glass-Steagall provisions of the Banking Act of 1933 forbade commercial banks from acting as underwriters for corporate securities.

Funding: The raising of deposits, other liabilities, or capital to support a bank's lending and other income-producing activities. To maintain profitability a bank generally seeks to minimize the various costs and risks associated with its funding operations.

Gearing: A synonym for financial leverage.

Geographic segmentation: The splitting of a financial market by governmental regulation along geographic lines. The federal McFadden Act segmented the U.S. market by restricting interstate branching by banks.

Government securities: Bonds or other marketable instruments issued by an official agency of government.

Grandfathering: The practice of exempting established institutions from newly adopted rules or policies. Avoids the problem of retroactivity.

Holding company: An institution whose principal function is to hold shares in the subsidiaries and affiliates of a parent company. Tax, regulatory, or other advantages may encourage the setting up of holding companies.

Intermediation: The function performed by banks when they take many small, short-term deposits, pool them, and lend or invest them at longer term.

Interstate banking: The operation of a bank in a U.S. state other than the one in which it was originally incorporated. Traditionally restricted under provisions of the federal McFadden Act, the Bank Holding Company Act, and the laws of various states.

Investment banking: Mainly, the provision of underwriting and other financial services in connection with the raising or investing of corporate capital.

Leasing company: A firm providing financial services in connection with (usually) the renting of a physical asset, such as equipment, vehicles, or other fixed assets.

Lender of last resort: An entity, usually a government agency or national central bank, that is committed to providing back-up support to financial institutions in the event of sudden, significant withdrawals of funds.

Lending limit: A limit set by a government or by a bank itself on the amount (or proportion) of its loan commitments to individual borrowers or to certain categories of borrowers.

Letter of comfort: Written assurance provided to regulatory authorities by a parent bank committing the parent to stand behind the obligations of a subsidiary, affiliate, or branch. A letter of comfort is less formal than a full guarantee and therefore may not have to be carried on the parent bank's balance sheet as a contingent liability.

Leverage: The relationship between a firm's liabilities (or assets) and its capital base. Higher leverage, that is, a higher ratio between liabilities and capital (or assets and capital), may result in higher earnings but also entails higher risks.

Liabilities: In general, claims on the assets of a company other than the claims of shareholders. In a bank, liabilities are mainly deposits and other cost-incurring commitments on the balance sheet.

Liquidity: The ability of a firm readily to convert assets into cash. In banking, liquidity is often calculated as the excess of a bank's very short-term assets over its most pressing liabilities. A bank and its regulators must use judgment in deciding how liquid to keep the bank's books. Generally, there is a cost in maintaining too much liquidity in that assets might earn more if placed for a longer term. Too little liquidity, on the other hand, may leave a bank unable to meet sudden demands for cash by depositors.

Macroeconomic policies: A government's fiscal and monetary policies aimed at the promotion of stable, noninflationary growth in the economy at large.

Merchant bank: A wide range of companies mainly providing investment banking services and/or other corporate financing services.

Merger: The voluntary or involuntary joining together of two separate institutions (usually) by a pooling of ownership interests, by an outright purchase, or by consolidation.

Middle market: That segment of a bank's business involving transactions with medium-sized clients, that is, not small retail clients or large corporate clients.

Money-center banks: Any of the very large commercial banks maintaining head offices in New York, Chicago, or other major U.S. cities. More generally, comparable large financial institutions based in major international financial centers such as New York, Tokyo, and London.

Money markets: Formalized markets where negotiable, usually short-term, financial instruments are traded. Often distinguished from capital markets, where longer-term instruments are bought and sold.

Money-market corporation: A nonbank financial institution in Australia mainly operating in the short-term money market.

Moral suasion: A tool of monetary policy involving an informal communication of intentions by monetary authorities to financial institutions in the expectation that appropriate implementing measures will be taken.

Mutual bank: A bank owned, but not necessarily managed, by its depositors.

National treatment: A commitment on the part of a government to the effect that, for legal, regulatory, and other purposes, it will treat a company whose head office is located in another country exactly as it would treat a like-situated domestic company. National treatment entails a commitment not to discriminate between competing companies on the basis of the nationality of shareholders or management.

Near-bank: Any one of a broad group of companies in Canada, such as a finance company or leasing company, providing certain banklike financial services, but not regulated by government in the same way as banks. A near-bank is usually not able simultaneously to accept a range of deposits and make loans.

Nonbank financial institution (NBFI): Institutions in Australia similar to Canadian near-banks. Often refers mainly to merchant banks.

OECD: The Paris-based Organization for Economic Co-operation and Development, founded in 1960 to promote multilateral economic growth and cooperation among advanced market-economy countries.

Off-shore banking: Banking activities treated by governments for regulatory purposes as if they occurred outside the domestic banking market. To attract certain types of wholesale business, such as lending to nonresident corporations, governments may provide incentives to domestic and foreign banks in the form of regulatory exemptions and tax concessions. Euromarkets are generally considered to be off-shore banking markets.

Overbanking: Highly competitive conditions in a local banking market believed to lead to unwise banking practices, unwarranted risk taking, and consequent market instability. The term is ill-defined and can serve as an excuse for restraining competition.

Parent company: A company that directly or indirectly owns or controls subsidiaries and/or affiliates.

Primary market: A market where securities, such as stocks and bonds, are first sold. Companies often raise capital by selling new stock through an investment bank in a primary market.

Prudential issues: Concerns related to the safety and stability of a bank or of a banking market as a whole, which constitute a principal rationale for governmental regulation.

Representative office: An office of a bank set up for purposes of liaison, information gathering, and so on, often in a foreign country. Representative offices are usually not permitted to engage directly in the provision of banking services, such as deposit taking and lending.

Reserves: Funds set aside by a bank out of current earnings or other resources to cover potential losses or other contingencies. Governments usually require banks to maintain a certain level of reserves proportionate to outstanding liabilities. Part of these reserves are often required to be in the form of central bank deposits.

Retail banking: The provision of banking services at the level of the individual or small company. Usually involves at least taking deposits from the general public and making small-denomination loans.

Savings bank: A financial institution specializing in longer-term activities such as residential mortgage lending. Savings banks are often limited in the types of deposits they can take and the types of loans they can make.

Schedule A: The first schedule attached to the Canadian Bank Act specifying those institutions that are chartered to carry on the business of banking in Canada and whose shareholders are limited in the amount of shares they may hold. The shares of Schedule A banks are widely held predominantly by Canadian individuals and institutions.

Schedule B: The second schedule attached to the Canadian Bank Act specifying those institutions that are chartered to carry on the business of banking in Canada and whose shareholders may hold controlling shares. The subsidiaries of foreign parent banks in Canada are therefore often referred to as Schedule B's.

Secondary market: A market where already-issued financial instruments, such as stocks and bonds, may be traded.

Securities company: A financial institution providing investment banking services.

Securitization: The process by which the dominant mode of corporate financing shifts from commercial banking markets to securities markets. Includes lenders' packaging as securities traditional financial assets, such as loans, for onward sale in a secondary market, thus freeing their own capital to support other activities.

Solvency: The possession by a bank or company of adequate resources to maintain itself as a going concern.

Spread: The difference between the price a bank pays for its deposits and the price it charges on its loans.

Strict reciprocity: Policy insisting on a quantitative and/or qualitative identity between two countries' regulatory treatment of each other's nationals.

Subsidiary: A firm whose capital is more than 50 percent owned by another firm. A parent company usually controls, and is responsible for, the operations of a subsidiary.

Swap: A financial transaction whereby one party exchanges with another comparable financial obligations. In foreign exchange, a swap may entail a bank's bringing into a foreign country an amount of its home currency, exchanging it into the currency of its host country, and lending the proceeds to local borrowers.

Trading banks: Any of the large national commercial banks of Australia.

Transparency: An expectation that the true intent and effect of regulations imposed by a government should be obvious to those affected by them.

Trust company: A financial institution that provides fiduciary services for individuals or other institutions, such as administering pension funds, handling stock registration and transfer, and investing funds held in trust.

Underwriting: A commitment, usually on the part of an investment bank, to purchase or attempt to sell new securities issued by a company.

Unit banking: A banking system in which banks are geographically restricted to one place of business. Such a restriction is usually intended to promote the establishment of many small, locally responsive banks and to discourage the growth of large banks through branching.

Universal bank: A bank permitted by its regulators to engage in both commercial and investment banking. Common in Continental Europe.

Wholesale banking: Financial activity mainly involving large-scale transactions between banks, governments, and major corporations.

# Notes

ABBREVIATIONS FOR FREQUENTLY CITED PERIODICALS

| | | | |
|---|---|---|---|
| AEN | Asahi Evening News | GM | Globe and Mail (Toronto) |
| AFR | Australian Financial Review | JT | Japan Times |
| AWSJ | Asian Wall Street Journal | JEJ | Japan Economic Journal |
| BL | The Banker (London) | LJ | Look Japan |
| BRW | Business Review Weekly | MDN | Mainichi Daily News |
| BW | Business Week | NKS | Nihon Keizai Shimbun |
| DY | Daily Yomiuri | NYT | New York Times |
| EC | The Economist | OE | Oriental Economist |
| EU | Euromoney | OJEC | Official Journal of the |
| FEER | Far Eastern Economic | | European Communities |
| | Review | SMH | Sydney Morning Herald |
| FP | Financial Post | TS | Toronto Star |
| FT | Financial Times (London) | WSJ | Wall Street Journal |

CHAPTER 1. *Banking, Politics, and Rules*

1. Marcus Wallenberg, "The Reciprocal Treatment of Branches of Foreign Banks in Different Countries," League of Nations, Provisional Economic and Financial Committee, E.F.S. 80, A.46 (1921 II).

2. By the early 1980s, for example, the ratio of foreign bank assets to total bank assets ranged from nearly 50 percent in Belgium to almost 4 percent in Japan. Starting from a smaller base, the rate of growth of foreign bank assets often outstripped that of domestic bank assets—even in those countries, like Germany and Japan, where overall penetration remained low. R. M. Pecchioli, *The Internationalization of Banking* (Paris: OECD, 1983), annex 2.

3. See OECD, *International Trade in Services—Banking* (Paris: OECD, 1984), 12–13. Iceland remained the sole exception.

4. The 1976 OECD "Declaration on International Investment and Multinational Enterprises" included the following summary of the national treatment standard: "Member countries should, consistent with their needs to maintain public order, to protect their essential security interests and to fulfil commitments relating to international peace and security, accord to enterprises operating in their territories, and owned or controlled directly or indirectly by nationals of another Member country, treatment under their laws, regulations and administrative practices no less favorable than that accorded in like situations to domestic enterprises." OECD, *National Treatment for Foreign-controlled Enterprises Established in OECD Countries* (Paris: OECD, 1978), 33–34. A description of how the principle applies to the banking sector is included in the introduction to U.S. Department of the Treasury, *Report to Congress on Foreign Government Treatment of U.S. Commercial Banking Organizations* (Washington, D.C.: Department of the Treasury, September 1979).

5. I am viewing the nondiscrimination or national treatment standard as an ideal policy goal. In reality, no governments provide unarguably equal treatment to foreign and domestic banks. But most OECD governments have appeared over time to approach the standard. Whether a country moves from closure to limited openness on the basis of strict reciprocity, or from limited openness to loosely regulated openness on a more nearly nondiscriminatory basis, the standard being approached may rightly be labeled "national treatment." A purely liberal regulatory environment would not penalize banks because of the nationality of their shareholders. Note that the point toward which cross-national policies converge is not in the final analysis some degree of openness that can be measured or compared in any quantitative sense. Convergence is seen to occur, rather, if effective regulatory policies are moving in the direction of creating roughly equivalent competitive opportunities, for foreign and domestic banks, that is, if governments, allowing for structural differences between their national markets, permit foreign and domestic banks to compete for available opportunities on an essentially comparable basis. In such an environment, the relative success or failure of specific institutions should be the result of competitive advantages not principally attributable to ostensibly unfair governmental favor.

6. This acquiescence was one of the most far-reaching changes of position since the creation of the postwar international economic order. It seemed to symbolize the rise of pressures for a purer liberalism than the moderated liberalism that characterized the early postwar years. See John G. Ruggie, "International Regimes, Transactions, and Change: Embedded Liberalism in the Post-War Economic Order," *International Organization* 36 (Spring 1982), 379–415.

7. See Benjamin J. Cohen, "Balance of Payments Financing: Evolution of a Regime," *International Organization* 36 (Spring 1982); Kenneth W. Dam, *The Rules of the Game* (Chicago: University of Chicago Press, 1982), ch. 9; and Thomas D. Willett, *International Liquidity Issues* (Washington, D.C.: American Enterprise Institute, 1980).

8. See Herbert G. Grubel, "The New International Banking," *Banca Nazionale del Lavoro Quarterly Review* (September 1983); Ian Giddy, "The Theory of Industrial Organization and International Banking," in Robert G. Hawkins et al., eds., *The Internationalization of Financial Markets and*

*National Economic Policy* (Greenwich, Conn.: JAI Press, 1983); and Dwight B. Crane and Samuel L. Hayes III, "The Evolution of International Banking Competition and Its Implications for Regulation," *Journal of Bank Research* (Spring 1983).

9. See Ralph C. Bryant, *International Financial Intermediation* (Washington, D.C.: Brookings, 1987). The author makes the point that most governments have tended to move more rapidly toward nondiscriminatory policies with respect to the international activities of foreign banks than with respect to their domestic activities, the United States being the notable exception at the national regulatory level. The evidence of the present study offers some support for this assertion, but it also shows how nondiscriminatory policies have in fact broadened considerably over time.

CHAPTER 2. *Foreign Banking in Four Countries: The Regulatory Contexts of Policy Making*

1. The dispute over jurisdiction originally related closely to the well-known confrontation between Thomas Jefferson and Alexander Hamilton over the appropriate balance between political decentralization and financial efficiency, a dispute that set the stage for Andrew Jackson's struggle against the Second Bank of the United States in 1832. Later in the nineteenth century, a major challenge to the ascendancy of states' rights in bank regulation came when Congress passed the National Currency and Banking Acts. These acts, passed during the Civil War, reinvigorated a two-tiered or dual banking system by providing for the federal chartering of national banks and by creating the Office of the Comptroller of the Currency to supervise the new institutions.

2. See Department of the Treasury, *Geographic Restraints in Commercial Banking in the United States: The Report of the President* (Washington, D.C.: Department of the Treasury, January 1981). A significant and long-standing exception to these geographic restrictions was embodied in the 1919 Edge Act, which allowed banks to set up offices in other states to provide services related strictly to foreign trade.

3. The Securities Act of 1933 and the Securities Exchange Act of 1934 created the Securities and Exchange Commission to oversee the newly segmented investment banking business. The 1956 act heightened the wall separating commercial banking from other sectors of the economy by forbidding bank holding companies from owning more than 5 percent of the shares of nonbanking companies.

4. Unlike its counterparts in other developed countries, the Federal Reserve is itself a decentralized institution consisting of twelve separately incorporated Reserve Banks and a Board of Governors in Washington.

5. Three other agencies may have an indirect effect on bank activities: the Securities and Exchange Commission, the Federal Home Loan Bank Board (which oversees federally chartered thrift institutions), and the National Credit Union Administration.

6. The long history of the dual banking system has created powerful impediments to centralizing initiatives. Even in the early 1980s approximately 70 percent of all American banking assets remained on the

balance sheets of state-chartered institutions. See Lynn W. Zempel, *The Dual American Banking System* (Washington, D.C.: The Government Research Corporation, April 7, 1982), 9; and Andrew S. Carron, *Reforming the Bank Regulatory System* (Washington, D.C.: Brookings, 1983).

7. Henry C. Wallich and Mable I. Wallich, "Banking and Finance," in Hugh Patrick and Henry Rosovsky, eds., *Asia's New Giant* (Washington, D.C.: Brookings, 1976); and Eisuke Sakakibara et al., *The Japanese Financial System in Comparative Perspective* (Washington, D.C.: GPO, 1982).

8. The Bank is legally distinct from the government and is expected to provide independent advice. The actual connection has, however, been quite close. Top personnel, for example, often come from the Ministry of Finance.

9. Aggressive lobbying, personnel exchanges, and a peculiar system of bureaucratic retirement (*amakudari*) have modified conventional "statist" views of ministry power. See James Horne, *Japan's Financial Markets* (Sydney: George Allen & Unwin, 1985), ch. 8; and Yung H. Park, *Bureaucrats and Ministers in Contemporary Japanese Government* (Berkeley, Calif.: University of California, Institute of East Asian Studies, 1986).

10. The cabinet too usually prefers to keep such matters out of the Diet because of the possibility that opposition members may use them to embarrass the government. See Mike Masato Mochizuki, *Managing and Influencing the Japanese Legislative Process* (Ann Arbor, Mich.: University Microfilms International, 1982).

11. The International Finance Bureau is the ministry's window to the outside world and is staffed by its polished, often multilingual diplomats. Most foreign bank contact with the ministry therefore takes place through the bureau.

12. Interview, Ministry of Finance, Tokyo, July 1985.

13. At this point, only primary industries, mining, petroleum, and leather-processing were fully excepted. In addition, certain banking and securities transactions abroad by residents and investments by nonresidents in land and certain insurance activities were reserved. See OECD, *Controls and Impediments Affecting Inward Direct Investment in OECD Member Countries* (Paris: OECD, 1982), 30; and annexes to the OECD Capital Movements and Invisibles Codes.

14. See Kiyoshi Kojima, *Japanese Foreign Direct Investment* (Tokyo: Charles E. Tuttle, 1978); and James C. Abegglen and George Stalk, Jr., *Kaisha, the Japanese Corporation* (New York: Basic Books, 1985).

15. Roughly half of the incoming direct investment came from the United States, mainly in the manufacturing sector. A third came from Europe, mainly in commercial ventures. Investments from other Asian countries have recently grown rapidly. Peat, Marwick, Mitchell & Co., *Investment in Japan,* 2nd ed. (Tokyo: Peat Marwick, 1983), 9.

16. Don Fenno Henderson, *Foreign Enterprise in Japan* (Tokyo: Charles E. Tuttle, 1975), 237–90.

17. Like Section 92 of the British North America Act, the first Bank Act failed to provide an operational definition of banking; instead it referred to a specific list of chartered banks and delimited entry conditions for

future additions. The narrowness of this approach left room for a provincial role in overall financial regulation.

18. The CBA has a unique status for what is essentially now a lobbying organization. Established by an act of Parliament in 1891, membership was made mandatory for all chartered banks.

19. Ronald Shearer et al., *The Economics of the Canadian Financial System* (Scarborough, Ontario: Prentice-Hall Canada, 1984), 292.

20. Government of Canada, *1964 Report of the Royal Commission on Banking and Finance* (Ottawa: The Queen's Printer, 1965).

21. The foreign banking recommendation in particular had an international political dimension, which was at the time readily outweighed by more basic domestic considerations. Canada was a founding member of the International Monetary Fund and the World Bank. It was also a signatory of the GATT and an active member of the OECD. In the OECD, however, it acceded originally to the Code of Liberalization of Current Invisible Operations but not to the Code of Liberalization of Capital Movements, principally because domestic political considerations were occasionally deemed to require deliberate checks on certain types of capital inflow, especially foreign direct investment.

22. In the mid-1980s the Big Five accounted for nearly 85 percent of Canada's banking assets (calculated from the annual reports of the Royal Bank of Canada, Bank of Montreal, Canadian Imperial Bank of Commerce, Bank of Nova Scotia, and Toronto-Dominion Bank and the *Bank of Canada Review* table of banking assets). For debate on the potential consequences of this concentration, see Standing Committee on Finance, Trade, and Economic Affairs, *Seventeenth Report*, February 25, 1982; and New Democratic Party, *Report on the Inquiry into Chartered Bank Profits,* July 1982.

23. External debt figures are from Reserve Bank of Australia, *Bulletin* (December 1984), 334; (December 1986), S102. Debt service calculations are from Reserve Bank of Australia, *Bulletin* (December 1984/January 1985), 374. GDP figures (at current prices) are from International Monetary Fund, *International Financial Statistics*, various issues.

24. H. W. Arndt, "Foreign Investment," in J. P. Nieuwenhuysen and J. Drake, eds., *Australian Economic Policy* (Melbourne: Melbourne University Press, 1977), 133–34.

25. Commonwealth of Australia, *Report of the Committee of Economic Enquiry*, 1 (May 1965), paras. 11.76, 11.91, 11.92, 11.94.

26. Ibid., paras., 11.85–11.87. The connection between Australian and Canadian concerns was close at this time. In one section of its report (para. 17.108), the committee commented favorably on Canadian attempts to increase domestic ownership and control of local industries. Such ideas led it to recommend (paras. 17.104–17.114) establishment of new policy advisory structures to supplement the existing virtual monopoly maintained by the Treasury Department. A strongly proforeign investment prime minister (Menzies) and an obviously interested Treasury subsequently ensured that the report was shelved. See R. N. Spann, *Public Administration in Australia* (New South Wales: Government Printer, 1973), 343.

27. *The Australian Financial Review* (October 2, 6, 9, 10–12, 24; November 7, 1972).

28. Department of the Treasury, *Australia's Foreign Investment Policy* (Canberra: AGPS, 1982), v.

29. Ibid., 37–42.

30. See Australian Labor Party, *Platform, Constitution, and Rules,* as approved by the 35th National Conference, Canberra, 1982, 44–45. Also, Office of the Treasurer, Press Release, No. 152, December 20, 1983.

31. See N. G. Butlin et al., *Government and Capitalism: Public and Private Choice in Twentieth-Century Australia* (Sydney: George Allen & Unwin, 1982), 332–37; and Peter Loveday, "Corporatist Trends in Australia," *Politics* 19 (May 1984), 46–51.

32. Butlin, *Government and Capitalism,* 325. Although the authors do not develop this point, it seems plausible that one factor encouraging the continued level of involvement of the state was a perception of vulnerability to an expanding international economy. See Peter J. Katzenstein, *Small States in World Markets* (Ithaca, N.Y.: Cornell University Press, 1985).

33. In reality, the Treasury both guided and accepted the policy decisions of cabinet; its influence under such a system was inversely related to the technical simplicity and political sensitivity of particular issues. Conversely, the Reserve Bank (formally established only in 1959) had responsibility for the day-to-day implementation of policy decisions, which often involved transmitting requests informally to the managing directors of the trading banks.

34. Ian R. Harper, in "Why Financial Deregulation?" *Australian Economic Review* (1st Quarter 1986), 37–49, argues convincingly that economic changes associated with inflation and government deficits, technological advances, and expanded linkages between domestic and international financial markets together shifted public and private perceptions of the benefits of the postwar structure of financial regulation. In turn, the increasing substitutability of financial products allowed economic actors to alter their behavior in the marketplace in line with such changed perceptions.

35. As inflation rates rose throughout the 1970s, total government deficits grew from 1.6 percent of GDP in 1971 to 6 percent in 1978. Australian Financial System Inquiry, *Interim Report* (Canberra: Australian Government Printing Service, 1980), 55. Both inflation and deficits strained exchange and interest rate controls, and recurrent crises necessitated high-profile and politically painful decisions.

CHAPTER 3. *The United States*

1. Foreign assets and earnings of U.S. banks from R. M. Pecchioli, *The Internationalization of Banking* (Paris: OECD 1983), 19, 47. U.S. assets of foreign banks from Jane d'Arista, *International Banking,* Staff Report of the Committee on Banking, Currency, and Housing, U.S. House of Representatives, 94th Cong., 2nd sess. (Washington, 1976), 13; and Jack Zwick, *Foreign Banking in the United States,* U.S. Congress Joint Economic Committee Print (Washington, 1966), 1.

2. Over the period 1960 to 1983, the number of foreign bank branches went from 5 to 329; over a ten-year period beginning in 1973 foreign bank assets as a percentage of aggregate U.S. banking assets rose from 4 percent

to 14.6 percent; in New York that percentage rose from 13 percent to 42 percent over the same period, and in California from 10 percent to 33 percent. Zwick, *Foreign Banking in the United States;* and *Federal Reserve Call Reports* (May 1984).

3. New York amended its banking laws to permit foreign agencies in 1911; within two years twenty-one such offices were established. See Francis A. Lees, *Foreign Banking and Investment in the United States* (New York: John Wiley & Sons, 1976), 11.

4. Proponents of the bill argued that continued discrimination against foreign parent banks was no longer tenable, that the effects of foreign retaliation against overseas American operations were serious, that New York stood to gain prestige as an international financial center, and that increased foreign competition would bring domestic benefits, such as expanded access to trade financing. Zwick, *Foreign Banking in the United States,* 4.

5. The debate in California was not simply about market protection. The superintendent of banks, for instance, opposed foreign branching because of the difficulty of ensuring that foreign parent banks continually met certain prudential standards; separately capitalized subsidiaries were easier to control in this regard. The eventual compromise permitted continuation of this organizational form. Ibid., 25.

6. Lees, *Foreign Banking and Investment in the United States,* 14. In most cases it was ambiguous whether the targets of such prohibitions were foreign banks or simply all out-of-state banks. The majority of states have simply left a statutory void, thus providing no legal basis for foreign operations within their borders. There was a reciprocal pattern with regard to location. The largest share of U.S. banks expanding abroad related to banks from New York, Illinois, and California; most foreign banks in the United States initially expanded in the same states. See Fred H. Klopstock, "Foreign Banks in the United States: Scope and Growth of Operations," *Federal Reserve Bank of New York Monthly Review* (June 1973), 144–53.

7. Zwick, *Foreign Banking in the United States,* 27.

8. In a report completed in 1967, the American Bankers' Association gave its opinion on the reciprocity proposals in the following aside to its main line of investigation: "It should also be noted that insistence on the principle of reciprocity by licensing authorities in the United States may not always be in the best interest of U.S. banks operating overseas. . . . For U.S. authorities to insist on the principle might very well hinder rather than assist U.S. banks in local negotiations abroad." American Bankers' Association, *Foreign Government Restraints on United States Bank Operations Abroad,* U.S. Congress Joint Economic Committee Print (Washington, 1967), 24–25.

9. H.R. 6778, 91st Cong., 1st sess., February 17, 1969.

10. Rosalyn Retkwa, "The Foreign Bank Lobby," *Euromoney (EU)* (August 1983).

11. Federal Reserve, Press Release, June 1, 1973. Although the Fed lacked statutory authority for such a request, virtually all foreign banks complied.

12. H.R. 11440, 93d Cong., 1st sess., November 13, 1973 (entitled the Foreign Bank Control Act); H.R. 11590, 93d Cong., 1st sess., September 1973. See Patman speech, *Congressional Record, House,* November 15, 1973, 10089–90. Fed officials were convinced that the bills represented

attempts to preempt the Mitchell Committee and set the tone for debate. Conversely, congressional sources claim the Fed was reacting to their initiatives. In any event, relations between Patman and the Fed were often tense.

13. Letter from Burns to Patman, February 16, 1974, subsequently released. Burns continued, "In the Board's opinion, adoption of the general principle of non-discrimination by the major industrial countries of the world is the best means of achieving true reciprocity in international banking regulations."

14. Letter from Patman to Burns, February 25, 1974, subsequently released. Furthermore, wrote Patman, the bill would "help insure that U.S.-based entities of foreign banks—however complex in structure or global in outlook—would respond to public policy at both the state and national level."

15. Letter dated March 6, 1974 to Arthur Burns and Treasury Secretary George Shultz, subsequently released. In part, the letter stated, "The members of the New York Clearing House believe that the present dual banking system is functioning well, that no federal legislation is required at this time and that the major issue of concern—interstate banking—is fundamentally a state issue which is best left to the states to resolve. . . . The absence of any restrictions on foreign branches and agencies in those states which allow them is the result of public policy decisions by the states involved. . . . Any change in the existing system of regulation, particularly if it restricted the current U.S. activities of foreign banking organizations, would very likely result in a reexamination of current policies abroad governing the development of international banking, potentially giving rise to retaliation by foreign regulatory authorities." At the time, the Clearing House comprised Bank of New York, Chase Manhattan, First National City Bank, Chemical Bank, Morgan Guaranty, Manufacturers Hanover, Irving Trust, Marine Midland, United States Trust, National Bank of North America, and Franklin National.

16. The interests of U.S. banks in this and other policy areas were far from homogeneous. The plethora of banking lobbies that have emerged over the years indicates divergent political needs, goals, and strategies. The largest lobby (representing thirteen thousand banks) and oldest (1875) is the American Bankers' Association. Partly because it is so large, a number of specialized lobbies have broken away from it. Some of the larger banks belong to a number of associations, and, in addition, some maintain their own lobbying offices in Washington.

17. The Fed originally proposed December 4, 1974, the date of its submission of a draft bill to Congress, as the cut-off date for grandfathering. Between 1972 and 1975 foreign bank assets had more than doubled from a base of $25 billion. Henry S. Terrell and John Lemoine, "The U.S. Activities of Foreign-owned Banking Organizations," *Columbia Journal of World Business* (Winter 1975), 87–97.

18. Interview, Washington, October 1984. It was well known at the time that Chase Manhattan, in particular, was intentionally building its profile as a strong supporter of foreign banks, at least partly as a means of increasing its correspondent banking business with them.

19. By 1975 BAFT included 140 voting domestic members, mainly regional and small banks engaged in trade financing, and 68 nonvoting foreign members.

20. Henry S. Reuss, "The Legislative Outlook for Foreign Banks Operating in the United States," address delivered at the Banking Law Institute, New York, May 3, 1974.

21. At this point the position of the CSBS was still in a formative stage. New York regulators, while opposing the aggrandizing proposals of the Fed, could in 1974 still support limited changes in federal law. See *American Banker,* June 24, 1974. The New York Fed was frequently viewed as a principal supporter of the major New York banks. The Board in Washington, however, would eventually win this internecine struggle. See Reuss, "The Legislative Outlook," 3. Reuss himself, who replaced Wright Patman as chairman of the House Banking Committee in 1975, supported the Mitchell proposals with several reservations.

22. The draft legislation was deliberately based on New York's banking law but without New York's reciprocity requirement. The handle for federal control was to be the Bank Holding Company Act.

23. Michele Sindona owned 21 percent of Franklin's shares. Because the bank was the twentieth largest in the country and a member of the Clearing House, its collapse had far-reaching repercussions and focused attention on the question of bank safety in increasingly integrated financial markets. Ironically, the eventual solution to the Franklin crisis came in October 1974 when federal authorities, though concerned about a negative reaction in Congress, nevertheless permitted a consortium of European banks to acquire most of the assets and liabilities of the failed bank. See Joan Spero, *The Failure of the Franklin National Bank* (New York: Columbia University Press, 1980).

24. See U.S. Congress, House, Committee on Banking, Currency, and Housing, Subcommittee on Financial Institutions Supervision, Regulation, and Insurance, *Minutes* (Washington, December 2, 1975).

25. Using 1975 data, the study listed 43 foreign bank interstate networks, comprising some 319 offices and $43 million in (branch) assets. Almost two-thirds of the offices were located in New York, one-fifth in California, one-tenth in Illinois, and the rest scattered over eight U.S. states or territories. It identified 19 foreign parent banks as owning significant shares of American securities firms. The study also listed almost two-thousand overseas offices of U.S. banks, including many engaged in securities and other nonbanking operations forbidden to them within the United States but permitted by local foreign laws. American branch assets overseas were then over $165 million. U.S. Congress, House, Committee on Banking, Currency, and Housing, *Financial Institutions and the Nation's Economy* (Washington, 1976), 13–23, 213–70.

26. U.S. Congress, Senate, Committee on Banking, Housing and Urban Affairs, Subcommittee on Financial Institutions, *Foreign Bank Act of 1975 (S.958),* Hearings, 94th Cong., 2nd sess. (Washington, January 28–30, 1976), (hereafter cited as Hearings, 1976). In fact, McIntyre was a proponent of increasing liberalization for domestic banks, and observers widely noted the lack of urgency with which he approached the foreign bank issue.

27. Hearings, 1976, 2.

28. Mitchell and his staff visited the central banks of Britain, France, Belgium, Switzerland, the Netherlands, Italy, and Germany in 1974. Later discussions were held with Japan. During 1975 Treasury and State organized a report on the regulation of U.S. banks in five countries. Only Switzerland maintained a fairly strict reciprocity requirement, although occasional problems were noted in Italy. Hearings, 1976, 226–31.

29. Gardner indicated his initial hesitation about a grandfathering provision because the continued existence of "nonstandard" banking offices could cause problems later. Nevertheless, owing to their relatively small size, Treasury would go along with either permanent grandfathering or a divestiture period of at least ten years. Ibid., 17–18.

30. In 1976 forty-four FCN treaties were in force. According to the State Department, "The executive branch has long regarded these treaties as an important element in promoting our national interest and a strong world economy. . . . From the viewpoint of economic foreign policy, one goal of FCNs was the desire to establish agreed legal conditions favorable to private investment. The heart of 'modern' (i.e., post–World War II) FCN treaties (and those with our OECD partners are generally of this type) is the provision relating to the establishment and operation of companies. This provision includes a right of establishment, governed by the national treatment standard, and nondiscrimination after establishment." Ibid., 235–42.

31. Ibid., 305–6.

32. Ibid., 423–34. New York strongly favored mandatory federal coverage. Other states preferred to keep the coverage optional.

33. Ibid., 437. Later the representative mentioned that BAFT favored amending S.958 to make Fed membership and FDIC coverage optional for foreign banks. He acknowledged "a difficult time getting a consensus on the need for legislation," but held that BAFT now considered passage to be an "urgent" matter.

34. H.R. 13876 (originally H.R. 13211), 94th Cong., 2nd sess., 1976. See U.S. Congress, House, *Report No. 94-1193* (Washington, 1976). For the debate and relevant votes, see *Congressional Record, House,* July 29, 1976, 24392–421.

35. Section 5[a] of the bill forbade further foreign interstate branching until such time as Congress changed the McFadden Act and the Douglas Amendment to the Bank Holding Company Act.

36. U.S. Congress, Senate, Committee on Banking, Housing, and Urban Affairs, Subcommittee on Financial Institutions, *International Banking Act of 1976 (H.R. 13876),* Hearings, 94th Cong., 2nd sess. (Washington, August 31, 1976).

37. The Securities and Exchange Commission, for its part, wanted to see a more comprehensive review of financial regulation before adoption of the IBA. Ibid., 157–59.

38. Two responses by delegates to questions capture the essence of the carefully crafted European position on the retaliation issue: "I dislike the word [retaliation] and I dislike the concept. Of course I cannot exclude that some bad reaction . . . might come up in this or that European country. . . . Just as I would regret the passing of this bill by the Senate, I would regret any action taken by any European country to retaliate . . . because I feel this is detrimental to the Atlantic spirit by which we all live."

NOTES TO CHAPTER 3

"We are just bankers and if you talk about consequences which may happen in this country or another country, you're really thinking of your own or the foreign parliamentarians who can also be aroused to excitement and protectionism." Ibid., 379.

39. Ibid., 336.

40. Ibid., 377.

41. The Clearing House representative cited press coverage of the IBA in Britain and Germany. Reports in several European newspapers confirmed discussions on retaliatory measures in Continental banking circles. The *New York Times* printed a similar story on August 31, 1976, the day of the Senate hearing. Ibid., 394–95.

42. Data derived from Henry Terrell and Sydney J. Key, "The Activities of Foreign Banks: An Analytic Survey," in Federal Reserve Bank of Boston, *Key Issues in International Banking,* Conference Series No. 18, 1977, tables 1, 2, 5, 6, and 7. Over the same period, Japan's share of total foreign banking assets in the United States fell from 52 percent to 38 percent and Canada's from 19 percent to 9 percent; conversely, Europe's share rose from 24 percent to 46 percent. See "Recent Growth in Activities of U.S. Offices of Foreign Banks," *Federal Reserve Bulletin* (October 1976), 815–24.

43. The portion of foreign investment in the United States directly attributable to the establishment of foreign financial institutions themselves was less than 8 percent during the 1970s. Seung H. Kim and Stephen W. Miller, *Competitive Structure of the International Banking Industry* (Lexington: D.C. Heath, 1983), 11.

44. High U.S. reserve requirements still encouraged the bulk of such transactions to be booked outside the country, but booking options were valuable to many existing or potential clients.

45. H.R. 7325, 95th Cong., 1st sess., May 23, 1977.

46. U.S. Congress, House, Committee on Banking, Finance, and Urban Affairs, Subcommittee on Financial Institutions Supervision, Regulation and Insurance, *International Banking Act of 1977,* Hearings, 95th Cong., 1st sess. (Washington, July 12, 13, 19, 1977), 2, 35, 36 (hereafter cited as Hearings, 1977).

47. The explicitly acknowledged lack of unanimity among the governors on this score is noteworthy. No federal agencies enthusiastically supported grandfathering; all reluctantly viewed it as a necessary evil.

48. As it stood, the bill permanently grandfathered existing multistate banking offices established before May 1, 1976, and nonbanking operations (except securities affiliates) established before December 3, 1974. Securities affiliates opened before December 3, 1974, were grandfathered only until December 31, 1985, after which time foreign ownership would have to be reduced below 5 percent.

49. Hearings, 1977, 101–11. While remaining opposed to continued interstate branching, Governor Gardner did suggest in his testimony that foreign banks could be allowed to open agencies in other states empowered only to transact international business in a manner similar to domestic bank Edge Act corporations. This point would later be developed into a crucial compromise.

50. Ibid., 155.

51. The statement continued: "However, I want to advise the Committee that there is a group of about a dozen of our members who do not support

this legislation. This group . . . domiciled principally in New York . . . takes the position that the present regulatory environment is satisfactory, and that the proposed changes could lead to retaliation." In testimony, the spokesman (from the Philadelphia National Bank, a regional bank) followed up: "We have never heard retaliation mentioned in a serious way by any official authorities. It seems that we hear that primarily only from those groups whose interests would be furthered if you all would believe that there would be such retaliation." Ibid., 380.

52. In going through the testimony, it is not difficult for the reader to discern a greater degree of complexity to the BAFT position than its spokesmen explicitly articulated. The distinction between a political strategy designed to seek the same operating rights as other market participants and one attempting to preserve familiar and favorable regulatory restrictions can be exceedingly fine. BAFT's obsession with the foreign bank issue, and its continued opposition to the Clearing House, indicated deeper concerns about the disintegration of geographic barriers, which tended to protect smaller banks from the inroads of money-center institutions. In this light, the foreign banks were a stalking horse for the domestic deregulation favored by the large banks. The architects of the IBA understood this well. Interviews, Washington, October 1984 and April 1985.

53. The association cited forty-two foreign bank-owned securities companies active in the mid-1970s. Hearings, 1977, 254–56. From within the securities industry itself, however, came a partially contradictory view. Spokesmen for the Boston and Midwest Stock Exchanges, while agreeing in principle that commercial and investment banking should be kept separate, supported either exemptions for certain types of foreign securities activities or, at least, permanent grandfathering of existing foreign affiliates.

54. Ibid., 262.

55. The CSBS was united in its stance; even the New York Banking Department, which might have benefited from a more restrictive IBA because of the well-established dominance of New York City in international banking, argued against extending the interstate banking ban to foreign banks. Not all states wanted foreign banks to enter, however, even if they did oppose the IBA. Connecticut, for example, defeated in March 1977 a proposal by its banking commission to allow foreign entry. It was evident in this case that local bankers feared that foreign entry would eventually lead to the entry of money-center banks from New York. See *Econocast World Banker*, March 30, 1977, 6; and *American Banker*, August 3, 1977.

56. Obviously, the foreign banks remained concerned about the opportunities as well as the costs of doing business in the United States. For example, federal reserves had to be maintained in an interest-free form, whereas certain states allowed reserves to be held in interest-bearing accounts or securities. For some banks, freedom from FDIC premiums also lowered costs. BAFT had argued that these cost advantages partly accounted for the ability of foreign banks to build market shares by cutting rates charged on loans.

57. This view was reinforced by correspondence from the German Finance Ministry, which expressed its concern about the IBA's potential extraterritorial effects and about the temporary grandfathering provision for foreign securities affiliates. The ministry enclosed a position paper

drafted by the Association of German Banks that saw various other provisions of the IBA, such as the interstate branching prohibition, as violations of international reciprocity. The ministry concluded, "In the common interest of promoting closer economic ties between our two countries, the Federal Government feels it appropriate to support the position of the German banks should it become evident that, [contrary] to the declared objectives, the legislation turns out to result in discrimination." Hearings, 1977, 653.

58. Some of the organizations involved, such as the IFB, the Clearing House, and BAFT, had retained Washington law firms to represent them; others, such as the CSBS, maintained their own offices in the city. These lobbyists played critical roles in the formation of the eventual policy, and they had their greatest impact at the drafting stage. For the most part, their input was welcomed by key legislators and their staffs. Interviews, Washington, October 1984.

59. Correspondence from Reuss and St. Germain to Burns, October 25, 1977, House Banking Committee files.

60. Correspondence from Burns to Reuss and St. Germain January 25, 1978, House Banking Committee files.

61. U.S. Congress, House, Committee on Banking, Finance, and Urban Affairs, *International Banking Act of 1978 (H.R. 10899),* Committee Report No. 95-910, 95th Cong., 2nd sess. (Washington, February 23, 1978).

62. The Fed was also authorized to receive examination reports on state-chartered foreign banks but was forbidden to conduct its own direct examinations.

63. Ibid., 9-10.

64. *Congressional Record, House,* April 6, 1978, H.2551-75. Passage represented an explicit victory for the CSBS. Proponents stressed extensive correspondence received from twenty-seven state bank regulators (published in *Congressional Record, House,* April 13, 1978) and from the National Governors Association. The subject of entry guidelines was debated extensively. From the speeches of supporters of guidelines, it was clear that this provision, while not going so far as a reciprocity test, resulted from concerns about perceived unfair treatment of U.S. banks overseas, especially in Japan.

65. U.S. Congress, Senate, Committee on Banking, Housing, and Urban Affairs, Subcommittee on Financial Institutions, *International Banking Act of 1978 (H.R. 10899),* Hearings, 95th Cong., 2nd sess. (Washington, June 21, 1978), 1-2 (hereafter cited as Hearings, 1978). The senator also admitted, "One of the reasons I am more favorably inclined to this legislation than to past proposals is that the bill is less restrictive than earlier bills, particularly with respect to multistate operations. . . . If there is, indeed, a competitive imbalance [between foreign and domestic banks], . . . then it seems far more sensible to enable U.S. banks to better compete, rather than artificially imposing new restraints on foreign competition."

66. Ibid., 4-6.

67. *EU* (June 1978), 53.

68. Trade journals published during this period reflect an intense debate over respective funding advantages. For many foreign banks, the advantage

of more liberal reserve requirements was offset by the premium charged to "foreign names" in domestic money markets. See, for example, *Bank Letter,* June 19, 1978.

69. Comptroller General of the United States (General Accounting Office), "Considerable Increase in Foreign Banking in the United States since 1972," GGD-79-75 (Washington, August 1, 1979), iii. By 1979 it seemed apparent that the overall increase "could be attributed to anticipation of restrictive legislation." Ibid., i. Also see *Institutional Investor* (September 1977), 143; and *American Banker*, May 10, 1978.

70. *Congressional Record, House,* April 6, 1978, H.2563, 2569, 2571.

71. The New York State Banking Superintendent also testified along these lines but differed on the insurance question, contending that FDIC coverage should be mandatory. On the issue of interstate branching, the superintendent added, "There is a growing realization that the real issue in this connection is not competitive equality between foreign and domestic banks, but competitive equality between states." Hearings, 1978, 136. Around this time, the chairman of the House Banking Committee, Henry Reuss, came out publicly in support of the states on the supervision issue and accused the Fed of engaging in a "power grab." *American Banker,* June 26, 1978.

72. Hearings, 1978, 77–115.

73. Ibid., 356–57.

74. Ibid., 186, 191–92. Specifically, the IFB recommended (1) that section 5 apply only to foreign branches licensed federally or, if necessary, to state-licensed branches, but not to subsidiaries, investment companies, or agencies, (2) that FDIC coverage be optional or at least limited to domestic retail deposits, (3) that federal reserve requirements, if absolutely necessary, be applied only to branch operations, and (4) that prohibitions on nonbanking activities, after full and permanent grandfathering of existing offices, should carefully avoid any extraterritorial application. Complementary testimony was again given by the EEC Banking Federation. Representatives from Britain, France, and Germany appeared relieved by certain amendments to the original House bill, especially regarding the grandfathering of securities affiliates. They did not, however, hesitate to recommend that the grandfathering dates be moved forward to the date of enactment of any final bill in order not to "penalize investors who, in good faith, have invested in the U.S. economy." Ibid., 250–51.

75. Ibid., 56, 57, 77, 81.

76. The reasons for the hesitation of the CSBS, IFB, and EEC are obvious. Not so obvious is the opposition of the FDIC. Although still reluctant, the FDIC appeared to be resigning itself to the seemingly inevitable expansion of its duties; it therefore felt that its risks would be reduced by allowing maximum geographic diversification for the foreign banks it would have to insure.

77. U.S. Congress, Senate, Committee on Banking, Housing, and Urban Affairs, *International Banking Act of 1978 (H.R. 10899),* Report No. 95–1073, 95th Cong., 2nd sess. (Washington, August 18, 1978) (hereafter cited as Senate Report). Although the bill deferred to state law on the question of establishment, in subsequent practice, the comptroller took silence in state law as express permission. He also ignored reciprocity requirements stipulated in state law. The bill also required foreign bank

representative offices to register with the secretary of the treasury, but gave him no authority to prohibit their entry.

78. The home state was defined as the state where an initial deposit-taking office was established. Under later regulations, foreign banks were permitted to defer choosing a home state if they did not operate an unrestricted branch or deposit-taking subsidiary and also to change their home states once. Other regulations also permitted foreign and domestic Edge Act corporations to branch across state lines without state permission.

79. In the end, the committee was concerned that the inclusion of state-chartered subsidiaries, as recommended by the Fed, might jeopardize acceptance of the Stevenson amendment. See Transcript of Committee Mark-up, Senate Banking Committee files, 42. The entire picture would change when the Monetary Control Act of 1980 imposed federal reserve requirements on those banks, domestic as well as foreign, previously exempted.

80. The committee hoped the federal and state bank regulatory agencies would "cooperate with one another." Senate Report, 14. The Fed's residual authority enabled at least one federal agency to keep an eye on the national operations of a single parent bank. Significantly, this compromise also left the examination revenues derived by state regulators intact. See Transcript of Mark-up, 43. This solution made the supervisory apparatus no more, and no less, confusing than it was for domestic banks.

81. One intention was to prevent a, say, European bank from engaging in proscribed domestic activities by establishing a, say, financial subsidiary of a manufacturing firm owned by the bank itself. At the same time, they did not want to discourage investment by foreign companies in the United States. Accordingly, it enjoined the Fed to use Commerce Department Standard Industrial Classification (SIC) categories (at the four-digit level) to ensure that American subsidiaries of foreign companies were in lines of business closely related to their immediate parents. Senate Report, 16–17.

82. Ibid., 18. The only country specifically mentioned in the report as a source of concern in this respect was Japan. (Also see Transcript of Mark-up, 51.) The bill also mandated a review of McFadden Act prohibitions on full interstate branching. In truth, neither branch of government was particularly anxious to come to grips with the entrenched political interests involved in this matter. If nothing else, this provision respectably deferred action on the larger question while giving some hope to the large domestic and foreign banks that interstate branching barriers might be temporary.

83. As one authority on the subject put it, "In sum, foreign banks came out better than they could have reasonably expected when the process began in 1973; domestic banks received assurance that foreign banks would be under the same essential ground rules as they, without having their operations put under a retaliatory cloud; federal and state regulators each gained or retained enough authority to keep political balance; international banking in the U.S. received a strong Congressional boost through Edge Act changes and the latitude allowed foreign banks; interstate banking advocates were given new hope; and, Congress left enough unanswered questions to keep lawyers busy for years to come." Gary M. Welsh, "Legislative History of the International Banking Act of 1978," in Peter Hornbostel, ed., *The International Banking Act of 1978* (New York: Practicing Law Institute, 1979), 22–23.

84. *Congressional Record, Senate*, August 15, 1978, S.13387–96; *Congressional Record, House*, August 17, 1978, H.8827–29.

85. For example, Paul Volcker, in the *Federal Reserve Bank of New York Quarterly Review* (Summer 1979), 1, noted, "One of the more significant aspects of the long debate that led to the International Banking Act was the care of the Congress in responding to the expressed concerns of foreign banks—even in a situation in which those banks were defending some important competitive advantages inherited from the days prior to Federal legislation." On the rough balance of advantages achieved by the act, see Steven J. Weiss, "The Competitive Balance between Domestic and Foreign Banks in the U.S.," Office of the Comptroller of the Currency, Staff Paper (1980–13).

86. Sydney J. Key and James M. Brundy, "Implementation of the International Banking Act," *Federal Reserve Bulletin* (October 1979), 785, 790.

87. See U.S. Congress, Senate, Committee on Banking, Housing, and Urban Affairs, *Edge Corporation Branching; Foreign Bank Takeovers; and International Banking Facilities*, Hearings, 96th Cong., 1st sess. (Washington, July 16, 20, 1979) (hereafter cited as Senate Hearings, 1979). In subsequent years state adaptations to continuing market pressures would often attempt to preserve segmentation as it applied to the incursions of money-center banks and to enhance the competitiveness of small, regional, and sometimes foreign banks. Regional banking compacts created by state governments became the principal tool for so doing. See Donald T. Savage, "Interstate Banking Developments," *Federal Reserve Bulletin* (February 1987), 79–92.

88. Interview, New York, October 1984. On the need for foreign capital infusions at the time, see *American Banker*, August 1, 1978.

89. Correspondence from Muriel Siebert to Henry Reuss, February 16, 1979, subsequently released. Also see *American Banker*, March 19, 1979. The obstacles for domestic acquirers included the Douglas Amendment to the Bank Holding Company Act and antitrust statutes. Following the IBA, foreign banks were permitted to change their home states once; some took advantage of this provision to acquire existing banks in other states. Once this option was taken, however, all deposit-taking operations in the original home state had to be closed. HSBC, for example, had to sell a California subsidiary before regulators would approve the purchase of Marine.

90. Federal Reserve Board, Press Release, March 16, 1979.

91. The Office and Professional Employees Union (AFL-CIO), for example, petitioned the governor to prevent the takeover because of the fear that employee compensation would be reduced by foreign owners. See correspondence from union to Governor Hugh Carey, April 27, 1979, subsequently released. Similarly, there were concerns expressed by small banks to the effect that foreign owners would reduce employment opportunities for American workers. Correspondence from Chairman, Dollar Savings Bank, to Governor Hugh Carey, April 23, 1979, subsequently released.

92. New York State Banking Department, News Release, June 29, 1979.

93. Comptroller of the Currency, News Release, January 28, 1980. Ironically, the comptroller in office at the time, John Heimann, had been the previous New York State superintendent of banks. Seven-and-a-half

years later, HSBC would bid for full ownership of Marine without encountering political opposition. *Financial Times* (London), July 17, 1987.

94. Senate Hearings, 1979. Prominent in these hearings was the subject of international banking facilities, an idea first suggested by Citibank, Morgan Guaranty, and others in the mid-1970s. Essentially, it involved creating an offshore banking zone in New York City. At the time estimates of possible new jobs created ranged from nineteen hundred to three thousand. See *EU* (June 1978). The proposal was subsequently enacted.

95. S.J. Resolution 92, 96th Cong., 1st sess., June 26, 1979. Inasmuch as foreign acquisitions had been going on for years, there can be little doubt that this level of concern was related to the increasing volume of the transactions, the increasing size of the targets, and, in the case of HSBC, the exotic location of the parent's home base. Senator Heinz, for example, pointedly asked Muriel Siebert what would happen to Marine when the People's Republic of China took over Hong Kong; Siebert acknowledged her worries on this score. Senate Hearings, 1979, 119.

96. Ibid., 52–62. Siebert was apparently under pressure from major New York banks on this point. *EU* (July 1980), 65.

97. Senate Hearings, 1979, 113–118. It remained clear, however, that to many state authorities foreign acquisitions of ailing banks were preferable to takeovers by large out-of-state banks.

98. Ibid., 487–503. Also see *American Banker,* July 16 and 27, 1979. In later years, the independent bankers remained worried about the threat posed by foreign takeovers, and new legislation was periodically introduced by sympathetic congressmen. For example, see *Congressional Record, House,* June 6, 1984, E 2654.

99. *EC,* March 31, 1979.

100. In its brief against a move to extend the moratorium, the Fed argued that most recent acquisitions had been helpful to the economy and provided little evidence of serious regulatory or supervisory problems. Difficulties that might arise in the long run, such as the payment of excessive dividends to foreign parents, could be monitored and controlled under existing statutory authority. More importantly, in the Fed's view, the moratorium violated a "long tradition" of welcoming foreign investment and promoting free capital flows. See Board of Governors of the Federal Reserve System, *Foreign Takeovers of United States Banks,* Committee Print, Senate Committee on Banking, Housing, and Urban Affairs, 96th Cong., 2d sess. (Washington, July 1980)

101. U.S. Congress, House, Committee on Government Operations, Subcommittee on Commerce, Consumer, and Monetary Affairs, *Foreign Acquisitions of U.S. Banks and the Non-Banking Activities of Foreign Bank Holding Companies,* Hearings, 96th Cong., 2nd sess. (Washington, May 15 and June 25, 1980). Although all banking legislation must go through the Banking Committee, Government Operations had certain oversight responsibilities that were used to justify this involvement.

102. Comptroller General of the United States, "Despite Positive Effects, Further Foreign Acquisitions of U.S. Banks Should Be Limited until Policy Conflicts Are Fully Addressed," GGD-80-66, (Washington, D.C.: General Accounting Office, August 26, 1980).

103. Later published in book form as Comptroller of the Currency, *Foreign Acquisitions of U.S. Banks* (Richmond, Va.: Robert F. Dame, 1981).

104. A later study concludes similarly that long-term strategic considerations and regulatory factors determine foreign bank moves more than short-term or macroeconomic factors. See Lawrence G. Goldberg and Anthony Saunders, "Regulation and Foreign Market Growth by the International Banking Firm," Working Paper No. 252, Salomon Brothers Center, Graduate School of Business Administration, New York University, February 1982.

105. U.S. Congress, House, Committee on Government Operations, Subcommittee on Commerce, Consumer, and Monetary Affairs, *Foreign Government and Foreign Investor Control of U.S. Banks,* Hearing, 97th Cong., 2nd sess. (Washington, September 30, 1982).

106. Absolute growth for the foreign banks continued, but their rate of growth slowed markedly. In 1983 and 1984 the level of their relative share of the American banking market stayed near 15 percent. By 1986 the foreign share of the national market for corporate loans stood around 20 percent. *BL* (March 1986). Earnings problems caused by increased competition and overpayments for acquired banks are well examined in *WSJ,* June 19 and June 20, 1984. Midland Bank later sold Crocker back to domestic interests, an indication that acquisitions could go both ways.

107. State supervisors and the CSBS brought several federal approvals of foreign branch establishment to court. Although they insisted that the reciprocity tests specified in certain state laws should supersede the IBA, the courts held the opposite. See Thomas Amos Behney, Jr., "Federal and State Regulation of Foreign Bank Entry: Conference of State Bank Supervisors v. Conover," *Law and Policy in International Business* 15 (1983), 1223–58. In several states, notably New York and Texas, a process of loosening regulations in order better to compete with the potentially more attractive federal chartering option ensued. See, for example, *Laws of the State of New York,* 203rd sess., 883–22, December 1, 1980; 205th sess., 499–26, July 13, 1982; 207th sess., 306–51, October 8, 1984; *BL* (November 1985).

108. Department of the Treasury, *Report to Congress on Foreign Government Treatment of U.S. Commercial Banking Organizations* (Washington, D.C.: Department of the Treasury, September 17, 1979). One hundred and forty countries were included, all U.S. banks having overseas operations were surveyed, U.S. embassies abroad were asked for systematic input, and various consultations with foreign governments took place in the course of the study. The magnitude of the task and the speed with which it was completed (well ahead of the congressional deadline) testify to the priority given to it by the Carter administration. It would become an even higher priority for the Reagan administration.

109. In 1982 various bills were introduced in Congress that touched upon these matters, especially Senator Heinz's Reciprocity in Trade in Services and Investment Bill of 1982 and Senator Danforth's Reciprocal Trade and Investment Bill of 1982, the latter seeking to "establish reciprocal market access as a principle of U.S. trade policy." See *Congressional Record, Senate,* February 4 and 10, 1982; Danforth's News Release, February 10, 1982; and U.S. Congress, Senate, Committee on Finance, Subcommittees

on International Trade and on Taxation and Debt Management, *Trade in Services,* Hearing on S.2051 and S.2058, 97th Cong., 2nd sess. (Washington, May 14, 1982). (Note especially a letter from the IFB [288–91] objecting to reciprocity as a standard for trade in banking services.)

110. *Congressional Record, Senate,* November 18, 1983, S.17060.

111. Department of the Treasury, *Report on Foreign Government Treatment of U.S. Commercial Banking Organizations—1984 Update* (Washington, D.C.: Department of the Treasury, July 5, 1984).

112. See *BW,* May 14, 1984.

113. U.S. Congress, Senate, Committee on Banking, Housing, and Urban Affairs, *National Treatment of Banks,* Hearing (Washington, September 24, 1984).

114. The Federal Reserve was not represented at the hearing, but its chairman, Paul Volcker, was known to share the position put forward by Regan. Aside from its potentially protectionist implications, Volcker was concerned that a reciprocity bill could jeopardize progress toward greater multilateral cooperation on supervisory matters. Interviews, Washington, October 1984.

115. Department of the Treasury, *National Treatment Study: Report to Congress on Foreign Government Treatment of U.S. Commercial Banking and Securities Organization—1986 Update* (Washington, D.C.: Department of the Treasury, 1986).

116. Ibid., 23. Two OECD countries, Canada and Japan, were especially highlighted in this respect. It seemed evident that the authors were in the Canadian case trying to set the stage for coming bilateral negotiations on freer trade. In the Japanese case, the authors apparently were aiming to reinforce a continuing process of domestic financial liberalization.

117. Such contravention was particularly apparent in certain interstate regional banking pacts that permitted a degree of cross-border banking activity but restricted such rights to banks having the bulk of their deposits located within a specified region. Aimed principally at excluding domestic money-center banks, such restrictions often affected foreign-owned banks. Ibid., 921.

118. This expectation became ever more obvious in the debate on overarching trade policy as well as whenever foreign institutions broke new ground by, for example, investing in American securities companies or seeking to become primary dealers in U.S. government bonds. Japan remained the principal target of prominent efforts to make the expectation more explicit. See *BW,* December 22, 1986, 58; *Congressional Record, Senate,* April 28, 1987, S.5613–14; and *BNA's Banking Report* 48 (Washington, D.C.: Bureau of National Affairs, 1987), 589, 819–20.

## CHAPTER 4. *Japan*

1. "Banking Law" (Law No. 21, March 30, 1927), *EHS Law Bulletin Series* vi, 6050 (1969). Foreign banks are covered in Article 32, which permitted "special provisions to be made by ordinance" and allowed the finance minister to "place such limitations as may be necessary." Overall, the law originally codified a strongly centralized system of governmental

guidance in partial response to the tumultuous conditions prevailing in the banking sector during the 1920s. With authority thus conferred, the Ministry of Finance oversaw the consolidation of 1,541 commercial and savings banks in 1926 to 65 by 1945.

2. In the early 1970s, much to the ministry's chagrin, Japanese banks were forced to pay a premium for funds raised in the Euromarkets. This so-called Japan premium was related to the higher risk that Eurodollar depositors then associated with most Japanese financial institutions. In effect, the market perceived higher risks of default related to Japan's vulnerability to oil embargoes and price hikes.

3. The term *impact loan* is believed to have originated in postwar Italy, where incoming loans reduced the impact of a large balance-of-payments deficit. It later became associated with U.S. foreign aid programs and World Bank loans whose proceeds were used domestically.

4. Many foreign banks had been required to submit letters to the Ministry of Finance agreeing not to participate in retail markets. As part of a process of liberalization, the letters were later returned. Because swap limits were institution-specific and confidential, the ministry and the Bank of Japan had considerable flexibility to reward or punish individual banks as deemed necessary.

5. Swapping did carry an element of funding risk, probably one reason the Ministry of Finance permitted this situation. Much of the foreign currency brought into Japan came from international interbank markets. In the event of instability in those markets, foreign banks would bear the responsibility for supporting such funding operations.

6. In effect, the U.S. State Department and Defense Department dominated American policy toward Japan. Financial considerations remained secondary at least until the late 1970s.

7. Bank of Japan, *Economic Statistics Annual 1974*, cited in Christopher D. McFarlane, "The Role of Foreign Banks in Japan," *Bulletin* 59 (Tokyo: Sophia University Socio-Economic Institute, 1976), 4.

8. In such a context, foreign banks provided a needed safety valve. Domestic banks depended on the foreigners to meet exceptional requirements from their clients. Clients so introduced were also assisted by foreign banks in offshore operations. With the foreigners' role circumscribed in the domestic market, domestic banks had little fear that introductions would lead to any fundamental shifts in client loyalties.

9. A reciprocity test was applied flexibly in the case of a bank coming from a country that did not appear intentionally and specifically to limit the advance of Japanese banks, even if strict comparability of treatment was not available. In truth, it was rare that reciprocal treatment was not more than fully comparable inasmuch as Japan had a more highly restrictive domestic banking system than most of its major trading partners.

10. Representative offices, however, were not excluded. Only prior notification was required to open such an office, the functions of which were limited to intelligence gathering and liaison work for the head office. A rapid expansion in the number of representative offices dated from 1971 as internationalization became the vogue even for relatively small institutions.

11. The system of guarantees reflected a consideration of long-run interests. Banks, borrowers, and the government had their own interests in

convincing foreign capital markets of the risklessness of investments in core sectors of the Japanese economy. Aside from keeping the cost of borrowing down, the system aimed at protecting future access to foreign capital.

12. Correctly or not, foreign lenders often regarded the domestic banks that introduced impact loan clients as tacit guarantors.

13. Bank of Japan, *Economic Statistics Annual 1984* (Tokyo: Bank of Japan, March 1985), 10. GNP is calculated at constant (1975) prices. Industrial production actually fell by 4 percent in 1974 and 11 percent in 1975 (p. 6).

14. During prior years when the yen was weak and Japanese monetary policy tight, and opposite conditions prevailed in the United States, funds brought into Japan from head offices and swapped into yen gave foreign lenders (especially Americans) a very competitive local cost of funds. Facing a reversal of these conditions in the mid-1970s, the foreigners found their margins squeezed. Between 1975 and 1978 the yen rose 30 percent in value against the dollar. Ibid., 5.

15. *Oriental Economist (OE)* (March 1979), 8–16.

16. International Business Information (IBI), *The Future Role of Foreign Banks in Japan* (Tokyo: IBI, May 19, 1978), 11. In aggregate, foreign market share fell from 3.5 percent in 1976 to 2.8 percent in 1978 before recovering to 3.2 percent in 1979. Ministry of Finance sources, cited in Atsushi Hama, "The Yen-Dollar Relationship, Macro-Economic Policy, Financial and Capital Markets, and Related Issues," *Keidanren Papers* 10 (Tokyo: Keidanren, 1983), 91.

17. Andreas Prindl, *Japanese Finance* (New York: John Wiley & Sons, 1982), 71.

18. After 1975 impact loan portfolios declined by an average of 10 percent per year. Even worse, new impact loans booked after 1975 displayed the evidence of rising competition in their margins. The 1 to 1.5 percent spread common in the late 1960s fell to less than 0.6 percent as newly arrived foreign banks bid strongly for an initial market share in a declining market. *Japan Economic Journal (JEJ)*, June 13, 1978, 24.

19. Citibank, in particular, had a high public profile, which later included a publicized, but unsuccessful, request to the Ministry of Finance for permission to issue long-term yen debentures, a traditional prerogative of the long-term credit banks and the Bank of Tokyo. *JEJ*, June 27, 1985.

20. The dispute centered around the method foreign banks were using to cost funds brought in from overseas and reflected a lack of internal agreement between the tax, banking, and international finance bureaus of the Ministry of Finance. *Financial Times* (London) *(FT)*, May 27, June 8, 1976.

21. By the start of the 1980s, city banks earned over 10 percent of their total income overseas. In the United States, Japanese lenders had become the largest subgroup among foreign banks. In California alone, city banks owned six medium-sized banks outright and were capturing increasing shares of retail and wholesale markets. See Stephen Bronte, *Japanese Finance: Markets and Institutions* (London: Euromoney Publications, 1982), 27.

22. A small group of bankers did initiate a series of irregular and informal meetings to discuss the issues as early as 1976. Because of internal differences of opinion, however, the group made no progress. These

differences were compounded by the awareness, acquired early on in a banker's career in Tokyo, that an aroused ministry was capable of differentiating between competitors when it came to such things as swap limit increases. Interviews, Tokyo, July 1985.

23. The meeting came as a direct result of the earlier contact with disgruntled European bankers in Tokyo. The EEC had in fact maintained a financial attaché in Tokyo since 1964, but not until the late 1970s had the attaché's role involved detailed liaison regarding banking issues.

24. A telling instance of the conflicts thus engendered occurred in 1978 when American bankers were invited to the embassy in Tokyo to discuss their problems. Since his institution too was an American bank by virtue of its wholly owned subsidiary in California, a representative of the Bank of Tokyo was also invited.

25. American financial attachés in Tokyo came from the Treasury but overall management of the bilateral relationship with Japan remained under State Department authority. Even in 1978 economic issues did not have top priority. For its part, the Federal Reserve, concerned more about prudential than competitive issues and cognizant of the possibility of a backlash against America's peculiarly complex system of bank regulation, inclined against issue-specific negotiations with Japanese bank regulators. Interviews, Tokyo, June, July, 1985.

26. Shortly after President Reagan's first inauguration, an interdepartmental agreement gave the Treasury key responsibility for diplomacy on institutional banking issues.

27. U.S. Congress, House, Subcommittee on Trade, Committee on Ways and Means, *Task Force Report on United States-Japan Trade,* 95th Cong., 2nd sess. (Washington, January 2, 1979), 1, 26-28. The task force was established early in 1978 to monitor implementation of the so-called Strauss-Ushiba Agreement of January 13, 1978, on bilateral trade liberalization. The U.S. trade deficit with Japan totalled $1.7 billion in 1975, $5.3 billion in 1976, $8.1 billion in 1977, and $11.9 billion in 1978. The Strauss-Ushiba Agreement did not explicitly cover banking, but its spirit as well as that of the International Banking Act were invoked to justify the task force review.

28. *JEJ,* February 27, 1979.

29. Department of the Treasury, *Report to Congress on Foreign Government Treatment of U.S. Commercial Banking Operations* (Washington, D.C.: Department of the Treasury, 1979), 77, 132-33.

30. This was one reason why the Ministry of Finance kept pushing foreign bankers to establish a joint association. That the ministry liked the idea added to the bankers' reluctance. Informal and selective collaboration did continue, but there emerged no clear spokesmen.

31. One indication of the importance assigned by the council to the issue is that the foreign bankers' remarks and the relevant recommendations of the council are recounted in only 9 pages of a 950-page report. Kinyu Saido Chosukai (Financial System Research Council), *Futsuginko no arikatato ginko saido no kaisei* (Tokyo: Kinyu Saisei Jijo, September 1979), 32, 33, 38, 214-219. The council received, but did not publish, additional views from Chase Manhattan and other banks between December 1978 and February 1979.

32. Unpublished supplementary statement submitted to the Ministry of Finance, Committee on Financial Systems Research, December 4, 1978.

33. Kinyu Saido Chosukai, 1979, ch. 8, pt. 4, para. 3. The council in fact usually worked on the basis of drafts prepared by officials delegated from the Banking Bureau.

34. Ibid., ch. 9, pt. 4., para. 1. Japan had traditionally supervised foreign banks branch by branch; that is, each branch was treated as a separate bank. It had also looked to the capital base of the parent to support local assets, a convention now seen as risky in the wake of prominent fiascos in the Euromarkets.

35. *Nihon Keizai Shimbun (NKS)*, February 19, 1979.

36. Most foreign bankers simply did not understand the process of policy making within the ministry. A probable additional reason for the quiescence of the majority was a slight upturn in their fortunes during 1979. After the collapse of loan portfolios in 1978, aggregate loans grew from ¥3.2 billion to ¥3.9 billion in 1979 and ¥4.3 billion in 1980. Market share rose from 2.8 percent to 3.3 percent in 1979, and six new foreign banks entered the market in that year. Despite the rise, competitive loan pricing continued to hamper improvements in profitability. Ministry of Finance data, cited in Hama, "The Yen-Dollar Relationship," 91.

37. The Ministry of Finance cautiously controlled their foreign growth and occasionally curtailed expansion plans either for prudential or balance-of-payments reasons. Although it remained concerned that the nature of competition between the banks tended to make initial forays into new markets excessively aggressive, the ministry adopted a consistently permissive stance beginning in 1977. Until the mid-1980s, however, it still tried to control the extent to which the banks could engage externally in business activities restricted internally.

38. As should have been expected, the liberalization of swap limits also hurt the foreign banks, for it took away the arbitrage possibilities formerly present when demand exceeded supply. At base a problem akin to the prisoners dilemma of game theory was at work. It was rational for individual banks to push for increases in their own limits if all other limits stayed the same. In the extreme, the complete abolition of all limits meant that potential arbitrage gains disappeared.

39. Evidence of foreign lobbying can, however, be found in the way implementing ordinances interpreted the new law's requirement for the maintenance of prudential reserves by foreign banks. Foreign banks objected strongly to an initial proposal to require each branch of a single bank to hold such reserves. The Ministry of Finance subsequently amended the ordinance to allow for less costly maintenance on a consolidated basis. See M. Ichii, "The Japanese Banking Law of 1981," *The World of Banking* (September-October 1982), 32–34.

40. "The Banking Law," Law No. 59, June 1, 1981, published in translation in Government of Japan, *The Banking Law, Cabinet Order, and Ministry of Finance Ordinance* (Tokyo: Institute for Financial Affairs, 1982). Chapter 7 deals with foreign banks and spells out licensing requirements generally viewed as nondiscriminatory. Chapter 1 (art. 4, para. 3) specifies that foreign banks in the home country of a potential entrant must "enjoy a status equivalent in substance to the one allowed under this law."

41. The ministry's thinking appears to have been ahead of the banks here. It had in fact been adapting its policies to support the internationalization of the banking sector since around 1975. Throughout the rest of the decade, however, it received little pressure from the banks to do more at home to obviate the possibility of retaliation abroad.

42. The precedents of a 1971 law on foreign securities operations (Law No. 5, March 3, 1971), which was based on the national treatment standard, and the earlier economic treaties with other OECD countries were explicitly brought up in internal discussions. Even if the latter treaties specifically exempted domestic banking, the argument was that the sector no longer required protection and the spirit of the treaties should therefore apply.

43. The Ministry of Finance could, for example, argue that the cautious liberalization trajectory thereby formalized would over time provide increased opportunities for foreign banks. In this regard the Banking Law and the Foreign Exchange Law may be seen as complementary.

44. The United States, in particular, later hailed the law as a positive step toward "effective" national treatment. See Department of the Treasury, *Report to Congress on Foreign Government Treatment of U.S. Commercial Banking Operations—1984* (Washington, D.C.: Department of the Treasury, 1984), 22.

45. Average return on assets rose from 0.2 percent in 1979 to just over 0.5 percent in the middle of 1980. During the next three years, however, it fell back below its 1979 trough. International Business Information, quarterly data, cited in Eisuke Sakakibara and Yoriuki Nagao, *Study on the Tokyo Capital Market* (Tokyo: Japan Center for International Finance, 1985), 17; Hama, "The Yen-Dollar Relationship," 90, 91. Forty percent of the branches were North American; 35 percent, European; just over 20 percent, Asian.

46. Federation of Japanese Bankers Associations, *Banking System in Japan* (Tokyo: FJBA, 1984), 22. Almost half of international income, however, still came from foreign exchange operations in Tokyo.

47. Bruce R. MacIlwain (Lloyds Bank), Unpublished address to the Working Party on the Internationalization of the Tokyo Financial and Capital Markets, Tokyo, May 1985.

48. Department of the Treasury, *Report to Congress* (1984), 21.

49. Building market share is a common initial aim for any bank expanding into new fields, but the structure of Japanese banking powerfully reinforces long-term strategies on this basis. High leverage permitted by the Ministry of Finance, a perception in foreign money markets that an effective Bank of Japan guarantee exists, a preponderance of fixed costs at home because of the lifetime employment system, and the structure and expectations of bank shareholders all provide incentives for volume-oriented expansion strategies.

50. The enthusiasm for acquisitions was actually very low, principally because of the poor profitability performance of Japanese banks, their inadequate financial disclosure, and fear of staff hostility. Between 1979 and 1982, however, several foreign banks did make initial moves only to find that the shares of target banks simply were not tendered, no matter what the price.

51. Japanese bankers and officials added another question. Could foreign bankers actually hope to develop domestic business when few stayed longer than four years and even fewer spoke Japanese?

52. Prominent initiatives, accommodated by the new flexibility of the Ministry of Finance, included some branch expansion, establishment of consumer financing and leasing operations, and moves into the gray area between commercial and investment banking (e.g., government bond and investment advisory services).

53. *NKS,* February 28, 1982.

54. *Congressional Record, Senate,* February 4, 10, 1982.

55. The report signaled continuing disagreement within the administration as to analysis and approach. The Treasury, in particular, again objected to the inclusion of banking in broad policy recommendations covering all service industries. Interview, Tokyo, June 1985. Foreign bank leaders in Japan, recalling how the last round of bilateral diplomacy accelerated their loss of the impact loan monopoly, subsequently recorded their own disagreement with the tone and thrust of the report. *FT,* July 15, 1982.

56. Ministry of Finance, Banking Bureau, "Treatment of Foreign Banks, Securities Companies, and Insurance Companies in Japan," *Money and Finance,* 4, 35 (Tokyo: Institute for Financial Affairs, March 1982). Also see, Bank of Japan, Banking Department "The Policy of the Bank of Japan on the Activities of Foreign Banks in Japan," Tokyo, September 1982.

57. Members came from the ministry's banking, securities, and international finance bureaus, Dai Ichi Kangyo, Bank of Tokyo, Industrial Bank of Japan, Nomura Securities, and Yamaichi Securities. Their mandate was to explain the new Foreign Exchange and Banking Laws and the progress of liberalization measures. *JT,* July 26, 1982.

58. See Jeffrey A. Frankel, "The 1984 Campaign for Liberalization of Japanese Capital Markets," paper prepared for a symposium sponsored by the Ministry of Finance, Tokyo, August 27-28, 1984.

59. Securities companies in particular, lately targeting Japan in their expansion strategies, were facing some of the same sorts of barriers or "misunderstandings" that had hindered banks fifteen years earlier. The treasury secretary at the time was the former chairman of Merrill Lynch.

60. In January 1983 the Bankers Association for Foreign Trade (BAFT) compiled a new study on foreign barriers to U.S. banking. The section on Japan explicitly denied charges of discrimination and recounted regulatory measures that benefited foreign banks disproportionately. Remaining problems, it concluded, relate to the "closed nature of Japanese society.... For the most part, this is a barrier that foreign banks will have to try to overcome from inside Japan, and that cannot be mitigated by U.S. government initiative." BAFT, *Constraints on Foreign Bank Operations in OECD Countries* (Washington, D.C.: BAFT, 1983).

61. At this point European officials held their own diplomatic efforts in abeyance to wait and see what the Americans would achieve. Interview, Tokyo, June 1985.

62. "Joint U.S./Japan Communiqué on Monetary and Financial Issues," November 10, 1983, published in *Money and Finance,* 5, 53 (Tokyo: Institute for Financial Affairs, 1984). Among the eight items listed as initial subjects for discussion, those most directly relevant to foreign banks were

establishment of a yen bankers' acceptance market, improvements in the CD market, and an easing of regulations affecting Euroyen bond issuance.

63. Trust banks and insurance companies enjoyed the exclusive right to manage pension funds. Japan had a high savings rate, an aging population, and a reputedly inefficient trust banking sector comprised of few institutions. Of the major financial sectors in Japan, trust banking was one of the smallest (seven banks controlling 12 percent of the assets of the city banks) and weakest, financially and politically. All of these factors made it attractive.

64. Interview, Tokyo, June 1985.

65. This support represented a rare display of prime ministerial initiative in an area usually considered too technical and fraught with contentious vested interests. In part, it showed the pressure the prime minister was under after a setback in the December 1983 Lower House election, which left his Liberal Democratic party without a clear majority. With his continuing leadership in question, Nakasone needed a high-profile success in his economic diplomacy with the United States.

66. A lack of internal consensus was evident, and the ministry had in fact turned the issue over to the Financial System Research Council. *AEN,* January 13, 1984.

67. *JEJ,* February 21, 1984.

68. Transcript of remarks delivered at Tokyo American Center, March 24, 1984.

69. More specifically, for example, they offered to push for a promotion in voting status within the World Bank, something the government was known to want. They probably also threatened to hold up the pending acquisition of Bank of California by Mitsubishi Bank, a bluff in that the final decision belonged to a Federal Reserve Board known to be hostile to a stricter reciprocity policy. Despite the protests of an American bank that lost out in the maneuvering for Bank of California and despite concerns that Mitsubishi was overleveraged, the Fed approved the acquisition without regard to reciprocity considerations. *JT,* May 16, 1984; interview, Tokyo, June 1985.

70. The latter point was widely conceded by foreign banks themselves.

71. Within the Ministry of Finance strong resistance to the concessions remained, especially at lower levels. Senior officials were feeling the most pressure to reach a satisfactory agreement with the United States and probably saw the issue as a way to relieve that pressure without having to concede on much tougher matters, for instance, issuance of long-term yen debentures by foreign banks or rapid decontrol of domestic interest rates. Some also appeared genuinely convinced of the need for greater competition in the trust banking sector. They therefore spent a great deal of time trying to convince their doubting subordinates. Among other considerations, junior officials wondered how long they, as the generation likely to face the problem, would be able to deny to city banks a privilege now to be given to their foreign peers. Interviews, Tokyo, June 1985.

72. Japanese Ministry of Finance/U.S. Department of the Treasury, *Report on Yen/Dollar Exchange Rate Issues* (n.p.), May 1984, 22.

73. There were seven domestic trust banks and, on an exceptional basis, one city bank (Daiwa) in the market.

74. *JEJ,* July 2, 1985. The fact that no more than nine applied indicated new doubts among foreign bankers about the ultimate profitability of such ventures.

75. Again, the specificity of these changes reflected close coordination, mainly at the Treasury's initiative, between the U.S. negotiators and American financial institutions. Doubts remained within the foreign banking community in Tokyo, but head offices back home appeared generally to support the Treasury's approach. U.S. embassy officials also regularly consulted with their counterparts in other countries. However, no attempts were made to enlist the support of domestic interests who could expect to benefit from increased financial openness, such as domestic corporations. Unlike the case in other countries, foreign banks had no obvious domestic political allies, partly because their historical presence touched so few. Interviews, Tokyo, July 1985.

76. Department of the Treasury, *Report to Congress* (1984), 21–25.

77. *JEJ,* June 3, 1984.

78. There were rumors that Sumitomo did not request permission. Ministry officials deny the rumors and assert that they were informally consulted. It is possible that the Bank threatened to go ahead with the purchase even if the ministry demurred.

79. Interviews, Tokyo, June 1985. The problem did not arise to the same extent in the United States because the American securities operations of the major Swiss and German banks were grandfathered under the International Banking Act.

80. The securities companies argued that they should be given treatment equal to that provided in London to two U.S. brokers on an exceptional basis. British authorities obviously also wanted U.K. banks in Japan to have the same flexibility provided to Citibank.

81. *AWSJ,* March 27, 1985.

82. At this point, the EEC Commission played a passive role as separate national governments pursued their own agendas. Its only direct request to the ministry was that any regulatory changes be extended on a nondiscriminatory basis. Interview, Tokyo, June 1985.

83. Under a complex formula whereby new securities companies could be owned by international affiliates less than 50 percent owned by foreign parent banks, foreign institutions were provided treatment equal to that given Citibank while the Ministry of Finance technically avoided a direct breach of Article 65 of the Securities and Exchange Law.

84. Their growth also continued in the United States. In late 1986, for example, three Japanese securities companies were licensed by the Federal Reserve as primary dealers in U.S. government securities, despite vocal opposition from federal legislators and several American competitors. *WSJ,* October 7, 1986. The issue later resurfaced in trade bill debates.

85. The Bank for International Settlements reported that at the end of 1985, Japanese banks accounted for U.S.$640 billion in international assets. U.S. banks held $580 billion, French banks $221 billion, British banks $183 billion, and German banks $165 billion. *FT,* January 31, 1986.

86. One effect of the bilateral activity of 1983 and 1984 was to reinforce, at least in the minds of some bankers, the need for cooperation among the foreign banks in the search for solutions to their problems. Although most of the major banks stayed out (for their traditional reasons), over half of

the foreign banks active in Tokyo in 1985 were represented in a newly established Institute of Foreign Bankers. Building on social and information-sharing activities, its leaders hoped to mold it over time into a formal lobbying group. Interviews, Tokyo, June, July 1985.

87. Department of the Treasury, *National Treatment Study: Report to Congress on Foreign Government Treatment of U.S. Commercial Banking and Securities Organizations, 1986 Update* (Washington, D.C.: Department of the Treasury, December 18, 1986), 68; and Bank of Japan, "Financial Performance of Foreign Banks in Japan," unpublished paper, June 1985.

88. The U.S. Treasury's 1986 *National Treatment Study* noted that Japan continued to provide national treatment to foreign banks and to make progress in liberalizing operating conditions in its domestic market.

89. In 1984 the city banks earned an average of 18 percent of their gross profits from international transactions; the long-term credit banks, 13 percent; the trust banks, 13 percent; and smaller banks, 2.5 percent. Ministry of Finance, Financial Systems Research Council, *Creating a Suitable Environment for Further Progress of Liberalization,* June 5, 1985, appendix (Japanese only), table 13.

90. Morgan Guaranty, *World Financial Markets* (June 1984), 11, cited in Frankel, "The 1984 Campaign," 47.

91. The typical response to these questions was that several reforms (including fuller public financial disclosure and increased capital adequacy requirements for Japanese banks, complete interest rate deregulation in the domestic market to equalize the marginal costs of funds of domestic and foreign competitors, and an abandonment of outmoded rules of functional segmentation) would work to restore the natural order of things.

92. European banking officials, while never abandoning the national treatment standard in their talks, began introducing terms like "fully effective national treatment" and "balance of advantages." Britain began to put some legal force behind the expectations suggested in these phrases by building a discretionary and flexible reciprocity guideline into its deregulatory 1986 Financial Services Act. "Terms as favorable" as those prevailing in Britain for foreign institutions would henceforth be expected for British institutions abroad.

93. On U.K./Japan bilateral diplomacy, see *AWSJ,* February 18, 1987; *EU* (April 1987), 78–123; *EC,* April 11, 1987, 75–76. On talks with France, see *Banker International* (June 1987). On further U.S./Japan interaction that led to the granting of Japanese securities licenses to U.S. banks at a time when Japanese banks remained forbidden to undertake such activity both in Japan and the United States, see *EC,* August 6, 1986, 59–60; and *WSJ,* June 4, 1987.

94. Advisory councils to various bureaus of the Ministry of Finance set out agendas for a continued easing of restrictions on overseas expansion, the deepening of the Euroyen market, and the creation of an offshore banking market in Tokyo. By 1986 Japanese banks accounted for 32 percent of global Eurocurrency lending activity, compared to 19 percent for U.S. banks and 23 percent for British, French, and German banks combined. *BL,* March 1987.

CHAPTER 5. *Canada*

1. Data on the Mercantile Bank case, gathered principally from extensive press clipping files that Citibank maintained, is compiled in John Fayerweather, *The Mercantile Bank Affair* (New York: New York University Press, 1974). As we shall see, the book itself played a role in shaping the events of the 1980s.

2. Government of Canada, *Royal Commission on Canada's Economic Prospects—Report* (Ottawa: The Queen's Printer, 1957).

3. The Liberals remained in power for twenty years, except for a brief respite in 1979-80. One of Gordon's first actions as minister was to propose a budget that included a new tax on foreign takeovers of Canadian companies. The suggestion was later dropped because of unfavorable reaction at home and hostile reaction abroad.

4. See Walter L. Gordon, *A Political Memoir* (Toronto: McClelland & Stewart, 1977), 208-14, appendix 3.

5. The restriction was modeled on federal insurance and trust company legislation that limited the distribution of company shares to a maximum of 25 percent for any group of nonresidents and 10 percent for any individual investor. These regulations had the dual purpose of ensuring domestic control and preventing ownership concentration.

6. Government of Canada, *1964 Report of the Royal Commission on Banking and Finance* (Ottawa: The Queen's Printer, 1965).

7. In 1966 Mercantile, with assets of C$224.5 million, was the smallest of the eight chartered banks (one-tenth the size of the smallest of the Big Five) and had a gearing ratio of 22.5:1.

8. Fayerweather, *The Mercantile Bank Affair*, 78-79.

9. Ibid., 411-12.

10. Ibid., 419-21.

11. One chairman wrote, "It is a matter of considerable concern to us that the form of ownership restriction in the proposed new Act will effectively close Canada to new foreign banks, because we fear it will have adverse effects on our own important foreign business." Unpublished submission, July 15, 1965, Royal Bank of Canada archives.

12. Perceiving the costs of retaliation abroad to be higher than the costs of at least some increased competition at home, seven out of eight banks agreed in principle that some sort of reciprocal accommodation should be made. They were not able to agree, however, on what precise form the accommodation should take.

13. Ontario, heartland of Canada in terms of population and industry, and therefore the most obvious place for foreign banks to establish an initial presence, had a Conservative government throughout this period. Although the government had long been amenable to protectionist measures aimed at preserving its industrial base, it did not share the worldview of Walter Gordon and the Liberals when it came to the provincial financial market.

14. Even the Foreign Investment Review Agency (FIRA), created by the federal government in 1973 to screen incoming direct investment, was not empowered to stop their entry in this fashion because expansion by any firm in its existing line of business was not forbidden. At least one anomalous situation resulted. Many foreign banks carried on the leasing business in their home jurisdictions, and could therefore do so in Canada through

subsidiaries. But a section of the 1967 Bank Act prohibited domestic Canadian banks from competing with them by forbidding them to engage in the leasing business in their own home market.

15. Ronald A. Shearer et al., *The Economics of the Canadian Financial System,* 2d ed. (Scarborough: Prentice-Hall Canada, 1984), 367. Calculated at current prices.

16. From 1970 to 1975 the international activity of the Big Five grew by 18 percent per year, and from 1976 to 1982 it advanced by 26 percent per year. Average net income derived from international operations rose from 23.9 percent of total net income in 1975 to 48.8 percent in 1982 before declining steeply after 1983 as international loan losses hit and the domestic economy slid into severe recession. For all five, international assets as a percentage of total assets averaged 30 percent in 1976, 36 percent in 1980, and 38 percent in 1982. (The roughly comparable figure for 1967 was around 20 percent.) In terms of returns on assets, international operations actually proved more profitable than domestic activity until 1983. (Calculations from annual reports; P. Nagy, *The International Business of Canadian Banks* (Montreal: Centre for International Business Studies, École des Hautes Études Commerciales, 1983), 27; and E. Wayne Clendenning, *The Eurocurrency Markets and the International Activities of Canadian Banks* (Ottawa: The Economic Council of Canada, 1976).

17. By 1980, 556 banking offices had been established offshore, up from 256 offices fifteen years earlier. The geographic distribution of Canadian banks' international assets also changed over time. In 1965, 42 percent related to U.S. business, 21 percent to Europe, and 15 percent to Latin America. In 1980, 37 percent reflected European, 20 percent U.S., 11 percent Latin American, and 30 percent Asian business.

18. A limited precedent did exist in the federal Foreign Insurance Companies Act.

19. BNS, RBC, and BMO appear to have been the most internationally inclined of the group, an impression consistent with the pace and scale of their growth in overseas markets. Nevertheless, all tended toward a policy not of complete nondiscrimination but of bilateral reciprocity. This impression is documented, for example, in press accounts of public discussions of the issue that took place in 1974 and 1975. *GM* and *Montreal Gazette,* Business Sections, September 18, 1974; *Financial Post (FP),* September 21, 1974, and *Bank of Montreal Business Review,* supplement (December 1975).

20. See *Toronto Star (TS),* Business Section, November 11, 18, 1976. By that time, the split within the CBA was fully public, and it was widely noted that TD's prime market, southern Ontario, was the most vulnerable to expanded foreign competition.

21. Especially jealous of their right to regulate near-banks were Ontario and Quebec. In the run-up to a crucial provincial election in Quebec Prime Minister Trudeau and his cabinet did not want to fan the flames of French-Canadian nationalism. The separatist Parti Québécois succeeded anyway and turned the ruling Liberals out of power on November 15, 1976.

22. Only in the late 1970s did the government begin systematically to collect data on the extent of foreign operations. Representative offices were not required to register until 1980. Estimates of the number of foreign affiliates operating in the mid-1970s ranged from fifty to one hundred.

Their domestic assets are estimated to have increased from C$1.8 billion in 1974 to C$10.3 billion in 1980, amounts not inclusive of business solicited in Canada but booked off shore. Shearer et al., *Economics of the Canadian Financial System*, 371.

23. Economic Council of Canada, *Efficiency and Regulation* (Ottawa: Economic Council of Canada 1976), 89–90.

24. Government of Canada, "White Paper on the Revision of Canadian Banking Legislation," Ottawa, Department of Finance, August 1976. Although the paper also concerned establishment of a new payments clearing system, expansion of the business powers of banks (for example, into leasing), and various other regulatory matters, well over one-third of the paper (fifteen out of thirty-nine pages) dealt with aspects of the foreign bank issue.

25. Ibid., 25–26.

26. The government apparently took the suggestion made by BNS in 1974 that federal statutory authority for carrying the proposals into legislation be broadly interpreted. The drafters noted that the proposals were put forward on the basis of powers delegated by the BNA Act to the federal government over banking as well as over international trade and commerce, aliens, and the census. A wholly owned foreign subsidiary could be regulated in the same fashion as a small Canadian bank, and its own capital funds would supposedly provide an independent source of protection for Canadian depositors in the event of trouble in the parent organization. The subsidiaries themselves, however, could have their own branches within Canada.

27. Permission to stay was the carrot, this provision was the stick. Since the balance sheets of most affiliates were inadequate to attract low-priced money market funds on a stand-alone basis, parent guarantees typically assured the affiliates of access to funds at prices that allowed them to be competitive with the Canadian banks. Without the guarantees, their cost of funds would become prohibitive.

28. The latter rule would prevent data processing outside the country. Regulators claimed that the reason for this was prudential. Skeptics saw it as a mechanism for protecting Canadian data processing firms from American competition.

29. This provision became the Canadian version of a loose reciprocity requirement. Not as liberal as the U.S. approach, it nevertheless represented a step away from the decidedly illiberal policy of the past. It was also more conducive to increasing openness than the alternative of a strict one-for-one reciprocity interpreted on a bilateral basis.

30. The paper deftly stepped around the constitutional issue raised by the potential abridgment of provincial authority by carefully avoiding any attempt to define banking, thus permitting continued provincial licensing of near-banks. The paper did propose, however, to bring certain types of provincially licensed entities into a new national check-clearing system, which would entail the maintenance of reserves with the Bank of Canada.

31. Gross fixed capital formation (at 1971 prices) rose from C$18,904 million in 1970 to C$27,731 million in 1976 before falling to C$27,606 million and C$27,585 million in 1977 and 1978, respectively. Only in 1979 would it recover to C$29,448 million. United Nations, *National Account*

*Statistics: Main Aggregates and Tables* (New York: United Nations, 1985), 185–215.

32. Ibid.

33. Canadian Bankers' Association, "Presentation on the White Paper," (n.p.), October 15, 1976.

34. Toronto-Dominion Bank, "Foreign Banks in Canada," a submission to the Minister of Finance, November 1, 1976. The bank pointed out that an identical volume of assets generated in each other's country by Canadian and American banks would leave the Americans with 20 percent of the Canadian market and Canadians with only 3 percent of the U.S. market. If there were more fundamental reasons for TD's position, they have never been made public. Aside from speculation about the vulnerability of the bank's southern Ontario base, however, plausible explanations circulating at the time within the financial community rested on the trauma caused senior TD executives by the overtures made in 1963 by Chase Manhattan and on the wholesale nature of the bank's burgeoning international operations, which mitigated the need for physical expansion. TD's position was not obviously related to the relative distribution of its assets or income. Indeed, although the smallest of the Big Five in terms of assets, from 1976 to 1982 it consistently ranked second in terms of the proportional share of net earnings contributed by international operations. According to data compiled in annual reports, between those years TD's international assets as a percentage of total assets rose from 25 percent to 44 percent, significantly lagging behind only the Bank of Nova Scotia.

35. At least one near-bank considered legal action on the grounds that the federal government was exceeding its constitutional authority by contending that provincially licensed business firms could be classed as aliens. The idea was dropped in light of the expectation of serious negative publicity. Interview, Toronto, July 1984.

36. Individual bankers did, however, occasionally inject their views. David Rockefeller, for example, made another trip to Canada in 1978 and publicly defended the value of freer competition in Canadian financial markets. *TS*, January 24, 1978.

37. Citibank, despite its continuing but slightly diluted control of the Mercantile, had already begun preparing to apply for a federal charter in 1977. *FP*, August 13, 1977. Its public posture remained aggressive during the initial period of the Bank Act revision process but noticeably shifted to a more accommodating one in 1979 when the presidency of its own near-bank affiliate changed hands. *Institutional Investor* (February 1980).

38. The official U.S. governmental position later depicted the proposals as they stood in 1978 as "a welcome step toward more equal treatment of foreign banks." Department of the Treasury, *Report to Congress* (1979), 50. An exceptional moment of intervention in the Canadian debate occurred in August 1979 when the New York superintendent of banks wrote a letter to the chairman of the Commons Finance Committee that argued that Canadian banks had greater freedom in the United States than U.S. banks had in Canada. The chairman made the letter public and called it a "discreet reminder that our banks are hostages in the U.S. to our treatment of U.S. banks here." Other parliamentarians took offense at this interference, but it never generated the heat evident in the previous decade. *GM*, August 21, 1979. Also contrary to earlier experience, senior

bureaucrats working on the new Bank Act claim not to have felt significant pressure from their counterparts in Washington or other national capitals. Interviews, Ottawa, July 1984.

39. Pending conclusive action by Parliament, the old Bank Act was simply renewed on a yearly basis.

40. See, for example, *TS*, March 8, December 8, 1977; January 7, July 21, 1978. Note that the *Star*, consistent with its stance ten years earlier, took a strongly negative editorial line on the issue. Typical editorial titles were: "Let's keep our banks Canadian," "Stop the sell-out to foreign banks," "We may regret opening the door to foreign banks," and "We don't need foreign banks here."

41. *GM*, November 21, 1978.

42. *TS*, November 22; *GM*, November 29, 30, 1978. Not all of the foreign bank testimony was critical. In fact the general tone of their remarks was one of praise for a step in the right direction, which provided needed legitimacy for their continued operation in Canada. *GM*, February 1, 1979.

43. See Parliament of Canada, *Minutes of Proceedings and Evidence of the Standing Committee on Finance, Trade, and Economic Affairs*, October 1978–January 1979. Less than a year later, following the lead of RBC and BMO, TD announced a major expansion of its U.S. operations. *GM*, December 4, 1979.

44. *FP*, December 13, 1978. In fact, the specter of a loss of monetary control from the on-shore operations of foreign institutions has long been discredited in central banking circles. Even the more plausible concern about retaining control in the face of expanding offshore money markets was then becoming outmoded.

45. The turbulence had a strong economic content, and accusations of fiscal mismanagement by the federal government were frequently heard. Between 1978 and 1979 the federal budget deficit rose from C$577 million to C$2.6 billion. United Nations, 1985, 185–215.

46. The perceived weakness of Conservative leadership, a disastrously unpopular budget proposal, and the planned referendum on quasi-separation in Quebec aided the Liberals.

47. Abbie Dann, "New Rules of the Game: The Bank Act Hearings, 1978–79," *Parliamentary Government* (Autumn 1980). Elite-level has been the traditional style of lobbying in Canada, especially on legislation as technical as the Bank Act, where the degree of intricacy left wide drafting flexibility to key bureaucrats. Dann contends that it was a mistake to underestimate the influence of individual MPs, especially members of the Finance Committee. Another reason for the lack of cooperation among foreign bankers was the reluctance of European and Japanese bankers to associate themselves too closely with Americans. As one European banker put it, "They don't realize how much their pushy style rubs Canadians the wrong way" (p. 7).

48. Several of the changes were consonant with suggestions from foreign banks. For example, the explicit number of allowable Canadian branches for foreign subsidiaries was removed and left to the discretion of the finance minister; the C$500 million ceiling on individual bank assets was scrapped (Citibank's subsidiary already exceeded that figure); a slight increase in aggregate foreign assets was incorporated by changing the ceiling from 15

percent of domestic bank commercial loans to 8 percent of their total domestic assets; there was to be no limit on international assets booked by the new banks, but they were not allowed to operate offshore branches.

49. In the end, the principal NDP goal was to enact amendments that would compel foreign banks to disclose more information about the extent of their activities in Canada. Their amendments failed. *GM,* July 16, 1980. The Liberal government did, however, attempt to mollify the NDP and was reluctant to force closure in the face of its often strident opposition. The 8-percent ceiling on foreign bank growth, for example, emerged from cabinet partly because of the expectation that it would be psychologically somewhat easier for the party to accept.

50. The act passed overwhelmingly, the NDP the only opposition. For the full text, see Parliament of Canada, *Banks and Banking Law Revision Act 1980,* 29 Elizabeth II (Ottawa: Ministry of Supply and Services, 1980–81).

51. Other major conditions included: annual license review for five years, and every five years thereafter; discretionary limits on the establishment of domestic branches; prohibitions on foreign branches; reciprocity for Canadian banks in the home country of parent institutions; and data processing and storage in Canada. (The latter applied also to Schedule A's.) In addition, the act forbade any institutions owned by foreign banks from raising funds under parent guarantee unless they were licensed as Schedule B's. The Schedule B's were requested by the inspector general to provide "letters of comfort" from their parents committing full support for liabilities incurred in Canada.

52. This bureaucratic discretion, deemed necessary to ensure orderly market conditions, represented a notable innovation in Canadian bank regulation and a step away from its traditional rule-orientation.

53. Canadian regulators contended that the act reflected desires to maintain orderly markets while an evolutionary liberalization took place. Foreign bankers, conversely, were quick to label the cautious conditionality of their new status as regulatory overkill. Officially, the government maintained, "Canada's policy on foreign banks is designed to achieve a balance between the objectives of maximizing competition and ensuring that the control of our financial system remains predominantly in Canadian hands." Government of Canada, "Exchange of Information Pursuant to the Ministerial Decision on Services," General Agreement on Tariffs and Trade, January 18, 1984.

54. The inspector general went to Japan in January 1981 to negotiate an agreement that would allow all the Schedule A banks to establish branches there. Unlike in the Australian case where the number of available licenses would initially be limited, little difficulty was encountered. A similar agreement was reached with Swiss authorities. Consistent with earlier proposals from the Canadian banks, the International Policy Committee of the CBA kept the inspector general up-to-date on Canadian bank treatment abroad.

55. The banks included eighteen American-owned banks, six Japanese, six British, five French, three Swiss, three Israeli, two German, six other European, and seven other Asian.

56. Office of the Inspector General of Banks, "The Status of Foreign Bank Subsidiaries," prepared for the House of Commons, Ottawa, 1983,

5–12. The report also noted that the banks had accounted for C$1 billion in capital imports during their start-up period.

57. It was unclear whether the statutory requirement for all chartered banks to join the CBA applied to the foreign banks. Many new entrants felt their interests would be ill-represented in an organization where weighted voting arrangements would ensure Canadian bank dominance. In a survey taken after the eventual decision, 51 percent of the bank spokesmen said that they joined in order to "work within the system" and 41 percent said either that the inspector general asked them to join or that they felt legally bound. Once inside the CBA, however, the new banks established their own permanent secretariat to look after collective interests. See H.B.W. Metcalfe, *Foreign Banks in Canada* (St. Catharine's, Ontario: Brock University, March 1984), 12–14.

58. Regulators contended that only the 8-percent ceiling was aimed at constraining growth. The two discretionary limits were seen as prudential and more generous in percentage terms than similar limitations on domestic banks. (Domestic banks at the time, owing to their strong retail deposit bases at home, funded less than 3 percent of their Canadian dollar assets off shore.) Foreign banks, like domestic banks, also disliked the prohibition on offshore data processing.

59. A typical strategy was to expand assets rapidly to gear up to twenty times initial capital, possibly by aggressively discounting loan rates or by buying short-term securities at fine margins, then to request an increase in deemed capital, then to resume expanding assets, and so on, until the inspector general would have no more deemed capital to allocate.

60. The subsidiaries of Citibank, Chase, Morgan Guaranty, Continental-Illinois, and Barclays were especially prominent.

61. In 1981 both the executive and the legislative branches of the U.S. government initiated studies on the ceiling and other restrictions on the expansion of American banks in Canada. *Business Week (BW)*, February 2, 1981. The U.S. Treasury, the focal point for banking diplomacy within the executive branch, already maintained a financial attaché in Ottawa, who was conveniently placed to work with American bankers on the issue.

62. American Bankers' Association, "White Paper on the Treatment of U.S. Banks in Canada," (n.p.), May 1982. The paper also labeled the Canadian restrictions "onerous" and the 1980 Bank Act "self-serving" and "protectionist." The input of American Schedule B executives was obvious.

63. Unpublished correspondence dated June 29 and July 23, 1982. Foreign bank executives characterized their continuing communications with government officials as "friendly, open, and frank." Interviews, Toronto, July 1984.

64. Executives of Barclays became especially prominent. *Business Journal* (June 1982). One senior American banker very active in the lobbying effort admitted having read John Fayerweather's book on the Mercantile affair and having come away from it determined to avoid the mistakes of the 1960s. Interview, Toronto, July 1984.

65. As the president of Citibank Canada put it at the time, "We hope that once we can demonstrate that we're making a real contribution, the restrictions will be lifted." *Business Journal* (June 1982), 21.

66. For example, *TS*, August 3, December 10, 1982; *GM*, December 30, 1982; *Canadian Banker and ICB Review* (December 1982), 5.

67. Canadian officials conceded that their delegation at the OECD in particular was feeling pressure. The matter was continually raised, for example, in the OECD committee responsible for monitoring the capital movements code; because Canada had not acceded to the code, it could not respond in an official capacity. Interviews, Toronto and Ottawa, July 1984.

68. *FT*, February 21, 1983, 38. The bankers were told that the U.S. government would not treat the issue as a political priority until the 8-percent ceiling had been reached and that Treasury officials in Ottawa were following matters closely.

69. Here such groups as the Small Business Federation and various chambers of commerce were targeted. The goal of this activity was to create a domestic constituency for required legislative change. Interviews, Toronto and Ottawa, July 1984; Washington, April 1985.

70. *GM*, February 14, July 12, 1983.

71. Gross domestic product (at constant 1971 prices) actually fell from C$139 billion in 1981 to C$133 billion in 1982 before beginning a slow recovery in 1983. OECD, *Quarterly National Accounts* (Paris: OECD, 1985). Unemployment rose from 7.5 percent in 1981 to 11.9 percent in 1983 before falling slightly to 11.3 percent in 1984. OECD, *Main Economic Indicators* (Paris: OECD, February 1986).

72. Antirecessionary government spending pushed the federal deficit (at current prices) from C$9.58 billion in 1981 to C$27.17 billion in 1983. Total national debt owed to foreigners ballooned. Stable at around C$700 to $800 million during the early 1970s, the figure rose to C$1.8 billion in 1976, C$6.4 billion in 1978, C$10.2 billion in 1981, and C$17 billion in 1984. International Monetary Fund, *International Financial Statistics Yearbook*, 1985. In addition, the extent of negative foreign reaction to both the Foreign Investment Review Agency and the National Energy Program of the late 1970s had been seriously misjudged. In 1983 the GATT formally ruled against Canada on a U.S. complaint about FIRA. *New York Times*, July 14, 1983. The provincial premiers provided important additional pressure for policy modification when they unanimously called for increased foreign investment in Canada. *GM*, August 12, 1983.

73. OECD, *Code of Liberalisation of Capital Movements* (Paris: OECD, March 1982). The code dates from 1961. Most member countries acceded early; Australia in 1971 and New Zealand in 1977. Only Canada remained completely outside. (Iceland and Turkey were temporarily exempted in 1962; others maintained certain reservations.) The code calls for progressively abolishing restrictions on capital movements to the extent necessary for effective cooperation, the treating of all nonresident-owned assets in the same way regardless of the date of their formation, and avoidance of exchange restrictions. The code is legally binding on signatories, but the sole sanction for breaches is public censure.

74. According to one American banker, the effort to win official approval now went so far as to permit the inspector general to vet much of the correspondence between the American Schedule B's and Washington. Interviews, Ottawa and Toronto, July 1984.

75. Office of the Inspector General of Banks, "The Status of Foreign Bank Subsidiaries," 1983.

76. Research Staff, House of Commons Standing Committee on Finance, Trade, and Economic Affairs, *Foreign Bank Subsidiaries in Canada*

(Ottawa: Library of Parliament, September 1983). Although it considered a range of problems, the report found that Canada's legislated ceiling was unique within the OECD and the extent of foreign penetration low by international standards, with the notable exception of Japan. It concluded that the ceiling was unnecessary, for the inspector general possessed the discretionary power to limit bank growth, even without an explicit aggregate limit.

77. Canadian Gallup Organization, "Report on Attitudes to Schedule B Foreign Banks," April 1983.

78. Submissions in Standing Committee files dated September 8, 1983, September 1983, and August 23, 1983, respectively. RBC, Canada's largest bank, contended that in view of the "positive contribution" of the foreign banks, all statutory restrictions should be removed, but discretion should still be available to ensure reciprocity-in-fact for Canadian banks overseas. The Executive Committee cited their strengthening of Canada's international image, their job creation, and their acquiescence to continuing discretionary control after abolition of the explicit ceiling. The Trust Companies Association put forward no objection to removal of the ceiling, but pressed for expeditious review of their own now-outmoded legislation perhaps before the foreign banks were satisfied. Initially one might have expected smaller domestic financial institutions to oppose further foreign bank expansion. That opposition did not develop partly because of some deliberate alliance building by foreign banks, but more importantly because most foreign banks were not initially geared to compete for small business and their wholesale activity was perceived by smaller institutions to divert the attentions of larger domestic banks. The Canadian Federation of Independent Business, a loose association of small businesses and one intensively courted by the foreign bank Executive Committee, also informally made known its support for the foreign bank position. Interviews, Toronto and Ottawa, July 1984.

79. The amendment would in fact be the first since 1924. Nevertheless, the position was regarded by outraged foreign bankers as self-serving, especially as later developments unfolded.

80. Congressional and administration officials were in contact with the Standing Committee; and there was no ambiguity in the American position on the Canadian situation, although it was apparently put forward with tact. Interview, Montreal, July 1984.

81. *GM*, September 28, 1983.

82. Interestingly, after an opening statement by the Frenchman, almost all of the committee's questions were directed to the Americans—the presidents of Citibank Canada and Manufacturers Hanover Canada. Parliament of Canada, *Minutes of Proceedings and Evidence of the Standing Committee on Trade, Finance, and Economic Affairs* 153, October 6, 1983.

83. *TS*, November 19, 1983. In *Maclean's*, December 12, 1983, 58, Peter Newman, a leading business commentator, wrote that the Canadian banks were "joyfully participating in their own demise."

84. *GM*, November 1, 1983.

85. Details of the bank's meetings in Washington were never made public. However, around the same time the chairman of the Commons Standing Committee made a trip to the U.S. capital and reported when he

returned that the Harris acquisition and the removal of the 8-percent ceiling "were certainly not considered independently" by the American regulators. "In a very kind and gentle way," he continued, "I was led to believe that action on the foreign banks would not work contrary to the interests of Canadian banks in the United States." *GM*, February 13, 1984.

86. A grand jury investigating drug smuggling ordered the Miami branch of BNS to hand over confidential documents from the bank's Cayman Islands branch. BNS refused on the grounds that compliance would have involved a violation of Cayman law. The U.S. court subsequently imposed stiff financial penalties on the bank. In the ensuing diplomatic struggle, the U.S. State Department and Justice Department took opposite sides.

87. Interviews, Toronto, July 1984.

88. For the first time on foreign bank matters, the president of the CBA was able to express publicly a consensus view in support of the bill. *TS*, April 12, 1984

89. The pending update of the 1979 U.S. Treasury study on commercial bank treatment abroad and Senator Garn's reciprocity amendment to the International Banking Act indicated continuing American interest in the Canadian situation among others. As C-30 was being drafted in the Finance Department, U.S. Treasury officials quietly let their counterparts know that two separate versions of the Canadian chapter of their update had been prepared. If C-30 passed, the more favorable version, praising Canadian progress toward national treatment, would be included. A favorable report remained important to Canadian banks operating in the United States. Interviews, Ottawa, July 1984; Washington, April 1985; *American Banker*, July 5, 1984.

90. The bill was introduced on the eve of the spring meeting of the IMF in Washington and the spring ministerial session of the OECD. On his way to Washington, Lalonde gave a speech in New York that highlighted the bill. It was widely rumored that he was then campaigning (ultimately unsuccessfully) for the job of OECD secretary general.

91. The statement continued, "Unless and until the foreign banks show that they are serious about serving the financial needs of small business . . . , [we] will vigorously oppose any further entries into Canada." New Democratic Party, Press Release, May 9, 1984.

92. "Statement by the Honourable A. J. MacEachen, Deputy Prime Minister and Secretary of State for External Affairs of Canada," OECD Ministerial Meeting, Paris, May 1984. The minister noted, "Canada supports the principle of international capital mobility. Our important role as a capital importer and exporter argues in favour of participation in a Code that discusses policies and norms related to capital movements to promote effective economic cooperation. . . . Our intention to adhere to the Code reflects our desire to participate actively in OECD work in this area." As other governments had done, the federal government acceded with reservations, especially in the area of inward direct investment.

93. Interviews, Ottawa, July 1984; Paris, February 1986. Canada committed itself in general to progressively liberalizing inward and outward capital flows. Subsequent OECD reviews of the Canadian reservation covering inward direct investment aimed at refining and limiting the extent to which it was applicable. An indication of the evolution in Canadian

thinking, despite apparent continued caution, was the acceptance in 1986 of a new paragraph in the code (Annex B) that obliquely codifies a right of establishment insofar as such a right is necessary to foster capital mobility. The relevance of such a right to the banking sector is evident.

94. For example, early in the administration of Prime Minister Brian Mulroney, the Foreign Investment Review Agency was transformed into Investment Canada, an agency whose primary aim was to promote increased foreign investment in Canada.

95. The 1984 near-collapse of the Continental-Illinois Bank in the United States, for instance, convinced regulators that they were right to require parent banks to inject substantial capital into their Canadian subsidiaries before starting up. The point was debatable. Perceptions of the appropriateness of forcing foreign banks into the middle market depended on where one sat. To foreign bankers, it seemed a way to raise their costs and make them less competitive in the corporate market. To Canadian bankers, by preventing foreign banks from competing only for the most desirable business, it seemed an entirely fair way of ensuring that overall a level playing field was maintained. To regulators, it represented an equitable means of fostering balanced (and therefore safer) portfolios in local banks while also meeting political commitments to extend the benefits of increased competition to smaller businesses and consumers.

96. The deposit squeeze following these failures brought two other smaller institutions to the brink of insolvency; the Mercantile, no longer controlled by Citibank, was one of them, and in 1986 it was acquired by the National Bank. The political controversy following the failures revived discussion about complementing the traditional rule-oriented approach to regulation with enhanced discretionary powers in the inspector general's office. The reform and upgrading of that office ensued. See Willard Z. Estey, *Report of the Inquiry into the Collapse of the CCB and Northland Banks* (Ottawa: Minister of Supply and Services, 1986).

CHAPTER 6. *Australia*

1. Not until 1976 did the last descendant of these "imperial" banks, the Australia and New Zealand Bank, formally switch its domicile from Britain to Australia. The first indigenous bank, the Bank of New South Wales, dates from 1817.

2. Recounted in A. F. W. Plumptre, *Central Banking in the Dominions* (Toronto: University of Toronto Press, 1947), 74. Plumptre himself added, "Australian bankers, like others in the Dominions, look unfavorably upon foreign intruders, particularly because they are likely to skim off some of the most profitable business without assuming any responsibility for the general financial well-being of the country."

3. The prewar Associated Banks of Victoria was superseded by the Australian Bankers' Association in 1954. The system of limited competition was bolstered during and after World War II by a wide range of governmental controls over the pricing and terms of deposits and loans.

4. Ministerial discretion, not legislation, underpinned the policy. The first Bank Act (1945) specified no formal licensing requirement and made no reference to foreign banks. The principal mechanism for administration

was quiet treasury discouragement of inquiries, a perfect example of the capacity of a Westminster system of government to formulate and implement policy on the basis of implied cabinet authority, precedent, tacit understandings, and the institutional memory of a permanent civil service.

5. Cited in Kevin Davis and Mervyn Lewis, "Foreign Banks and the Financial System," in *Australian Financial System Inquiry* (AFSI), *Commissioned Studies and Selected Papers* I (Canberra: Australian Government Publishing Service [AGPS], 1982), 523.

6. Department of the Treasury, *Overseas Investment in Australia* (Canberra: AGPS, 1972). In 1971 ministers declared a "special interest" in the banking sector. See Commonwealth of Australia, *Parliamentary Debates, Representatives*, 27th Parliament, 2d sess., October 27, 1971, 2588.

7. As in other countries the precise definition of banking is legally problematic. Even when banking regulations were codified in 1945, 1953, and 1959, lawmakers included no precise definition and instead referred to a schedule of existing banks. See Commonwealth of Australia, *Banking Act, 1959*, pt. I, sec. 5. Banking powers gave listed domestic institutions considerable advantages in terms of access to the payments system, availability of low-cost funding, and an assured revenue stream under a regime of exchange control. The debate over extending these powers to foreign banks was therefore highly substantive; it was not simply about ratifying the market positions built up by foreign banks through representative offices and NBFIs.

8. The bank was the Anglo-Australian Corporation, jointly founded by Morgan Grenfell and Lazard Brothers, both of London. The first American foray came in 1961 when Morgan Guaranty took a minority position in Australian United Corporation.

9. AFSI, *Interim Report* (Canberra: AGPS, May 1980), 94–96.

10. Because of its possession of a banking license, the Bank of Queensland (then under a different name) was the target of similar attempts in 1958. Adverse reaction from Canberra discouraged them.

11. The history of Labor, Australia's oldest party, was profoundly shaped by its reaction to domestic and international financial forces—the "money power." Aside from consistently opposing encroachments by foreign financial institutions, the party has long struggled with the domestic banks over credit allocation, loan pricing, profitability, and related matters. During periods of parliamentary control this hostility led the party to several highly significant actions. In 1911 it created the Commonwealth Bank, later split into Australia's central bank (the Reserve Bank) and the government-owned Commonwealth Banking Corporation; in 1945 it extended wartime controls to curb interest rate increases and provide a direct means of affecting monetary aggregates; two years later the same Labor government nationalized all private domestic banks, an action overturned only by an appeal to the Privy Council in London after an intensely bitter fight; finally, in 1975 the party laid on the private banks part of the blame for its unorthodox dismissal from office following the turbulent Whitlam years.

12. Treasury officials argued that merely having the potential power to impose controls would effectively enable the government to limit NBFI activities. There were also technical difficulties in monitoring specifically

legislated controls on this sector. The existence of Part IV had the perverse effect of actually accelerating the growth of many NBFIs in the short term. Fearing imposition of growth restraints, merchant banks, for example, competed strenuously to increase market penetration levels before limits were assigned.

13. Citibank's loans to IAC peaked at $125 million, the largest financial rescue in Australia's history to that time. Responses to continuing problems raised Citibank's shareholding to 61 percent in early 1977 and 100 percent in September 1977, subject to the condition that it sell off 10 percent to the Australian public within six years and 25 percent within ten.

14. AFSI, *Interim Report,* 1980, 96. Of the thirty-two major finance companies registered in 1979, nineteen had at least one foreign shareholder. Of the thirty-three major merchant banks, also called money-market corporations, thirty had at least one foreign shareholder. (Some were in fact joint ventures between foreign banks and domestic banks, which were also precluded from owning merchant banks outright.)

15. "Overseas Operations of Australian Banks," in Reserve Bank of Australia, *Statistical Bulletin* (February 1981), 417.

16. Fraser's personal stance was difficult to gauge. Exchange crises in 1976 and 1977 and other problems led him to create and chair a new cabinet committee to oversee monetary policy; the same difficulties and increasing disillusionment with treasury advice prompted his greater reliance on private advisers, the Department of the Prime Minister and Cabinet, and other outsiders to the traditional process of financial policy making. An innate caution, however, prevented him from following through with piecemeal changes made in regard to the exchange rate and government financing mechanism. Despite tensions in the relationship, the Treasury appears successfully to have reinforced this caution. Interviews, Canberra, August; Melbourne, September 1985.

17. The AuBA developed over the years into the key political lobbying group for the banking community as a whole. A research directorate within the association facilitated consensus building and had been working on issues related to the effects of government controls since the mid-1960s. Not until 1979 did member banks begin establishing their own complementary lobbying offices in Canberra.

18. ANZ Banking Group Ltd., "Discussion Paper for Member Banks of the Australian Bankers' Association and the Commonwealth Trading Bank on Future Prospects for Trading and Savings Banks," March 1978.

19. Howard was also under pressure to respond to the 1978 collapse of the Bank of Adelaide by proclaiming controls over NBFIs, something he was loath to do because of a conviction that their contribution to Australia on balance was positive.

20. The chairman of a major real estate developer and of a merchant bank, Keith Campbell, headed the committee. Members included a senior insurance executive, a private financial adviser, the chairman of a small public bank, an official of the Reserve Bank, and, as secretary, an official from the Treasury.

21. Treasurer, Press Release, No. 6, Canberra, January 18, 1979, 1. The terms of reference were drafted by officials in the Department of the Prime Minister and Cabinet and the treasurer's office. The Treasury reasserted

itself when the review appeared inevitable and provided the committee with a secretariat and staff.

22. Ibid., 2.

23. In addition to presenting formal submissions to the committee, the banks provided much supporting information. Committee staffers came to rely heavily on the banks for technical advice.

24. Typically a draft policy position would be hammered out by such a special committee, or by the AuBA research directorate itself, and would then be forwarded to the managing directors of the member banks for approval. When no consensus existed, the AuBA would take no official position.

25. Australian Bankers' Association, *Submission to the Committee of Inquiry into the Australian Financial System,* 1979, para. 1.0.21. Conditional entry implied a limited number of new entrants gradually introduced to the market and subject to certain operating requirements to ensure the absence of cost advantages.

26. Postwar exchange control arrangements stifled the development of a forward exchange market, where Australian dollars could be purchased or sold for future delivery. A fixed exchange rate was meant to obviate the need for such transactions. With international instability in the 1970s came an increased demand for facilities to hedge foreign claims. Innovative merchant banks, prohibited from directly trading in foreign exchange, began to meet this demand informally in the mid-1970s by matching customers with offsetting currency requirements. In January 1979 the Commonwealth government acceded to the creation of a private currency futures market, and in June 1979 the domestic banks received permission to compete in this activity. Subsequently, merchant bankers stepped up pressure for full foreign exchange trading licenses, but the domestic banks insisted that such operations should only be undertaken by institutions recognized as banks. Historically the banks depended on foreign exchange profits to subsidize less profitable operations in their extensive branch networks.

27. Australia and New Zealand Banking Group Limited, *Submission to the Inquiry into the Australian Financial System,* July 1979, paras. 4.36–4.39. In passing, ANZ stated that the issue of "reciprocal entry rights for Australian banks into overseas markets has to a large extent been overstated."

28. Bank of New South Wales, *Submission to the Committee of Inquiry into the Financial System,* June 30, 1979, 4. Perhaps anticipating later developments, the bank added, "It should be accepted at the outset that, whatever the safeguards imposed, free access to foreign banks could impose severe structural adjustment upon the smaller Australian banks. More than one such bank may be compelled to merge to remain viable against major foreign competitors."

29. Commonwealth Banking Corporation, *Submission to the Inquiry into the Australian Financial System,* August 1979, 7.

30. Commercial Banking Company of Sydney, *Submission to the Australian Financial System Inquiry,* 1979, 9. The contradiction reflected dissension within the bank itself.

31. AFSI, *Transcript of Proceedings,* Sydney, October 17, 1979, 942–45.

32. Ibid., October 18, 1979, 1114. Martin's "savage dogs" subsequently entered the political vocabulary. A few years later the local representative of the Bank of Tokyo claimed that the entry of his bank represented a case not of allowing in a savage dog but of "Lassie come home." *The Age,* September 12, 1984. The perception of foreign bank aggressiveness was also captured in a joke that circulated widely at the time. "An Australian banker tells of a New York banker surfing at Bondi Beach when, as occasionally happens, several sharks approached him. 'It was terrible,' the Australian reported, 'the New York banker ate two of the sharks and the third only narrowly escaped.'" *AFR*, November 3, 1980.

33. AuBA, *Supplementary Submissions to the Australian Financial System Inquiry,* April 1981, A17, A53, A80–86. The writers did not, however, stress the fact that on an aggregate basis the domestic banks' market share had declined only from 44.5 percent in 1970 to 44.2 percent in 1978 (A16).

34. In addition to new foreign entrants with retail banking aspirations, the principal targets here were such domestic rivals as building societies. Although often couched in terms of prudential stability, technological efficiency, and past investments, the banks' concerns were apparently with preserving privileged access to the relatively high level of interest-free deposits associated with the clearing system. Estimates put these deposits at around 40 percent of the total deposits of trading banks in 1980 and 30 percent in 1983. See Westpac Banking Corporation, *Submission to the Group Established to Report on the Structure of the Australian Financial System,* August 1983, 25.

35. The possibility of additional mergers had actually been mooted since 1969 when the ANZ merged with the ES&A Bank. The government briefly considered the possibility of allowing a foreign takeover of the Bank of Adelaide, but this plan was probably aimed at heightening pressure on ANZ.

36. U.S. Department of the Treasury, *Report to Congress on Foreign Government Treatment of U.S. Commercial Banking Organizations* (Washington, D.C.: Department of the Treasury, September 17, 1979), 35–37. Campbell staffers were aware of the report, as were officials within the Australian Treasury. In neither quarter did it generate much concern, partly because it noted that a review of the situation was underway and partly because it made no direct threats. The Australians were also well aware that any potential American demands on this score would be tempered by other overriding considerations within the American government. U.S. Treasury concerns were typically submerged in a broader strategic relationship managed especially by the State Department and Defense Department.

37. See, for example, AFSI, *Transcript of Proceedings,* Sydney, November 8, 1979, 1705–32. Some of the banks also indicated a willingness to develop retail branch networks, but as the domestic banks feared, most expressed a desire to concentrate on wholesale business, which did not entail expensive establishment costs and local infrastructure.

38. AMBA, *Submission to the Campbell Committee of Inquiry into the Australian Financial System,* 1979; *Second Submission to the Campbell Committee,* March 1980.

39. Australian Bank Employees' Union and Commonwealth Bank Offi-cers' Association, *Submission to the Australian Financial System Inquiry*, 1979; AFSI, *Transcript of Proceedings*, Melbourne, October 1, 1979. The bank unions were two of Australia's largest labor groups. The ABEU represented seventy-eight thousand members from the private banks, and the CBOA, thirty-one thousand in the Commonwealth Bank.

40. As matters subsequently developed — the two largest insurers entered the banking markets through joint ventures with foreign banks — it would seem that the insurance companies were already concluding that their best chance to diversify would come as a result of foreign entry. It is significant that a senior executive of the second largest insurer was a member of the Campbell Committee.

41. The submissions were from the two mining companies CSR and CRA. These two giants enjoyed close relationships directly with the head offices of major foreign banks; indeed, CRA's lead banker was an American institution. In any event, taxation and exchange rates constituted far more important issues for the companies.

42. Davis and Lewis, "Foreign Banks and the Financial System."

43. Such concerns were surprisingly never even expressed to a delegation from the committee that visited several Western governments and international organizations during 1980 to explore prudential and supervisory issues. Interviews, Sydney and Canberra, August 1985.

44. AFSI, *Final Report* (Canberra: AGPS 1981), 439–44.

45. In the context of negotiations over a treaty on closer economic relations, New Zealand's prime minister, for one, increased the pressure for greater reciprocal financial openness. Australian banks already dominated New Zealand, and beginning in 1979, Prime Minister Muldoon called for the licensing of the National Bank of New Zealand in Australia. In 1981 he was quoted as saying, "I am knocking back foreign banks which want to start up in New Zealand, including Citibank recently, but when I say no, I'm protecting the Wales, and the Commercial and the ANZ as well as the Bank of New Zealand. On that basis, we feel we should fairly be allowed access to Australia." *AFR*, February 2, 1981.

46. This view further divided them from the National Farmers' Federation (NFF), which continued to favor financial liberalization. NFF leaders actually had already begun meeting with foreign banks to explore mutual interests.

47. In supplementary correspondence with the committee, the Treasury contended that foreign bank entry would "increase the potential for destabilizing capital flows" and could "add significantly to the difficulty of administering the exchange rate and exchange control system in a manner consistent with the intent and sovereignty of domestic monetary policy." *AFR*, June 10, 1981.

48. During 1980 a range of administrative amendments eased restrictions on inward and outward capital flows, raised the maximum permissible shareholding of domestic banks in NBFIs (to 60 percent), reduced maturity controls on bank certificates of deposit (to a minimum of thirty days), introduced incremental changes in the marketing of government debt, and, most significantly, completely removed interest rate ceilings on bank deposits. It appears that many cabinet members were not aware of the implications of these changes, although Howard and his

advisers certainly were. Deregulating one side of the banks' balance sheets, for example, would make it more difficult to maintain controls on the other side.

49. *Parliamentary Hansard, Representatives,* November 17, 1981.

50. The working party included two proderegulatory senior advisers to the cabinet. The report itself spawned a minor industry in academic and financial circles. Symposia, analytical papers, and books abounded and undoubtedly helped sustain a broader political interest in a seemingly arcane subject.

51. For instance, in an effort to move toward the decontrol of interest rates on loans, the treasurer engaged in intensive bargaining with the domestic banks. In March he announced a resulting package of measures, which slightly relaxed maturity and pricing controls and provided tax concessions for mortgage holders in exchange for bank commitments to increase housing loans. (Banks could now sell certificates of deposit with a minimum maturity of fourteen days, a serious threat to the funding bases of merchant banks.) In June, the treasurer also announced changes in government deficit financing. A price-sensitive tender system now provided a basis for replacement of direct monetary controls on the banks.

52. Difficulties in the United States centered on Chicago, where in 1981 the ANZ opened a limited branch under federal authority in apparent contravention of reciprocity provisions in Illinois state law. The other trading banks followed in 1982 and 1983, but not before Illinois had taken ANZ to court in an effort to force closure of its branch. Protracted litigation ensued. The traditional American battle over federal and state prerogatives lay at the core of the dispute, and eventually the federal government won. Its policy of extending national treatment to foreign banks regardless of reciprocity stood, but the Australian banks (who argued that U.S. banks enjoyed de facto reciprocity in Australia) came to realize the delicacy of their position.

53. Many banks were also complementing low-key lobbying in Canberra with efforts to build connections with nontraditional clients (for example, in the rural sector) and potential domestic partners in the hope that this would increase chances for a license.

54. *SMH,* October 12, 1982. The vice-chairman evidently made the same demand, in the same tone, directly to the prime minister in a meeting that followed his public speech.

55. The treasury proposal attempted to limit foreign entry by insisting on 50-percent local equity in any new banks. The proposal would have had the double effect of constraining their relative size and their numbers because few Australian companies would be willing or able to make such substantial equity commitments. Another challenge faced by Howard was the prime minister's ambivalence on the issue. Some who worked with him felt that he had reconciled himself to the entry of five or six foreign banks; others discerned a fundamental opposition. With an election call in the offing, Fraser in fact had doubts about the reaction of the electorate to the issue. Interviews, Sydney, Canberra, and Melbourne, August–September 1985.

56. Australian Labor Party, *Platform, Constitution, and Rules,* as approved at the 35th National Conference, Canberra, 1982, 40.

57. Ibid., 44. Labor parliamentarians are not technically bound by the platform, as they are by formal decisions of the parliamentary caucus. But by tradition the platform is taken quite seriously and delegates are expected to hold elected officials accountable. The time between national conferences is short, and parliamentarians are therefore extremely reluctant to flout sensitive planks, although they sometimes find ways to stretch interpretations.

58. At most, the lobbying generally confirmed Howard in his course. One adviser to the treasurer commented at the time that any decisions on foreign entry could be taken only after extensive public justification, and lobbying would win no one a license. *AFR*, January 21, 1983.

59. The turnaround in popularity was also reflected in public opinion polls. The coalition's approval rating recovered from its nadir of 41 percent in November to 43 percent in mid-December and 44 percent in mid-January, while the ALP dropped from 50 percent to 48 percent. At the same time, Fraser's personal popularity recovered from an all-time low of 33 percent to 39 percent in January. *Bulletin*, January 28, 1983.

60. Treasurer, Press Release, No. 3, Canberra, January 13, 1983.

61. *AFR*, January 18, 20, 21, 1983.

62. A subsidiary element in Howard's own calculations related to his plans to attend a meeting of the Interim Committee of the IMF in Washington late in January and subsequently to meet with Japanese Prime Minister Nakasone in Tokyo. The foreign bank issue had previously come up in such meetings, and the treasurer wanted good news to announce to the international community. *AFR*, January 19, 1983.

63. A spokesman for the Australian Democrats gave some indication of his party's view when he called foreign bank entry a "bargain basement sale of Australia's future [to] rapacious and irresponsible juggernauts." *AFR*, January 19, 1983.

64. On January 26 Howard stated that contrary to initial expectations, the Bank (Shareholdings) Act did not require amendment and permission to allow foreign banks to hold more than 10 percent of a new bank could be granted without new legislative authority. Treasurer, Press Release, No. 15, January 26, 1983.

65. *AFR*, February 10, 1983.

66. In November 1982 ABEU leaders met with Howard to press their case against the foreign banks. Core arguments focused on the loss of jobs from branch closure in a heightened competitive environment and from the introduction of new technology, a reputed antiunion attitude in several large multinational banks, and antipathy to objectionable operating practices by the same banks. (Here Citibank became the principal symbol.)

67. ABEU, Press Releases, January 14, March 1, 1983. Full page advertisements ran in the major newspapers under the headline "They've sold the farm — now they're selling the mortgage." *AFR*, March 4, 1983.

68. In a parliamentary debate much later, Keating claimed that he and Hawke had argued in favor of foreign entry within the party caucus as early as the time of publication of the Campbell Report. *Parliamentary Hansard, Representatives*, May 7, 1985, 1764.

69. Very early on in the new administration, the treasurer told a stunned treasury official, who had strongly supported the Campbell recommendations and was now in despair, that his party would implement

the recommendations much more decisively and quickly than the former Liberal government. The same message filtered through to the banking community. Interviews, Sydney and Canberra, August 1985.

70. Treasurer, Press Releases, Nos. 25 and 33, May 29, June 2, 1983. These objectives explicitly included an adequate and reasonably priced supply of finance for housing, rural, and small business sectors, and an efficient and stable financial system. A treasury official, a Reserve Bank official, and an academic were also appointed to the committee.

71. The complex deal involved the rationalization of shareholdings in several merchant banks, with Citibank eventually ending up completely owning a vehicle that it planned to build into a major institution. Notwithstanding the fact that the proposed vehicle, Grindlays Australia, was already owned outright by foreigners, the treasurer, on the strong advice of the Treasury, decided that Citibank's expansion plans represented a violation of the spirit of existing restrictions on foreign banking. After prolonged negotiations and pressure from purely domestic interests who were tangled in the affair, the government finally compromised and allowed Citibank to establish a new wholly owned merchant bank with the proviso that it sell down to a 50-percent share within six years.

72. ABEU, Press Release, December 21, 1983. By this time, much of the union's attention had clearly become focused on Citibank. Prominently circulated by the union was International Federation of Commercial, Clerical, Professional, and Technical Employees (FIET), *An International Trade Union Report on Citibank* (n.p., 1983), which alleged poor management practices and antiunion activity in the bank's global operations.

73. AuBA, *Submission to the Group Reporting on the Structure of the Australian Banking System*, August 1983. The Commonwealth was now formally a member of the AuBA.

74. Westpac Banking Corporation, *Submission to the Group Established to Report on the Structure of the Australian Financial System*, August 1983. After earlier opposing the Liberals' foreign bank plan, early in 1983 the head of Westpac called on the new Labor government to continue with deregulation, including some foreign bank entry. Within Westpac an aggressive new strategy involving rapid international expansion was being implemented, and the concerns of the international division were finally coming to the fore. Admitting only a few foreign banks to Australia appeared to limit the opportunities for Australian banks, especially in Japan because of Japan's assumed preference for one-for-one reciprocity in such cases. Also specifically mentioned as a special case for government assistance was New Zealand, where all new Australian investment proposals had recently been frozen by Prime Minister Muldoon until this and related investment issues had been resolved. Muldoon later even threatened to expel Westpac and ANZ over the issue.

75. (Martin Group), *Australian Financial System, Report of the Review Group* (Canberra: AGPS, 1984), ch. 5.

76. Between 1978 and 1983, merchant banks as a group grew by an average of 26 percent per year, the trading banks by 16 percent. During the same period, foreign ownership of aggregate Australian financial assets rose from 14 percent to 16 percent. By June 1983, 66 percent of the merchant banking sector was foreign owned. Ibid., 10–12.

77. The AMBA, as well as the trading banks, had been pushing strongly for this.

78. The AuBA responded with less enthusiasm. It agreed that four to six banks might eventually be appropriate but again requested 100-percent shareholdings, a reflection of increasing concerns about reciprocal treatment overseas as well as continued concern about the entry of domestic insurance companies. During the next year the reciprocity issue would temper Westpac's enthusiasm for the report as its foreign expansion plans proceeded.

79. Andrew Theophanous, *The Martin Report: Implications for the Economy and ALP Policy,* (n.p., March 1, 1984).

80. Having lost a series of court rulings to the U.S. comptroller and therefore unable to force closure of the Australian bank offices in Chicago, Illinois began assessing a special fine in lieu of effective reciprocity. The affected banks subsequently went back to court to challenge the constitutionality of the levies.

81. During that same period another Citibank vice-chairman journeyed to Canberra to request a banking license without equity restrictions, although he did indicate a new degree of flexibility on the subject. One month earlier, Senator Garn of the Banking Committee had come to Australia to press the U.S. case for increased openness. The visit was intentionally low-key (and involved other countries), but his initially tough stance was apparently softened somewhat by a firsthand introduction to the true intent of the Australian government and to the political realities facing it. Interviews, Canberra, August 1985.

82. Treasurer, Press Release, No. 23, February 22, 1984.

83. The decisions were nicely balanced from a political point of view, and the foreign exchange decision was evidently delayed to coincide with deposit deregulation. Complete deposit freedom for the domestic banks would severely damage the relative funding position of merchant banks. Foreign exchange licenses might help compensate. The merchant banks could hardly complain, for they had long been seeking foreign exchange licenses, but many were now skeptical about the profitability of this activity; in addition, some were reluctant to lose what they saw as a lever to obtaining full banking licenses.

84. Formal opposition, instead of quiet support, reflected a delicate balancing act within the ACTU. ACTU was closely associated with the present government (Hawke had formerly headed the organization) and wanted to maintain its influence. On the other hand, it was gradually shifting its base from blue-collar to white-collar unions and had no desire to offend the ABEU. Also, within the ACTU, several state conferences, notably Queensland and Victoria, were pushing vigorously to keep foreign banks out.

85. Participants in the discussions claimed that the banking issues were handled on their own and not tied to deals on any other contentious subjects to be addressed by the conference. Interviews, Sydney and Canberra, August 1985.

86. Australian Labor Party, *Minutes of the 36th Biennial National Conference,* Canberra, July 9, 1984, 142–86. The obvious shallowness of most of the speeches reflected the difficulty of defining interests and costs clearly in such an arcane subject area once the attempt was made to go

beyond symbolism. The technical complexity of banking issues evidently undercut the effort of Left leaders to rally troops more emotionally engaged by other issues. This also helps explain why the issue slipped quickly from the Left's agenda after the conference ended.

87. The premier of New South Wales, who was serving as conference chairman, supported this view. It is interesting to note how a heightened rivalry between the state premiers in attracting the jobs and prestige associated with new foreign bank head offices completely overwhelmed concerns on their part to protect the positions of their own state-owned banks. The reciprocity issue also surfaced briefly in the debates, in particular in a speech by the prime minister.

88. Australian Labor Party, *Platform, Constitution and Rules as Approved by the 36th National Conference,* Canberra, 1984, ch. 7.

89. The ABEU was now in a difficult position. Having not been formally affiliated with the ALP and having annoyed the government with its strident opposition, it lacked leverage to affect the terms of entry. Its credibility with the government was also hurt when an embarrassing account of a meeting between its leaders and the treasurer was leaked to the press and discussed in Parliament. *Parliamentary Hansard, Representatives,* October 8, 1984, 1785–87, 1811–12. Furthermore, soon after the conference several potential new entrants initiated talks with a rival and more conservative union, the Federated Clerks.

90. The most prominent example of this expansion was ANZ's acquisition of Grindlay's Bank of the United Kingdom. ANZ apparently first considered bidding for an American bank but ultimately decided to acquire the global base of Grindlay's, which, significantly, included a large branch in Japan.

91. The secretary's differences with the government went much deeper than the foreign bank question. More important disputes involved a perceived politicization of the civil service and the overall trajectory of economic policy.

92. Treasurer, Press Release, No. 142, September 10, 1984.

93. The ALP Left scarcely reacted to the announcement. Having been defeated in conference, its more vocal leaders took refuge in the need to maintain party unity. Ironically, it was now clear that the domestic banks had been the beneficiaries of their former intransigence, which effectively granted them a three-year reprieve from direct foreign competition.

94. In Washington, Keating also announced policy changes to enable foreign stockbrokers to raise their stakes in Australian brokerage houses from 15 to 50 percent.

95. In what would turn out to be a tactical maneuver apparently to stimulate strong applications, which would improve his bargaining position in cabinet, the treasurer had let the banks know that only six to eight licenses were likely. Interviews, Washington, October 1984; Canberra, August 1985.

96. The first moves to establish a foreign bankers association came from within this group. Originators focused initially on social matters and the sharing of market intelligence but hoped to broaden their scope eventually to encompass political lobbying on issues of common concern. Larger banks stayed away partly to avoid the appearance of collusion, partly because they preferred their own direct channels to government, and partly to avoid

possible labor law consequences if the organization came to be viewed as a bargaining agent for all foreign banks. For them, the bank licensing process ensured that competitive pressures still outweighed any perceived need to collaborate.

97. Only eleven of the forty-two included any provision for local equity. Some banks provided alternative applications, a preferred one at 100 percent and one with a provision for local equity.

98. Treasurer, Press Release, No. 20, February 27, 1985. The treasurer also noted that although "some Australians may not have local access to the new banks at the outset . . ., all Australians will benefit from the better services and innovation stimulated by the new banking competition."

99. Three promised some local equity in the future. To enable high initial shareholdings, the government decided to amend the Bank (Shareholdings) Act. South Australia and Western Australia succeeded in attracting one bank each, Victoria attracted four, and the balance went to New South Wales. In the final decision-making process, the interventions of the state premiers were apparent. An additional license went to the Bank of China following separate negotiations dating back to February 1984.

100. In January 1985 officials in the treasurer's office quietly let it be known that up to twenty new entrants was a possibility. The absence of opposition convinced them of the feasibility of exceeding previous expectations. Keating was later asked if he had perhaps interpreted his conference mandate too liberally or if he had in fact tricked the delegates. He responded, "One is not bound to be frank always." *AFR*, February 28, 1985.

101. Formal discussions took place with Hong Kong over the entry of Hongkong and Shanghai Bank. The new government in New Zealand of Prime Minister Lange had dropped its predecessor's investment sanctions but continued to push for the entry of the National Bank. Even though that bank was now owned by Lloyds Bank of the United Kingdom, it was still a nationally managed and staffed institution. Somewhat surprisingly, similar considerations did not lead to the entry of a Swiss or South Korean bank. Although the Swiss were evidently next on the list, the government did not react favorably to very blunt pressure exerted just prior to the final decision. The Swiss thought they had an undoubted claim to a license in view of the existence of an ANZ/Grindlay's operation in Switzerland. To the chagrin of Australian bankers, South Korean banks, apparently deterred by the small number of entrants initially envisaged, did not apply.

102. For example, the decision to give in to Citibank's demand for a full license without local equity may be attributed to several factors. The bank's own diplomacy had noticeably moderated during the run-up to the final decision; its application was extensively detailed and well received; its existing involvement in both wholesale and retail markets (A\$4 billion in assets, thirteen hundred staff — by far the largest foreign NBFI operation) promised an effective competitive challenge for the domestic banks in a very short period of time. In addition, government officials argued that in the absence of compelling reasons it would have been embarrassing to exclude Citibank from a list that comprised its major U.S. rivals. There is no evidence to suggest that any overt pressure from the American government entered into the decision.

103. Aside from their inability directly to participate in the domestic payments system and a marginal funding disadvantage, the new merchant banks were more than just reinforced representative offices. Their upgraded presence represented a basic policy shift and a deliberate stimulus to the institutional integration of domestic and international financial markets.

104. ABEU, Media Release, February 28, 1985. An attempt by some in the membership to call a protest strike was quickly scotched by the leadership. The focus had now shifted to maximizing any potential benefits of foreign entry for the union and its members.

105. Little credence was given to the domestic bank reaction, which was in any case muted. During fiscal 1984, the total assets of the major trading banks rose by 17 percent (compared to 10 percent the previous year) while net earnings shot up by 43 percent. During that same year, the net earnings of merchant banks grew by only 1 percent and overall returns fell. Peat Marwick, *1985 Survey of Financial Institutions* (Sydney: Peat Marwick, March 15, 1985). As their own operations expanded across geographical (and functional) borders, the trading banks would later complain that the government should have let in more banks from countries of interest to themselves.

106. Some of the new entrants, but not all, considered the bank overly cautious, particularly in its insistence that during start-up the new banks maintain a higher capital ratio (6.5 percent) than the domestic banks (5 percent but rising under Reserve Bank pressure). According to the governor, such prudential caution was decidedly "not designed to thwart competitive aspirations." *AFR*, July 19, 1985.

107. A broad reservation concerning inward direct investment remained. The OECD secretariat and key trading partners subsequently argued for limiting the reservation since actual Australian policies were now markedly less restrictive. Interview, Paris, February 1986.

108. See Government of Australia, "Australia's Position on the New Round of Trade Negotiations," submitted to GATT, August 1985.

CHAPTER 7. *Converging Policies and Developing Norms*

1. Charles P. Kindleberger, *A Financial History of Western Europe* (London: George Allen & Unwin, 1984), 262.

2. *Foreign* here refers both to banks from another member state and to banks from nonmember states.

3. See Paolo Clarotti, "Progress and Future Development of Establishment and Services in the EC in Relation to Banking," *Journal of Common Market Studies* 22 (March 1984), 199–226.

4. "Council Directive (73/183/EEC) of June 28, 1973," *Official Journal of the European Communities* (hereafter *OJEC*) 16 (July 16, 1973), 1–5. A directive, as opposed to a regulation, which immediately supersedes national laws, is technically binding as to policy result but leaves the amendment and coordination of specific national legislation to member states themselves. In this case, the directive explicitly noted specific national restrictions on banking to be abolished. Until the 1986 amendments to community rule making, directives had to be unanimously adopted by the

Council of Ministers. After the changes, directives affecting policy areas such as banking may be adopted after a majority vote.

5. Certain countries, notably Britain, effectively extended such rights to branches, but member countries were technically left free to insist on reciprocity before allowing branch establishment. There has been a movement since 1973 to abolish such a requirement. For banks from relatively open countries, it poses no problem. Moreover, although the expense involved may be higher, banks from any country not providing reciprocity can still establish in subsidiary form. German regulators claim that their traditional maintenance of such a requirement was largely symbolic and designed to encourage openness in countries less open than Germany, especially developing nations. Interviews, Frankfurt and Bonn, February 1986.

6. *European Report* 122 (March 16, 1974), 1–2.

7. *European Report* 170 (September 21, 1974), 5. The reasons for the slowness of European banks in this regard are much debated. If tacit barriers constituted major problems, European bankers did not seriously avail themselves of remedies potentially available through the European Community judicial system. Strategic design, banking traditions, and cautious assessments of competitive conditions abroad should not be discounted. Perhaps more important were persistent impediments to the free flow of capital throughout the community.

8. "First Council Directive (77/780/EEC) of 12 December 1977 on the Coordination of Laws, Regulations, and Administrative Practices Relating to the Taking up and Pursuit of the Business of Credit Institutions," *OJEC* 30 (December 17, 1977).

9. Interview, Brussels, February 1986.

10. "Council Directive (83/350/EEC) on the Supervision of Credit Institutions on a Consolidated Basis," *OJEC* L193 (July 18, 1983).

11. For varying political and technical reasons, Belgium, Italy, and Greece (after 1981) had difficulty in so doing but by and large soon brought their regulatory practice into conformity. Italy, Ireland, France, Denmark, and later Greece took advantage of an escape clause in the directive that permitted retention of economic need criteria for decisions on new entries for maximum periods of twelve years. See Commission of the European Communities, "Commission Report (77/780/EEC) to the Council," May 9, 1984.

12. In the mid-1980s, commission strategies shifted once again, this time from stimulating gradual alignment to fostering mutual recognition of idiosyncratic national regulatory policies. A concept borrowed from the traded goods sector, where it was seen as a way of overcoming subtle trade barriers put up by unique national certification standards, it implied that a bank authorized to engage in certain activities in its home country would automatically be permitted to engage in the same activities in host countries, regardless of the host's own regulatory conventions. The benefit was that mutual recognition obviated the arduous task of fully harmonizing national laws and practices. Consistent with such an ideal was the proposal that the EEC itself eventually charter banks to operate directly across all internal frontiers. See Commission of the European Communities, "Completing the Internal Market," White Paper (COM[85]310), June 28–29, 1985.

13. Prior to joining the community, Spain and Portugal had not kept pace with community nations in this regard, but both made significant moves toward openness in the early 1980s. Within the community as a whole, a particularly sticky problem remained in housing finance. Compared to the rest of the world, however, the community remained far ahead in even attempting to extend openness to a traditionally highly localized part of the banking industry.

14. In Britain, to cite the most obvious example, Japanese banks had captured by the middle of the 1980s 23 percent of the total banking assets booked in the country, a proportion just surpassing U.S. banks as a group and fractionally falling short of the share controlled by the British clearing banks. *FT,* February 12, 1986.

15. In London the number of jobs directly associated with the Euromarkets grew from nine thousand in 1968 to over thirty-eight thousand fifteen years later. *EU* (September 1983), 140–45.

16. Pessimistic assessments of potential profitability in a more competitive Swedish market discouraged applications. In the end, only fourteen foreign banks requested licenses (five French, three Norwegian, three Finnish, two American, and one Dutch). *BL* (December 1985).

17. Webster's *Third International Dictionary* defines bellwether as "one that takes the lead or initiative." The word is derived from the Middle English term for the leading sheep of a flock around whose neck a bell was hung. The word seems particularly appropriate in the field of banking, where sheeplike behavior is frequently observed.

18. The explicit priority given to reciprocity in the Canadian position partly contradicted the preference of the United States and others to give priority to the norm of nondiscrimination. Despite the fear that reciprocity would turn into a tool for protectionism, however, the Canadian case well illustrates the force of reciprocity in expanding openness when it is flexibly interpreted and applied within systems traditionally closed.

19. In "International Debt: The Behavior of Banks in a Politicized Environment," *International Organization* 39, 3 (1985), 454, Philip Wellons makes such an argument and cites the failure of Chase Manhattan to set up a retail network in Germany during the early 1980s as evidence of subtle protectionism administered by the major German banks themselves. Other banks, including Citibank and several Japanese banks in industrialized areas of Germany, have, however, faced the same problems with somewhat more success. More generally, the evidence discussed in the present study cautions against using a policy label that obscures a general trend toward openness and makes remaining differences in actual national policies more difficult to assess.

20. Lon L. Fuller "Human Interaction and the Law," *The American Journal of Jurisprudence* 14 (1969), 24.

21. Lon L. Fuller, *Anatomy of Law* (Harmondsworth: Penguin, 1971), 105. Fuller continued with an enlightening simile, "Customary law is like a play improvised from the beginning; if in the end it achieves unity and coherence, these qualities are not imposed on it by any single deliberate decision, but emerge from the interplay of the parts as they are acted out."

22. See, for example, John L. Comaroff and Simon Roberts, *Rules and Processes* (Chicago: University of Chicago Press, 1981). Comparable approaches have been advanced in the field of international relations. See

Robert Axelrod and Robert O. Keohane, "Achieving Cooperation under Anarchy: Strategies and Institutions," *World Politics* 38 (October 1985).

23. In this context, the reciprocity involved comes close to what Robert Keohane calls "diffuse reciprocity," where state interaction is premised not on a strict tit-for-tat foundation (as in situations of specific reciprocity), but on a basis of shared interests adequate to ensure a rough equivalence of values. Norms underpinning such interaction may, in Keohane's convincing view, constitute standards of behavior regarded simply as legitimate by the interacting parties and do not necessarily embody ethical principles that override self-interest. See "Reciprocity in International Relations," *International Organization* 40, 1 (1986), 21. In banking circles, national treatment, equivalent access, and reciprocity are sometimes seen as exclusive concepts. In reality, all three are necessarily intertwined.

24. Within the OECD, national treatment tends to be more liberal than alternatives. Red tape is eliminated; artificial advantages for certain classes of institutions are reduced, thereby increasing efficiency in markets; and effective reciprocation is easier to gauge. All of this, of course, depends upon a reasonable level of confidence that foreign governments will respond in an acceptable manner and that foreign markets hold out roughly equivalent opportunities for domestic institutions. These conditions are generally met within the advanced industrial world, and national treatment policies therefore tend to liberalize markets. Problems begin, however, when national treatment is applied in countries where the domestic market is highly controlled, as in some developing nations. In these cases, national treatment may actually restrict opportunities for foreign institutions, whereas strict reciprocity would tend to open the more restricted market. Charles Lipson describes an example of this in *Standing Guard: Protecting Foreign Capital in the Nineteenth and Twentieth Centuries* (Berkeley and Los Angeles: University of California Press, 1985), 260–62.

25. To this extent, such a standard also rests on what Jock Finlayson and Mark Zacher, in their analysis of the GATT regime, have termed a "liberalization" norm. See "The GATT and the Regulation of Trade Barriers: Regime Dynamics and Functions," in Stephen D. Kasner, ed., *International Regimes* (Ithaca: Cornell University Press, 1983), 282.

26. See Palitha T. B. Kohona, *The Regulation of International Economic Relations through Law* (Dordrecht, Netherlands: Nijhoff, 1985).

27. See Robert R. Wilson, *United States Commercial Treaties and International Law* (New Orleans: Hauser Printing, 1960). Because FCN-style treaties are unattractive to many developing countries, the United States began in the early 1980s to negotiate comparable bilateral investment treaties.

28. On broader trade issues, analysts have noted a similar movement in recent years. In 1982, Charles Lipson, for example, noted a bifurcation in the global trading order. A liberal core retained scope for nondiscrimination internally even as it sought to manage external relations with newly industrializing states on a different basis. See "The Transformation of Trade: The Sources and Effects of Regime Change," *International Organization* 36 (Spring 1982); Stephen D. Krasner, *Structural Conflict: The Third World against Global Liberalism* (Berkeley: University of California Press, 1985); and Miles Kahler, "European Protectionism in Theory and Practice," *World Politics* 37 (1985).

# Selected Bibliography

On conceptual and methodological matters raised in the preface, see Brian Barry, *Sociologists, Economists, and Democracy* (Chicago: University of Chicago Press, 1978); Alexander L. George, "Case Studies and Theory Development," in Paul Gordon Lauren, ed. *Diplomacy* (New York: Free Press, 1979); Peter Gourevitch, *Politics in Hard Times* (Ithaca: Cornell University Press, 1986); Philip Jessup, *Transnational Law* (New Haven: Yale University Press, 1956); Lon L. Fuller, *Anatomy of Law* (Harmondsworth: Penguin, 1971); Sally Falk Moore, *Law as Process* (London: Routledge & Kegan Paul, 1978); and Friedrich Kratochwil and John Gerard Ruggie, "International Organization: A State of the Art on an Art of the State," *International Organization* 40 (Autumn 1986).

On the broader environment in which foreign bank regulation evolves, see Philip A. Wellons, *Passing the Buck: Banks, Governments, and Third World Debt* (Boston: Harvard Business School Press, 1987); J. Andrew Spindler, *The Politics of International Credit* (Washington, D.C.: Brookings, 1984); R. M. Pecchioli, *The Internationalization of Banking* (Paris: OECD, 1983); OECD, Committee on Financial Markets, *Trends in Banking in OECD Countries* (Paris: OECD, 1985); Richard Dale, *The Regulation of Banking* (Cambridge: Woodhead-Faulkner, 1984); Janet Kelly, *Bankers and Borders* (Cambridge, Mass.: Ballinger, 1976); Jonathan David Aronson, *Money and Power: Banks and the World Monetary System* (Beverly Hills: Sage, 1977); A.E. Safarian, *Governments and Multinationals: Policies in the Developed Countries* (Washington, D.C.: British North America Committee, 1981); Jonathan David Aronson and Peter F. Cowhey, *Trade in Services: A Case for Open Markets* (Washington, D.C.: American Enterprise Institute, 1984); Brigid Gavin, "A GATT for International Banking?" *Journal of World Trade Law* 19 (March–April 1985); and Ingo Walter, *Barriers to Trade in Banking and Financial Services* (London: Trade Policy Research Centre, 1985). For associated economic analysis, see Richard N. Cooper, *Economic Mobility and National Economic Policy* (Stockholm: Almqvist & Wiksell International, 1973); Gunter Dufey and Ian H. Giddy, *The International Money Market* (Englewood Cliffs, N.J.: Prentice-Hall, 1978); Robert Z. Aliber, "The Integration of the Offshore and Domestic Banking System," *Journal of Monetary Economics* 6 (1980); Adrian Tschoegl, *The Regulation of Foreign Banks* (New York: New York University Graduate School of Business Administration, 1981); and Ralph C. Bryant, *International Financial Intermediation* (Washington, D.C.: Brookings, 1987).

On the U.S. case, see Benjamin G. Cohen, *In Whose Interest? International Banking and American Foreign Policy* (New Haven: Yale University Press, 1987); Jeffry Frieden, *Banking on the World: The Politics of American International Finance* (New York: Harper & Row, 1987); George J. Benston, ed., *Financial Services: The Changing Institutions and Government Policy* (Englewood Cliffs, N.J.: Prentice-Hall, 1983); Michael J. Feinman, "National Treatment of Foreign Banks Operating in the United States: The International Banking Act of 1978," *Law and Policy in International Business* 11 (1979); James V. Houpt, "Foreign Ownership of U.S. Banks: Trends and Effects," *Journal of Bank Research* (Summer 1983); and Charles W. Hultman, "International Banking and U.S. Commercial Policy," *Journal of World Trade Law* 19 (May–June 1985).

On Japan, see Hugh T. Patrick, "Japan: 1868–1914," in Rondo Cameron, ed., *Banking in the Early Stages of Industrialization* (New York: Oxford University Press, 1967); Robert S. Ozaki, *The Control of Imports and Foreign Capital in Japan* (New York: Praeger, 1972); Gary R. Saxonhouse, "The Micro- and Macroeconomics of Foreign Sales to Japan," in William R. Cline, ed., *Trade Policy in the 1980s* (Washington, D.C.: Institute for International Economics, 1983); Yoshio Suzuki, *Money and Banking in Contemporary Japan* (New Haven: Yale University Press, 1980); Shoichi Royama, "The Japanese Financial System: Past, Present, and Future," *Japanese Economic Studies* (Winter 1983–84); and Frances McCall Rosenbluth, "The Politics of Japan's Financial Deregulation," diss., Columbia University, 1988.

On the Canadian case, see E. P. Neufeld, *The Financial System of Canada* (New York: St. Martin's, 1972); Kenneth J. Friedman, "The 1980 Canadian Banks and Banking Law Revision Act: Competitive Stimulus or Protectionist Barrier?" *Law and Policy in International Business* 13 (1981); Ontario Task Force on Financial Institutions, *Final Report* (Toronto: Queen's Printer, December 1985); Government of Canada, *New Directions for the Financial Sector* (Ottawa: Supply and Services, 1986); and *The Canada–U.S. Free Trade Agreement* (Ottawa: External Affairs, 1987).

On Australia, see A. L. May, *The Battle for the Banks* (Sydney: Sydney University Press, 1968); Peter Love, *Labour and the Money Power* (Melbourne: Melbourne University Press, 1974); Richard E. Caves and Lawrence B. Krause, eds., *The Australian Economy: A View from the North* (Washington, D.C.: Brookings, 1984); Ian R. Harper, "Why Financial Deregulation?" *Australian Economic Review* (1st Quarter 1986); Edna Carew, *Fast Money 2* (Sydney: Allen & Unwin, 1985); and Michael T. Skully, "Foreign Banks in Australia," *Bankers' Magazine of Australasia* (June 1979).

For relevant background to foreign banking in Europe, see Leon Lindberg, *The Political Dynamics of European Economic Integration* (Stanford: Stanford University Press, 1963); Ernst B. Haas, *The Uniting of Europe* (Stanford: Stanford University Press, 1968); J.-J. Servan-Schreiber, *The American Challenge* (New York: Atheneum, 1968); Charles P. Kindleberger, ed., *The International Corporation* (Cambridge: MIT Press, 1970); Stuart W. Robinson, Jr., *Multinational Banking* (Leiden: Sijthoff, 1972); Eric Stein, *Harmonization of European Company Laws* (Indianapolis: Bobbs-Merrill, 1971); Paolo Clarotti, "The Harmonization of Legislation Relating to Credit Institutions," *Common Market Law Review* 19 (1982); Peter Troberg, "Convergence of European Systems of Banking Supervision," *Netherlands Banking Digest* 6 (July 1979); Jane Welch, ed., *The Regulation of Banks in the Member States of the EEC* (The Hague: Nijhoff, 1981); and D. C. Kruse, *Monetary Integration in Western Europe* (Boston: Butterworths, 1980).

For theoretical works of general relevance to interstate policy coordination in the financial sector, see Robert O. Keohane and Joseph S. Nye, *Power and Interdependence* (Boston: Little, Brown, 1977); Hedley Bull, *The Anarchical Society* (New York: Columbia University Press, 1977); Peter J. Katzenstein, ed., *Between Power and Plenty* (Madison: University of Wisconsin Press, 1978); Robert Axelrod, *The Evolution of Cooperation* (New York: Basic Books, 1984); and Robert O. Keohane, *After Hegemony: Cooperation and Discord in the World Political Economy* (Princeton: Princeton University Press, 1984). On the development of international norms and rules, see Myres S. McDougal and associates, *Studies in World Public Order* (New Haven: Yale University Press, 1960); Louis Henkin, *How Nations Behave* (New York: Council on Foreign Relations, 1962); Michael Barkun, *Law without Sanctions* (New Haven: Yale University Press, 1968); Anthony A. D'Amato, *The Concept of Custom in International Law* (Ithaca: Cornell University Press, 1971); Oran Young, *Compliance and Public Authority* (Baltimore: Johns Hopkins University Press, 1979); Stephen Krasner, ed., *International Regimes* (Ithaca: Cornell University Press, 1983); Nicholas Greenwood Onuf, ed., *Law-Making in the Global Community* (Durham: Carolina Academic Press, 1982); Terry Nardin, *Law, Morality, and the Relations of States* (Princeton: Princeton University Press, 1983); Friedrich Kratochwil, "The Force of Prescriptions," *International Organization* 38 (Autumn 1984); and Robert Axelrod, "An Evolutionary Approach to Norms," *American Political Science Review* 80 (December 1986). For applicable anthropological and sociological research, see Sally Falk Moore, "Law and Anthropology," *Biennial Review of Anthropology* (1969); Leopold Pospisil, *Anthropology of Law: A Comparative Theory* (New York: Harper & Row, 1971); Francis G. Snyder, "Anthropology, Dispute Processes, and Law: A Critical Introduction," *British Journal of Law and Society* 8 (Winter 1981); Donald Black, ed., *Toward a General Theory of Social Control* (Orlando, Fla.: Academic Press, 1984); and Anthony Giddens, *The Constitution of Society* (Berkeley: University of California Press, 1984).

# Index

INDEX

Index

INDEX

INDEX

banking, Canadian (*cont.*)
overseas expansion, 18, 19
structure and regulation of, 18–21
banking, Japanese:
insurance companies and, 86
overseas expansion, 67, 72, 82,
214n21, 221n89, 221n94, 246n14
position of foreign banks, 70, 71, 91,
92, 216n36
securities companies and, 86, 91, 93
structure and regulation of, 12–15
trust companies and, 86–89, 219n63
banking, United States:
acquisitions, 51–54, 60, 61
antitrust policies and, 58
foreign bank growth, 44, 45, 51, 57,
60, 61, 202n25, 204n42
interstate branching, 52–55, 209n87
regional, 51, 59
state jurisdictions and, 29, 30, 35,
42, 43, 200n3, 200n5, 211n107
structure and regulation of, 9, 11, 36
Banking Act, Australia, 122
Banking Act, United States, 10
Banking Law, Japan:
of 1927, 67
of 1981, 78–82
Bank of Adelaide, 129, 234n19,
236n35
Bank of America, 29, 33, 67, 68, 76,
87
Bank of British Columbia, 117
Bank of California, 219n69
Bank of Canada, 19, 95, 101, 107,
111, 112
Bank of China, 120, 243n99
Bank of Japan, 14, 15, 68, 70, 73, 76,
91, 197n8
Bank of Montreal (BMO), 18, 97, 101,
106, 112–15
Bank of New South Wales (BNSW).
*See* Westpac Banking Corporation
Bank of New Zealand, 120
Bank of Nova Scotia (BNS), 18, 100,
106, 112, 115, 231n86
Bank of Queensland, 122
Bank of Tokyo, 67, 120, 122, 150,
215n24, 218n57
Bank (Shareholdings) Act, 122, 243n99
Banque Nationale de Paris, 120
Barclays Bank, 94, 149
bilateral investment treaties, 247n27
Bill C-30, Canada, 115–17
Boston, Port of, 42
Bretton Woods system, 4
Britain. *See* United Kingdom

British Chamber of Commerce in
Japan, 84
British North America Act, 18, 101,
197n17
Burns, Arthur, 34, 49

California, state of, 29, 30, 35, 43, 59,
200, 214n21
Campbell, Keith, 234n20
Campbell Committee, 125–35, 141–43,
167
Canadian Bankers Association:
establishment of, 19, 198n18
on foreign banks, 97, 99, 109, 110,
228n57
Canadian Federation of Independent
Business, 230n78
Canadian Imperial Bank of Commerce
(CIBC), 94, 101, 106, 112
capital adequacy, 184
capital allocation mechanism, Canada,
103, 108
capital mobility, 4
Carey, Hugh, 209n91
Cayman Islands, 230n86
Central Union Trust Company. *See*
Manufacturers Hanover Bank
certificates of deposit, 74, 79
Chartered Bank, United Kingdom, 66
Chase Manhattan Bank:
in Canada, 95, 225n34
and foreign banks, 29, 36, 201n18
in Japan, 67, 68, 215n31
Chemical Bank, 87
Citibank:
in Australia, 120–23, 137, 142, 149,
234n13, 239–43
in Canada, 95, 99, 118, 162, 163,
225n37
and foreign banks, 29, 36, 59
in Japan, 66, 68, 84, 87–90, 214n19
Commercial Bank of Australia, 126,
129
Committee of Foreign-Owned Banks,
32, 34
Commonwealth Banking Corporation,
128, 129, 233n11, 240n73
Commonwealth Bank Officers Association (CBOA), 132, 140, 237n39
Comptroller of the Currency, United
States:
and foreign banks, 53, 58–63
regulatory role of, 11, 12, 196n1
Conference of State Bank Supervisors
(CSBS):
and foreign bank issue, 36, 39, 42,
48–52, 205n55

252

Conference of State Bank Supervisors (CSBS) (*cont.*)
after International Banking Act, 56, 59, 211n107
Congress, United States, 155, 178
and American banks abroad, 22, 56, 57, 64
House Committee on Banking, Currency, and Housing, 36–41, 49, 58, 60
House Subcommittee on Financial Institutions Supervision, 36, 40, 46
Joint Economic Committee, 30
Senate Committee on Banking, Housing, and Urban Affairs, 37, 55, 59, 63
Senate Subcommittee on Financial Institutions, 37, 50, 60, 158
Connecticut, state of, 205n55
Continental Bank of Canada, 117
Continental-Illinois Bank, 232n95
Council on Financial System Research, 75, 80
CRA, Australia, 237n41
Crocker National Bank, 61, 211n106
CSR, Australia, 237n41
customary law, 182

Dai Ichi Kangyo Bank, 218n57
Daiwa Bank, 219n73
Danforth, John, 84, 85, 211n109
Denmark, 176
Department of Defense, United States, 236n36
Department of External Affairs, Canada, 96, 112, 116
Department of Finance, Canada, 19, 102, 113–16
Department of Justice, United States, 11
Department of State, United States:
foreign banks and, 39, 48, 231n86, 236n36
general banking matters and, 12, 65, 86, 96, 98
Department of the Treasury, Australia, 25, 26, 121–26, 135–38, 147–51, 168, 198n26, 199n33
Department of the Treasury, United States:
and American banks abroad, 12, 56, 62–65, 158, 179, 215n26, 220n75
and Australia, 131
and Canada, 115, 228n61
and foreign banks, 41, 48, 50
and Japan, 74, 89, 160, 215n25
Deutsche Bank, 76, 84, 150

Diet, Japan, 74, 76, 78

Economic Council of Canada, 102
economic nationalism:
in Australia, 24, 146
in Canada, 106, 107, 115, 117, 163
Edge Act, 35, 42, 52–59, 158, 196n2, 208n78, 208n83
equivalent access principle, 6, 164, 247n23
Eurocurrency markets, 33, 37, 89, 91, 176, 213n2, 219n62, 221n94, 246n15. *See also* offshore currency markets
Eurodollar market. *See* Eurocurrency markets
European-American Bank, 51
European banking, 170–77
European Economic Community (EEC), 5, 171, 184
Banking Federation of, 40, 42, 48, 106, 207n74
banking in member states of, 63, 176
and foreign banks, 172–75, 244n4
and Japan, 73, 74, 84, 215n23
Euroyen market, 85, 86, 89. *See also* Eurocurrency markets
exchange controls:
in Australia, 134, 144, 235n26
in Japan, 68
Export-Import Bank of Japan, 73

Federal Deposit Insurance Corporation (FDIC):
and California banking law, 29
and foreign banks, 34–44, 53–56
regulatory role of, 11, 12
Federal Home Loan Bank Board, 196n5
Federal Reserve Bank of New York, 36
Federal Reserve Bank of San Francisco, 73
Federal Reserve Board:
and foreign banks, 32–46, 49, 56, 58, 59, 61, 149, 155–58
and Japan, 215n25
Federal Reserve system:
foreign banks and, 34, 35, 55
regulatory role of, 11, 12, 196n4
Federated Clerks Union, Australia, 242n89
Financial Corporations Act, Australia, 123, 166
financial deregulation:
in Australia, 5, 6, 22, 141, 167
in Canada, 20, 118
in Japan, 78–80, 85

# Cornell Studies in Political Economy

EDITED BY PETER J. KATZENSTEIN

*Collapse of an Industry: Nuclear Power and the Contradictions of U.S. Policy*, by John L. Campbell

*Power, Purpose, and Collective Choice: Economic Strategy in Socialist States*, edited by Ellen Comisso and Laura D'Andrea Tyson

*The Political Economy of the New Asian Industrialism*, edited by Frederic C. Deyo

*Dislodging Multinationals: India's Strategy in Comparative Perspective*, by Dennis J. Encarnation

*Democracy and Markets: The Politics of Mixed Economies*, by John R. Freeman

*The Misunderstood Miracle: Industrial Development and Political Change in Japan*, by David Friedman

*Patchwork Protectionism: Textile Trade Policy in the United States, Japan, and West Germany*, by H. Richard Friman

*Politics in Hard Times: Comparative Responses to International Economic Crises*, by Peter Gourevitch

*Closing the Gold Window: Domestic Politics and the End of Bretton Woods*, by Joanne Gowa

*Cooperation among Nations: Europe, America, and Non-tariff Barriers to Trade*, by Joseph M. Grieco

*Pathways from the Periphery: The Politics of Growth in the Newly Industrializing Countries*, by Stephan Haggard

*The Philippine State and the Marcos Regime: The Politics of Export*, by Gary Hawes

*Reasons of State: Oil Politics and the Capacities of American Government*, by G. John Ikenberry

*The State and American Foreign Economic Policy*, edited by G. John Ikenberry, David A. Lake, and Michael Mastanduno

*Pipeline Politics: The Complex Political Economy of East-West Energy Trade*, by Bruce W. Jentleson

*The Politics of International Debt*, edited by Miles Kahler

*Corporatism and Change: Austria, Switzerland, and the Politics of Industry*, by Peter J. Katzenstein

*Industry and Politics in West Germany: Toward the Third Republic*, edited by Peter J. Katzenstein

*Small States in World Markets: Industrial Policy in Europe*, by Peter J. Katzenstein

*The Sovereign Entrepreneur: Oil Policies in Advanced and Less Developed Capitalist Countries*, by Merrie Gilbert Klapp

*International Regimes*, edited by Stephen D. Krasner

*Power, Protection, and Free Trade: International Sources of U.S. Commercial Strategy, 1887–1939*, by David A. Lake

*State Capitalism: Public Enterprise in Canada*, by Jeanne Kirk Laux and Maureen Appel Molot

*Opening Financial Markets: Banking Politics on the Pacific Rim*, by Louis W. Pauly

*The Fruits of Fascism: Postwar Prosperity in Historical Perspective*, by Simon Reich

*The Business of the Japanese State: Energy Markets in Comparative and Historical Perspective*, by Richard J. Samuels

*In the Dominions of Debt: Historical Perspectives on Dependent Development*, by Herman M. Schwartz

Library of Congress Cataloging-in-Publication Data

Pauly, Louis W.
  Opening financial markets.

  (Cornell studies in political economy)
  Bibliography: p.
  Includes index.
  1. Banks and banking, Foreign — United States.  2. Banks and banking, For-
eign — Japan.  3. Banks and banking, Foreign — Canada.  4. Banks and bank-
ing, Foreign — Australia.  I. Title.  II. Series.
HG2491.P38  1988        332.1'5        88-47740
ISBN 0-8014-2080-6 (alk. paper)